STAIRWAY
TO
HEAVEN

STAIRWAY
TO
HEAVEN

The Spiritual Roots of Rock 'n' Roll—
From the King and Little Richard
To Prince and Amy Grant

DAVIN SEAY
WITH
MARY NEELY

A Ballantine/Epiphany Book
Ballantine Books · New York

To Summer, at the threshold

REF.
ML
3534
.S428
1986
cpl.

A Ballantine/Epiphany Book

Copyright © 1986 by Davin Seay and Mary Neely

All rights reserved under International and Pan-American Copyright Conventions. Published in the United States by Ballantine Books, a division of Random House, Inc., New York, and simultaneously in Canada by Random House of Canada Limited, Toronto.

Due to limitations of space, permissions acknowledgments appear on the opposite page.

Library of Congress Catalog Card Number: 86-7951

ISBN: 0-345-33022-6

Design by Holly Johnson
Manufactured in the United States of America

First Edition: November 1986
10 9 8 7 6 5 4 3 2 1

Contents

Acknowledgments

Many others have taken the measure of rock 'n' roll's spiritual reach as they've sought to convey some of the joy, frustration, anger, and, yes, revelation that the music has brought them. To those "writers and critics who prophesy with your pens" and whose work figures so largely in this work: thanks.

This book would not have been possible without the vision, perseverance, and ever-present help of Mary Neely, who knew a good idea when she thought of one. Thanks also to Mike Roe, Daryl Zackman, Steve Scott, Jan Volz, Ruth Walden and the entire Warehouse staff and to Louis Neely, a wise man, for their prayers, support, and enormously helpful suggestions.

To Pastor Ken and Leslie Robillard, my appreciation for their intercessions and exhortations.

To Michelle Rapkin, for encouragement, understanding, and transcontinental psychoanalysis; a debt of heartfelt gratitude. For the timely help of Toni Simmons, many thanks.

Special thanks also to Stephen R. Tucker, Bill C. Malone, and Van K. Brock for their generous assistance in providing material for the Elvis and Jerry Lee chapter.

Thanks also to Gene Sculatti for his special gifts of proportion and perspective.

Segments on the Doors and the history of rock criticism in Chapter Ten appeared previously in the *L.A. Weekly*.

Finally, thanks and all love to Diane, under whose wings each word of this book found life.

—D.S.

Special thanks to Mike Roe for his work on "Rock Scope" and teaching me what I didn't already know about rock 'n' roll; Daryl Zackman, who was so much more than the engineer; Steve Scott and Jan Volz; to my supportive family; and most of all to Davin Seay for his powerful pen.

—M.N.

STAIRWAY
TO
HEAVEN

Introduction

Everybody's looking for the answers
How the story started and how it will end. . . .

—Prince

The sound is evocative, alluring. It throbs with echoes, curling like smoke, languid, sensuous. A dreamy babble of notes leaks from a saxophone, and a piano performs a delicate minuet with a string quartet. Somewhere, behind the steady, anchoring beat, angels' voices croon the chorus: "Everybody's looking for the ladder, Everybody's looking for salvation of the soul."

Confounding expectations; stretching limits; bursting

3

bubbles: for Prince, the latest member of that certified platinum fraternity of rock 'n' roll megastars, the unexpected was becoming something of a habit. He had, after all, built his reputation (and a phenomenally successful career) on a string of scandalous, sexually explicit hits. A sultry, bikini-clad Lothario, he unabashedly celebrated the joys of incest, wedding night seductions, and *Kama-sutra* kinkiness. His song titles told it all: "Controversy," "Dirty Mind," "Let's Pretend We're Married," the suitably suggestive "Little Red Corvette. . . ." It was music designed to shock. And sell millions of records. Unprecedented popularity was the payoff.

Then, in 1985, like the proverbial bolt from the blue, came *Around the World in a Day*. It was psychedelic, experimental, sentimental, and . . . well, mystical. "All thanks 2 God," read the LP's dedication, while among the now-regulation Prince chart toppers—"Raspberry Beret" and "Pop Life"—were cuts like "The Ladder," with lines like "The love of God's creation will undress you," or "Temptation," which proclaimed, "Temptation is useless; love is more important than sex." The evidence was clear: to steal the line Buddy Miles had growled fifteen years before, Prince was going through "them changes."

The pouting Prince of Pop had, it seemed, discovered Religion, or the Path, or the Truth, or the Answer. Or something. Prince suddenly seemed less interested in getting us hot than getting us enlightened. You could almost hear the hush falling round the world when, as his contribution to the Live Aid extravaganza to feed the hungry of Africa in July of that year, Prince offered an enraptured globe a video performance of an original song. Gazing earnestly into the camera, strumming an acoustic guitar, he sang, simply and affectingly, about a man who healed the blind and lame, a man who "died for the tears in your eyes."

Had Prince "found God?" In a world that reinvents itself as consistently and completely as does popular music, where the new and different are defined on a weekly basis, the notion of idol-turned-apostle must have seemed, indeed, quite the novelty to rock's fresh generation of camp followers. Yet, for once, Prince was opening no new vistas.

Twenty-eight years before Prince's satellite-beam confessional, a performer who had stunned popular music with his sexually ambiguous persona, towering pompadour, and frenzied musical assault was having his own moment of truth in a plane over Melbourne, Australia. "When it got dark and I could see the engines on the wings glowing red hot, I thought the plane was on fire," Little Richard told his biographer Charles White. "In my mind I pictured these angels flying up under the plane holding it up. It was like a sign to me." It was the next evening, in the middle of an outdoor concert, as he ripped through "Good Golly, Miss Molly," "Long Tall Sally," "Tutti Frutti"—the full stack of hits that had made him an international phenomenon, that he saw Sputnik winging its lonely way across the southern skies. "It looked as though the big ball of fire came directly over the stadium, . . ." the singer recounted. "It shook my mind. It really shook my mind. I got up from the piano and said, 'This is it. I am through. I am leaving show business to go back to God."

In 1970, thirteen years later, friends, business associates, and the simply curious pored through the personal effects of a left-handed guitarist with a frizzed afro halo and a monkey on his back. Among the last lines of rock-lyric–cum–poetry that Jimi Hendrix set to paper before suffocating in his own vomit—a drug casualty—was a strange stanza regarding an enigmatic figure wandering the desert only to die for the collective tears of humanity.

By thanking God, evoking Christ (or a reasonable facsimile), and climbing the ladder up his own spiritual quest, Prince, like Little Richard, Jimi Hendrix, and so many others, became part of a tradition that stretches back to the genesis of rock 'n' roll.

"God Only Knows," the Beach Boys crooned in that lilting and lovely song of the same name. Eric Clapton, in Blind Faith, evoked the thundering "Presence of the Lord," while George Harrison and his Krishna chorus extolled "My Sweet Lord" for the benefit of the unenlightened masses. "Saved," shouted Laverne Baker;" "Jesus Is Just All Right," echoed the Doobie Brothers, the Byrds, and others, while Lou Reed and the Velvet Underground called forth the "Jesus" of an aching heroin haze. It was, according to Norman Greenbaum, the "Spirit In The Sky"; for Genesis it was the "Watcher of the Sky," while for Jimi Hendrix it was a sassy "Scuze me while I kiss the sky." Paul Simon's mama loves him like "the Rock of Ages"; Edwin Hawkins celebrates "Oh Happy Day"; in a ganja dream Bob Marley conjures the "Natural Mystic"; U2 rallies to "Pride in the Name of Love." Whether in passing reference or fervent pronouncement, as an object of ridicule or adoration, God in many guises, the heavenly host, and the elusive meaning of life have all played pivotal roles in rock's journey of self-discovery.

When, in 1968, Procol Harum solemnly announced in their multilayered mood piece "Shine on Brightly" that "Life is a beanstalk, isn't it?" they were echoing a fascination with eternity that has maddened, mystified, and mesmerized rock writers and performers for nearly thirty years. When the Beatles invited us to "turn off your mind, relax, and float downstream" on the 1966 "Tomorrow Never Knows," they sent us drifting inevitably East, to a promised land of perpetual transcendence. It was into realms of magic and ritual that Jim Morrison and the Doors exhorted us to "Break on Through" one year later. In 1974,

6

when David Bowie assured us that "Somebody Up There Likes Me," he was reflecting the absorbing preoccupation with metaphysics that has led modern music down its most twisted and convoluted corridors. The Sex Pistols' Johnny Rotten snarling "Lord God have mercy, all crimes are paid" in the 1978 "God Save the Queen" played tellingly on rock's mordant fascination for Christ and the anti-Christ, while Black Sabbath, summoning the "Children of the Grave" in 1971's *Masters of Reality*, led the pack of heavy metalists reveling in rock's Faustian bargain with the dark powers. Brian Eno and David Byrne depicting "My Life in the Bush of Ghosts" in the 1981 album of the same name, coaxed African spirits from rock's own dim past. It would be a tall order to catalog all the references, allusions, and refrains of Old and New Testaments in the lyrics of Bob Dylan or Bruce Springsteen, from "When the Ship Comes In" to "The Promised Land." *Stairway to Heaven*, its title borrowed from a 1971 Led Zeppelin opus, perhaps the most famous of rock's forays into ethereal realms, is about those connections—some shadowy, some shining brightly.

To say that religion—and the quest for cosmic revelation—is an integral part of rock 'n' roll may seem to some to be widely missing the point. To millions of devoted fans, rock doesn't simply deal with religion. Rock *is* religion. The freedom, the power, the rebel thrills, and the fierce hopes that rock music promises (but does not always deliver) comprise a life-style that, for many, will always be more real than any truth revealed in a cathedral or ashram. A single note strummed from the Boss's guitar speaks more eloquently to them of life's joys and sorrows than all the parables of Jesus, Mohammed, and Buddha combined. For rock's true believers, church is a concert hall, a leather jacket the vestment, and the gospel, now and always, a joyous "Awop-Bop-a-Loo-Mop-Alop-Bam-Boom."

So if rock is a religion, what's the message? You needn't listen long to realize that the spectrum of popular music offers a dazzling catalog of meanings. And most of what rock has to tell us sounds strangely familiar. "There's nothing new under the sun"; dusty as it may be, the biblical chestnut has the ring of truth to it. Nihilist or optimist, epicurean or anarchist, demonic or divine; more often than not, and whether they like it or not, rock 'n' roll's prophets are the champions of causes lost and won long ago and many times before. Whether it's "get down with your bad self" or "everybody is a star," rock is music that embodies, celebrates, and mourns conditions of the human spirit—conditions familiar to saints and sinners throughout history.

But, like real religion, good rock is hardly a philosophical abstraction; it's a potent, vitalizing force, a continual source of excitement and pleasure, a soundtrack to our lives. In its ability to capture a moment, a mood or a message, it has an enduring and endearing quality.

At the same time, the flip side of rock's relation to religion is equally fascinating. For if rock is indeed a religion, it certainly has its share of false prophets, golden calves, and wacko cults. In a business where longevity is a three-week perch in the Top Ten, there is more than a touch of irony to rock's high priests straining toward immortality by drenching their music in overblown profundities. And more than a little delusion among rock's followers, hanging on every utterance of their guitar-slinging avatars. Pop music is a heady, treacherous, heartbreaking hall of mirrors in which countless well-meaning souls have lost their way. The awesome follies and often absurd pretense of rock culture comprise a cautionary parable.

Stairway to Heaven deals with that parable: It's about

8

Jerry Lee Lewis's wild race with destiny and John Lennon's popularity contest with Jesus. About Jim Morrison's deadly muse and the Grateful Dead's nirvana syndrome. About the Rolling Stones' sympathy for the devil and Bob Dylan's moment of truth. About punk prophets and Prince's ladder. It's a story about music, about people and about "changes"—good changes, bad changes, and changes still to come.

Like pith-helmeted Amazon explorers seeking the river's fabled source, musicologists are forever sticking their flags in history and proclaiming, "This is It. This is where rock 'n' roll began." And why not? Immortality awaits the lucky hunter who stumbles onto that seminal note, the scratchy backbeat at 78 RPM, the disembodied hiccups of the preeminent hip shaker, the original Gone Daddy.

Conventional musical wisdom pinpoints the origin of rock to a New Orleans–bred blues shouter named Roy Brown, who in 1947 wrote and recorded "Good Rockin' Tonight," a hit subsequently performed by everyone from Jackie Wilson to B. B. King to the King himself, Elvis Presley.

And it seems as good a place as any to start. With its loose-jointed rhythms and roadhouse raunch, "Good Rockin' Tonight" certainly sounds like it could be the first rock relic, part accident, part inspiration, part divine intervention. Besides, that magic word "rockin'" pops out of the title like a prophetic utterance. And if that's not enough, how about Roy Brown's legendary stage show, that eye-popping, knee-quaking extravaganza he and his band, the Mighty Men, cranked up and cut loose? It had to be the prototype for every overamped rock idol who ever laid claim to the charge of exhibitionism. No question about it; Roy Brown, the original Mighty, Mighty Man, was a bona fide catalytic converter: the granddaddy of rock 'n' roll.

Or was he? Thirteen years earlier, American music archivists John and Alan Lomax made a live recording of a song called "Run Old Jeremiah," in a backwoods southern church. The lyrics included the following exultation:

Oh my Lord! Oh, my Lordy! Well, well, well!
I've gotta rock! You gotta rock!

Could it be that these black brethren, back in '34, shaking the dusty floors of their wood-framed chapel with a spirit–filled two-step, were at the actual root of rock's family tree?

Or did the Graves brothers arrive first? It was in 1929 that these Hattiesburg, Mississippi, musicians recorded a series of raw, stomping gospel songs for Paramount Records. They were called rockin' and reelin' spirituals, fashioned after a rousing variety of congregational singing heard in Holiness denomination churches across the Deep South. By capturing the shuddering, singsong call and response of the "ring shout," a communal dance chant of African lineage, the Graves had tapped into elemental energies that would later sound to many like the birth pangs of rock 'n' roll.

Which would've made Trixie Smith the midwife. In 1922 she cut a very blue blues song called "My Daddy Rocks Me (With One Steady Roll)" for Black Swan Records. It inspired all sorts of rocking, rolling variations throughout that roaring decade, including Robert Johnson's "I'm a Steady Rolling Man," Lil' Johnson's "Rock That Thing," and the gospel rouser "Rock, Church, Rock" by Clara Smith.

The fact is, the farther one strays down the dusky byways of rock 'n' roll, the more treacherous the path becomes. Even the pair of verbs "rock" and "roll," separately or in mystical conjunction, seems to have no fixed historical address, although it is generally acknowledged that "rock 'n' roll" is a black euphemism for sexual inter- course. It's as good an explanation as any for the euphon- ious and mystical coupling of "rock" with "roll." But et- ymology aside, its the sound itself that embodies the mystique of today's most popular music genre. The *effects* of rock 'n' roll—those thrilling, dangerous crescendos of release, rebellion, and all-night ecstasy—are as old as the first time the first man pounded out a syncopated riff on a hollow log. Therein lies the key to rock's origins and its unique relationship to religion.

One can almost hear the chorus of boos and hisses rising like steam at the very suggestion. Rock 'n' roll is supposed to be about fun, not the somber verities of the hereafter. It runs no deeper than a passing fancy; it's as enduring as the age of sixteen. Rock's virtue is its disposability. Pop and profundity just don't mix.

But music and mystery do. Whatever rock 'n' roll grew up to be, its infancy is linked to spiritual impulses of pre- historic lineage. Robert Palmer, in *The Rolling Stone Illus trated History of Rock 'n' Roll*, writes "In a very real sense rock was implicit in the music of the first Africans brought to North America." And implicit in their music were cen- turies of accumulated rites, rituals, and religious fervor. The music of those first brutalized and bewildered slaves, ripped from cultures as old as the Pyramids, those ancient chants and tribal stomps, didn't simply evoke the spirits of the forest gods; they animated and immortalized them.

The spiritual potency of music in prehistoric life—camp- fire chants, sacrificial incantations, deathbed drum vigils— was as constant as the seasons. Music was the purveyor of tribal identity, a placater of local deities, a focus of en- ergy for the whole community. And as a means of com- municating, imparting truth, tradition, and the tools of survival, it spoke more than words could ever tell.

If music is, as sociologist Raymond Williams asserts, a way of "transmitting a description of experience," then its use to transmit the most significant and enduring experience in the whole human catalog, the religious experience, naturally follows.

But for primitive man, music was not merely *a* means of relating the joys and terrors of an encounter with the supernatural: it was the *only* means. In an age before religious canon, doctrine, and writ, spirituality and the brotherhood of common faith was expressed in song.

If the rain god or fire spirit or death demon needed summoning, flutes and finger pianos and drums called them forth. Music existed not to *describe* the fear and wonder of the invisible realms, it actually reached out and touched them: a sensual, tactile, and, finally, inexpressible religious encounter.

This nonverbal, fundamentally physical understanding of religion, with music at its center, is hardly exclusive to Africa. European society, at the time of its initial contact with blacks through the slave trade, had substantially lost touch with its preliterate past. Yet heathen ways lingered, if only in the half-remembered traditions of the peasant class. The enormously rich tapestry of pre-Christian European religious belief continued to express itself through musically enhanced ritual and tradition.

The modern notion that the medium of music can be separated from its message, like salt leached from seawater, would have been incomprehensible to those for whom song was the spiritual substance of their lives.

For centuries music and religion wound snugly around each other in an endless, nurturing cycle. Yet, by the time the New World was a going concern, teeming with visionaries and charlatans, explorers and entrepreneurs, masters and slaves, the cycle had shattered. The ancient symbiotic relationship between the spirit and song had fallen on hard times. The powerful God of Christianity was waging war with the pantheon of pagan spirits. It was in the heat of that battle that rock 'n' roll was forged.

Leadbelly

Chapter One

MOTHER GOSPEL, PAPA GEDE

The God spoken about in black songs is not the
same one in the white songs.

—LeRoi Jones

Children, we shall be free,
When the Lord shall appear.
He'll raise the dead from under the earth,
And give them permission to talk.

—Negro spiritual

W. E. B. Du Bois called them "sorrow songs," the music
of "an unhappy people, of the children of disappointment;
they tell of death and suffering and unvoiced longing toward a truer world, of misty wanderings and hidden
ways."

The first African captives sold into slavery in the New
World in the early 1600s carried with them an agonized
inspiration that would become the cornerstone for vir-

15

tually every American musical expression to follow. It is ironic that a country founded on the misty wanderings of utopian pioneers and promoted as the land of "liberty and justice for all," should find its truest, most original and innovative expression in the music of the dispossessed and betrayed. The unimaginable horrors endured by those first slaves were transfigured, over the course of centuries, into a music defined by its dignity, grace, and beauty. As an astonishing feat of creativity, and equally as a heroically sustained act of faith, it is without historical parallel. As a spiritual odyssey told through song, it is the stuff of legend.

And legend is largely all that remains. The traditionally bucolic images of antebellum plantation life—a Currier & Ives fantasy of a smoothly integrated social order—were only a wistful dream. The institution of slavery exacted a heavy price on the collective conscience of America, a burden of guilt that has yet to be fully reckoned. Yet neither the total supremacy of the white man nor the utter subjugation of the black was ever completely realized, even within so comprehensively cruel a way of life. White masters may have held the power of life and death over their chattels, but the human spirit proved indomitable. Music became not only a means of spiritual liberation but an expression of all the seething contradictions and conflicts generated by a titanic cultural clash. The terms of that clash were as much religious as they were economic or social, and it's the spiritual dimension that echoes with enduring clarity in the songs of the American Negro slave.

"Because the African[s] came from an intensely religious culture," writes LeRoi Jones in his landmark book *Blues People*, "a society where religion was a daily, minute-to-minute concern . . . [he] had to find other methods of worshipping gods when his white captors declared that he could no longer worship in the old ways."

The old ways, of course, encompassed a complex primitive theology, bristling with fetishes, totems, and magic. Yet, for most of the enlightened Christian landowners of Colonial America, the only thing more odious than allowing their slaves to continue in their pagan ways was to initiate them into the True Faith. Concepts of racial inferiority, which buttressed the system of slavery, precluded any attempt to impart the love of Jesus or fear of God into the savage black. The unstated justification was clear: a Christian can't be a heathen; only a heathen is fit for the subhuman status of slave. The best solution was to destroy the religious impulse completely.

It was an impossible task. The African, asserts Jones, "could not function as a human being without religion; he daily invoked . . . the mystical forces he thought controlled the world . . . just as we dial our phones for a weather report. . . .The common day-to-day stance of the African towards his gods could not be erased overnight."

By the early nineteenth century, under pressure from the Quakers and other puritan fundamentalists, plantation owners began reluctantly yielding to the concept of conversion among their properties. It was soon discovered that Christian tenets could be perverted to meet the slave owner's ends. A "heathen" was no longer an unbelieving soul but instead a "bad nigger," one who displeased the master by being lazy or getting into mischief. Slave catechisms were written to enforce the quasi-divine status of the master. To the question "What is the meaning of 'Thou shall not commit adultery,'" the black man was required to answer "To obey our heavenly Father, and our earthly master, obey our overseer, and not steal anything." "What did God make you for?" the liturgy asked. "To make a crop," was the answer.

The luminous truths of Christianity could not, however, be extinguished by such deceptions. Slaves would often steal away into the night forest to hold strange semblances of Christian worship. It was at these clandestine rendez-vous that the fully developed use of music as a means of spiritual fulfillment was first incorporated with the estab-lished and often bone-dry traditions of European faith.

"The spirit will not descend without a song." It was a saying the slaves carried with them from the motherland, and whether the spirit was of the corn, river, or clouds, or whether it was the Holy Ghost, the power in the singing remained the same. "From the beginning," writes Ben Sid-ran in his book, *Black Talk*, "black Christianity was poten-tially a non-Western, if not anti-Western, institution. . . . Worship was more for pleasure than for exorcism of guilt, more release of emotional energy than lesson-learning."

Perhaps. But the true, joyous and liberating potency of the earliest American expressions of Christianity had little to do with East or West, black or white. Even as slaves celebrated a powerful and personal new God in their se-cret, moon-dappled clearings, strange sects with their own patented methods for calling it down from above were attracting new followers.

The United Society of Believers in Christ's Second Com-ming were better known by a nickname they earned when gathered together in huge meeting halls for night-long ses-sions of dancing, wordless singing, and uncontrolled dis-plays of kick-out-the-jams spirit power. Shakers did just that: shake, quake, rattle, and roll in long, intricately cho-reographed snake-dancing lines, men on one side, ladies on the other. The music accompanying their great gallop-ing praise-and-worship marathons was, by all accounts, of an awesome and chill-inducing variety, a vast chorus of moans and otherworldly utterances, sung to the rhythm of a thousand hands clapping as one, a thousand feet shuf-fling to a step that Mother Ann, the Shakers' founder, claimed to have learned directly from the heavenly host.

18

Shakers, along with other Puritan splinter groups, practiced a free, and physical, expression of God's power. The Society of Friends were derisively termed Quakers after their habit of quaking and trembling during religious services. While musical similiarities between the early Christian rites of Negro slaves and the spectacular spiritual shindigs of the Shakers and others can only be guessed, there is no question that the unfettered, over-the-top exuberance they shared was from the same source. And to the same end.

King David, decked out in a linen ephod and dancing like a man possessed before the Ark of the Covenant, is an early example of what happens when all heaven breaks loose on the sons and daughters of the Most High. The majestic, cyclical history of religious revival can be traced by outbreaks of feverish music-making. The Reformation kicked off with Martin Luther and others putting Christian sentiment to the melodies of barroom ballads and brothel ditties. The Great Awakening of 1740 ushered in a whole new era of popular church music, culminating in Isaac Watts's state-of-the-art classic *Psalms, Hymns, and Spiritual Songs*. Watts, in time, would become known for perennials such as "Joy to the World," "When I Survey the Wonderous Cross," and "O God, Our Help in Ages Past," hymns notable for their lyric simplicity and doctrinal density. Music, it seems, has always been used to lift the faithful out of the rut of rote and dogma, plugging them back into the emotional currents that distinguish true religious fervor.

The Negro slave in America was less concerned with revival than survival. The necessary virtues of endurance, hope, and long-suffering transformed his encounter with Christianity in a manner nearly unique to the faith. The Hebrews' four centuries of sore vexation in Egypt; the Israelites' captivity in Babylon; Daniel in the lion's den; these

19

were the telling biblical accounts that connected the slave with Judeo-Christian tradition. The lyrical focus of their music was, according to James Cone, in his book, *Spirituals and the Blues: An Interpretation*, "on biblical passages that stress God's involvement in the liberation of oppressed people . . . on God's liberation of the weak from the oppression of the strong, the lowly and downtrodden from the proud and mighty." "How Long, O Lord?," "Go Down, Moses," "Oh, Freedom," "My Lord Delivered Daniel"; the heartcry of such Negro spirituals is achingly plain.

But there was much more to the Christian fervor of the enslaved than biblical identification with their plight. Through the music of their evolving faith, they rewove the tattered fabric of community, reasserted their individuality in God's eyes, and even reached back across the ocean to recapture their history.

The black man's first choices from the range of Christian ritual were those that rang most familiar to him, the shadows and reflections of the old ways. Baptism was particularly appealing to early slaves because, as LeRoi Jones points out, "in most of the religions of West Africa the river spirits were thought to be the most powerful of the deities, and the priests of the river cults were among the most powerful and influential men in African society." In much the same way, writes Sidran, "the musical-religious ritual became the most important single experience in the daily life of the slave, much as it had been in preslavery Africa." The early black church, often called the "praise house," was not only the focus of social life for the slave, it was the one place where he was free from the prying eyes of the master, where he could express himself—and his culture—with something approaching freedom.

Central to this religious life, and most reminiscent of African tradition, was the phenomena of spirit possession;

the ecstatic experience of "gettin' happy." It was inevitably accompanied by outbursts of music and dancing. Dancing in church was forbidden, but for the black man, dancing was narrowly and conveniently defined as "crossing the feet." Shuffles and ring shouts, where feet never actually made the taboo crossing, became vehicles through which the spirit was revealed. Shaking and shimmying all night long induced, on the far side of exhaustion, a spirit receptive to the supernatural.

It was in the wild release of a Holy Ghost visitation that the slave's Christianity fused with his musical heritage. An observer unfolds the following scene in a black church circa 1867: "Boys with tattered shirts and men's trousers, young girls bare-footed, all stand in the middle of the floor, and when the 'sperichil' is struck up begin first walking and by and by shuffling around, one after the other, in a ring. . . . Frequently a band, composed of some of the best singers . . . stand by the side of the room to 'base' the others. . . . Song and dance are alike extremely energetic and when the shout lasts into the middle of the night, the monotonous thud, thud of feet prevents sleep within half a mile of the praise house."

Karl Marx much later would claim that religion was "the sign of the oppressed creature, the heart of the heartless world . . . the spirit of a spiritless situation." And it was in that heartless spirit that the white masters passed along their Christianity. But the smug assumption that images of the all-pervasive Great White Father and parables of the suffering servant would anesthetize the black man were proved spectacularly mistaken. The spiritual inheritance of the African negated any religion that would rob him of his essential humanity. James Cone sums it up best: "Through a song, black people were able to affirm that Spirit who was continuous with their existence as free beings; and they created a new style of religious worship.

21

They shouted and they prayed; they preached and they sang, because *they had found something*. They encountered a new reality; a new God not enshrined in white churches and religious gatherings." The slave's new style of religious worship sparked a new understanding of Christian truth, an emotional, intensely personal revelation. A radical identification with Christ's death and resurrection; a new understanding of a God who breaks the bonds of sin and suffering; life as a passage; heaven as a homeland. These were the themes of the great Negro spirituals.

It was the huge tidal floes of humanity following the Civil War and the Reconstruction—from slavery to freedom, farm to city, South to North—that brought to the wellspring of black spirituals new influences and experiences, resulting in two distinct hybrids: the blues and gospel.

Blues, descended directly from the gut–level emotional fervor of the spirituals, was melded with the work songs sung in the fields. It expressed the high hopes and hard times of the emancipated black man as he as began to tentatively step out into a strange and hostile land. For the first time he had the freedom to seek what lay over the next hill, the ability to express dimensions in his life other than work and worship, and the sobering task of making a place for himself and his family in the white man's world. "I never had no money befo'," was the lament of one early blues song, "and now they want it everywhere I go."

The fortunate black man earned his way with his music. By the close of the nineteenth century, a professional caste of black musicians, primarily blues singers, had begun to make their creative mark in mainstream American music. Their songs contrasted sharply to the heavenly hymnody of the spirituals. Aside from celebrating a rediscovered sense of identity—through the exploits of such archetypal black heros as Staggerlee, John Henry, Dupree, and others—the blues themselves would quickly come to signify all the varieties of sin and suffering the flesh is heir to, from whiskey to unrequited love, from existential angst to being down on your luck. "Other 'priests' of the community began to emerge," writes James Cone, ". . . the blues men and women. . . . Like the preacher in the church, they proclaimed the Word of black existence, depicting its joy and sorrow, and the awesome burden of being 'free' in a racist society."

Like the blues, gospel grew out of historical upheaval; the social shifts of the late nineteenth century. "The spiritual was born in the rural setting of the camp meeting," writes Eileen Southern, in *The Music of Black Americans: A History*, "where thousands assembled under the stars amid the blaze of campfires and torch lights. . . . The gospel song evolved in urban settings, in huge temporary tents erected for revival meetings by touring evangelists, in football stadiums, and in mammoth tabernacles." Gospel was also a coolly calculated commercial endeavor designed to capitalize on the enormous appeal of the Negro spiritual stylings.

The term "gospel music" was coined in 1875 by hymn writer Ira Sankey, but its emergence in the 1920s as a lucrative form of church music is commonly attributed to one man: Thomas Dorsey, the fabled Father of Gospel Music. The Georgia-born son of an itinerant Baptist preacher, Dorsey got his earliest practical musical experience playing a pump organ on his father's rural church circuit and thumping piano in the thriving black vaudevillian theaters of Atlanta. Relocating to Chicago as a young man, he was known as Barrelhouse Tom and Georgia Tom, playing jazz in bars and saloons, touring with legendary blues diva Ma Rainey, writing raunchy tunes with Tampa Red and forming the Famous Hokum Boys. In 1921, after attending the National Baptist Convention and hearing the

Reverend A. W. Nix galvanize the crowd with his rendering of the hymn "I Do, Don't You," Dorsey saw the notes scrawled on the sheet music of destiny. He decided to write religious music, terming his output "Gospel."

In the late twenties he toured the Midwest and South peddling his songs from church to church while still picking up the occasional barroom stint as a blues pianist. Allowed to perform his songs in churches only after the worship service, when he would hawk his texts for a few pennies apiece, Dorsey soon discovered a unique sales technique: he hired a female trio to back up his vocalizing. He later expanded the group, creating the first female gospel quartet in history and a model for every R & B and sweet soul girl group to follow, from the Supremes to the Pointer Sisters.

With the Depression, the bottom dropped out of the jazz and blues market, and Dorsey shifted his attention entirely to religious music. In the early thirties he pioneered the comprehensive commercialization of black church music, founding Dorsey's House of Music, the first publishing firm devoted to the development and dissemination of the songs of black gospel performers. Dorsey himself wrote over a thousand tunes, including "There'll Be Peace in the Valley," "Search Me, Lord," "Hide Me in Thy Bosom," and "When I've Done My Best." It was music that not only reflected the preaching and testifying heard in black Baptist and Methodist churches as well as the growing number of "sanctified" congregations across the country. It also made brilliant and liberal use of the melodies, harmonies, and rhythms of Dorsey's blues and jazz background.

Dorsey and other early gospel composers—Lucie Campbell, Sallie Martin, Roberta Martin, and Herbert Brewster—were also brilliant molders of form and image, presenting carefully packaged gospel performers calculated to have the widest appeal both in and outside the church. Church and revival concert circuits were well established by the mid-thirties with two popular kinds of gospel acts emerging. Nattily attired, smoothly harmonizing "gospel quartets," such as the sensational Dixie Hummingbirds, featured four or five male singers performing a cappella and accompanying themselves with snapping fingers and slapped thighs. Shades of doowop. The "gospel chorus," exemplified by the angelic Clara Ward Singers, were all-female hand clappers, dressed in choir robes and backed by a thundering piano or organ.

By the end of the decade Dorsey's gospel empire was in full swing: he promoted gospel "battles of song," pitting well-known groups against each other in hot and heavy sing-offs. Professional gospel artists began to arise—Mahalia Jackson and the astonishing "Sister" Rosetta Tharpe who sang gospel music for the first time in a secular setting when she performed with Cab Calloway at the Cotton Club in Harlem in the early thirties. Tharpe, with a voice that could convert the wicked with its sheer paint-peeling power, was also the first gospel pro to record for a major record label—Decca, in 1938. By the forties and the beginning of the Second World War, gospel music was a booming business, spearheaded by savvy black musician/ entrepreneurs who parlayed the passion of slave spirituals into wads of mammon.

But the vitality of black music could hardly be corraled into the church, no matter how willing and able gospel writers were to borrow from jazz and blues. A distinctly different, decidedly dark strain of music had been quietly but inexorably taking root even as the first black slaves landed in chains in Jamestown: a mirror image of Christian virtue, nurtured in secretive rebellion and blossoming forth in beautiful and evil fruit.

Not every abused and humiliated black man sought the

25

comforts of the church to soothe his vengeful spirit. Nor did every black man find in Christianity the gentle persuasions of a heavenly reward. "Our father who art in heaven," ran one work song, "White man owe me eleven and pay me seven. Thy kingdom come, thy work be done; And if I hadn't took that, I wouldn't had none."

"A few nights ago," wrote Daniel Payne, bishop of the African Methodist Episcopal Church in 1852, ". . . a runaway slave came to the house where I live for safety and succor. I asked him if he was a Christian; 'no sir,' said he, 'white man treat us so bad in Mississippi that we can't be Christians.' I began to question the existence of the Almighty," continued the good bishop, ". . . and how could I do otherwise, while slavery's cruelties were pressing and grinding my soul in the dust?"

In 1831, Nat Turner was a black preacher who knew God's Word and knew it well. And it was God, he believed, who commanded him to rise up and throw off the cruel yoke of slavery. By the time his terrifed white masters had run him to the ground and dangled him by his neck, Nat Turner had led the largest slave revolt in American history, dispatching fifty-five of the hated oppressors to the pit of Sheol. There's no record of what, if anything, he sang on his way to the hanging tree, but one doubts that it was "My Lord Delivered Daniel."

Yet it wasn't simply the manifest injustice of slavery or the gruesome ironies of the white man's pious hypocrisies that stirred trouble in the black man's breast. For what he had brought with him in the music of Africa was more than old customs and battered cultural baggage. Despite the handy similarities between river ritual and baptism, spirit possession and Holy Ghost visitation, there was much in the old ways that wouldn't mesh with the white God of Christianity. All the crowding horde of spirits that inhabited the jungles of the Gold Coast had booked passage on the slave ships, paying their fare with rhythms and chants and smoky invocations. According to one account, a certain Bishop Fisher of Calcutta, while traveling through the heart of the Dark Continent, "heard natives sing a melody so closely resembling 'Swing Low, Sweet Chariot,' that he felt he had found it in its original form."

Vodoun was what it came to be called by the descendants of the over forty separate African tribes and subtribes that were brought to the island of Haiti alone; clans and kingdoms with names like Bambarra, Fantin, Cotocolis, Mandingue, Loango. Vodoun meant "spirit" or "deity" to the Fon-speaking peoples of Dahomey. The Ga tribes called in *wong*, the Tshi tribes *bohsum*, the Yoruba *orisha*. "Vodoun permeates the land," writes Harold Courlander in his classic account *Haiti Singing*, "and, in a sense, it springs from the land. It is not a system imposed from above, but one that pushes out from below. It is a thing of the family, a rich and complex inheritance from a man's own ancestors. It is not the priests of Vodoun who control or direct its course. They, like the lowest peasant, simply move about within it and make use of its resources. Vodoun is strong, it cannot die easily, and this is one thing missionaries do not seem to understand. You cannot readily destroy something with such deep and genuine roots. . . . You can't easily annihilate a man's belief that his ancestors do not completely die, that a spirit is something more than an abstraction. Especially, you can't do these things when you propose only to substitute something else less acceptable, less meaningful in the light of the inner history of the race."

Not, according to Courlander, "a cult, nor in the limiting sense a religion, and yet . . . both and more," Vodoun is "a highly formalized and sophisticated attitude toward life . . . an explanation of all human and natural phenomenon." He catalogs over 150 Vodoun *loas*, a word that can mean either "god" or "devil." Among them: *Gede Nimbo*, aka *Baron Samedi*, guardian of the cemetery, a smoker of cigars who takes and never returns and is never satisfied; *Legba Se*, god of fertility and amorous urges, a mischief maker and seducer of women; *Nananbouclou*, loa of herbs and medicine, a grandmother loa who can teach her priest to "speak a hundred tongues at once"; *Ibo Jerouge,* the evil, red-eyed goddess who demands the sacrifice of chickens and pigs.

"You men eat your dinner, eat your pork and beans," moaned Howlin' Wolf, Willie Dixon, and a hundred blues journeymen after them in "Back Door Man," "I eat more chicken any man ever seen." Bo Diddley sang,

> I walked forty-seven miles of barbed wire, I got a
>   cobra snake for a necktie,
> I got a brand new house by the roadside, made out
>   of rattlesnake hide.
> It's got a chimney, and a smokin' stove, made from
>   a human skull.
> C'mon 'darlin', take a walk with me and tell me
>   who do you love?
>
> I died nine times on a midnight train,
> been through the fire and the cold, dark rain.
> Tell me, who do you love?
> I got a gravestone hand and a tombstone mind,
> I'm just twenty-one and I don't mind dyin'.
> Tell me, who do you love?

"Mojo hand"; "Black Cat Bones"; "John the Conqueroo." Not all of the blues were vengeful voodoo incantations, but much of the best sounded that way. The old ways lived, breathing life into swaggering barroom ballads, the boasts of beggars, and the painful pleasure of lust. The hidden faith endured to find its voice again in the blues. Ben Sidran writes, "Following Emancipation, freedom was equated with mobility, and thousands of questing Negroes took to the roads. . . . The traveling musician, who had taken on the role of truth-teller from the black Preacher, the role of trickster, or 'bad nigger' from the Devil, became the ultimate symbol of freedom."

It was pride, defiance, and the sheer bloody-minded joy of being "born under a bad sign" that gave the blues its heady appeal. To overturn centuries of humiliation, mock a fruitless hope in the hereafter of the white Jesus, to sing loud and true of the pleasures of the world, the flesh and the devil; all this, no less than the freedom to evoke the ancient magic, to call forth the loas in song to do a sinful bidding—such was the scarifying lure of a music that had nothing but its roots in common with the sanctified spirit-pleasing of gospel.

And it was the musician who stood like the reincarnated *Damballa Wedo*, most ancient of Vodoun devil/gods, plumed patron of spring and rain, holding the power of fertility and virility. Free, sexually potent, the trickster saints took on their own magic names: Peg Leg Howell, Peetie Wheatstraw, Son House, Barbecue Bob, Bo-Weavil Jackson, Jaybird Coleman, Blind Lemon Jefferson, Leadbelly, Howlin' Wolf, Muddy Waters, The Mississippi Sheiks. . . .

In January of 1951 Little Esther Phillips, "the original bad, ba-ad girl" and a discovery of Johnny Otis's (who was later to pastor his own congregation in Los Angeles), recorded a song that would neatly set the whole Afro-Christian tradition on its ear. "The Deacon Moves In" is a duet between a lascivious church elder and a young parishioner known only as Sister Pigeon. The deacon, a singer whose identity is lost in time, attempts to seduce the seemingly innocent Little Esther with the lure of long-cherished

29

symbols of Christian sanctity. There is, perhaps, no more telling example in recording history of the hair-raising schism between the sacred and profane that had occurred in music following the Civil War.

"Look out, fat deacon," Little Esther begins the jivey, swinging tune in her throaty high-pitched warble, "do you really think I'm gonna weaken?"

"Hey there, Sister Pigeon," the deacon answers, "if you really want that true religion, you better do what I say and see this thing my way."

"Your eyes are glowin'. . . ."

"That's natural, baby. . . ."

"Think I really better be a-goin'."

"You musn't flit. I am gonna make you feel the Spirit. Just give me your heart and sit upon my knee."

"Should I start prayin'?" Little Esther asks.

"No," says the deacon, "I think I'll dim the lights . . ."

The banter continues, until, at one point, Sister Pigeon threatens, "If you kiss me once again, I'm gonna stick you with this pin."

"Well," crows the deacon, "go ahead and stick me, 'cause the Deacon is movin' in."

A sizzling instrumental break follows, during which the deacon announces that "the prayer meeting is downstairs."

In the last verse, Little Esther sighs, "Got that true religion. Pass me down that gin and kiss me once again. 'Cause the deacon, the deacon is movin' in."

Sin and salvation. Jesus and the loas. Good Christians and bad niggers. Songs like "The Deacon Is Moving In" may have encapsulated the conflict, but they didn't settle it. Not then, not now, and not by a long shot.

Chapter Two

GREAT TONGUES
OF FIRE

What does all this mean? Does it not presage the
end of time?

—A. G. Jeffries, Methodist preacher

Religion is a work of art.

—Charles T. Smith, philosopher

In 1937, William R. Calaway of the American Record Corporation heard a thirty-three-year-old Tennessee country
singer by the name of Roy Claxton Acuff sing a very
strange song. Its melody was reminiscent of an ancient
British folk tune called "I'm Thinking Tonight of My Blues
Eyes," but the song Acuff sang had nothing to do with
blue eyes, or, for that matter, anything else on this earth.
The son of a Missionary Baptist minister, Acuff had

hopes of becoming a professional baseball player, but a near-fatal case of sunstroke had ruined his chances in the big leagues. In 1932 he toured east Tennessee with a medicine show, performing in blackface and singing in the plaintive, unabashedly emotional warble that would later earn him the title King of Country Music. A year later he and his band, the Tennesse Crackerjacks, were playing regularly on a Knoxville country music radio show.

It was from another Knoxville group, Charlie Swain and the Black Shirts, that Acuff first heard the song: a composition of utterly unknown origin. Acuff, who later maintained he recalled snatches of the tune from his childhood, asked Swain to write down the lyrics for him. Swain charged fifty cents for the service. Calaway recorded Acuff's strange and confounding tune, and it became not only a big country hit but a favorite among certain southern and zealous Christian sects. For almost forty years afterward, Roy Acuff has sung his song. Often he stands on the stage of the Grand Ole Opry—a program he helped to make an institution—screws up his eyes, and openly weeps as the words pour forth; words based on Jeremiah 12:9: "Mine heritage is unto me as a speckled bird, the birds round about are against her."

"Great Speckled Bird," it is generally agreed, refers to the Church, the Bride of Christ, persecuted and despised but ultimately triumphant as she is caught up in the air to meet the Son of Man at the end of time. At any rate, that's what it *seems* to signify. Jeremiah 12:9 is, in fact, one of the more obscure passages of Holy Writ, which makes the perennial appeal of Roy Acuff's song all the more inexplicably mystical.

> When He cometh descending from heaven,
> On the clouds, as He writes in His Word.
> I'll be joyfully carried to meet Him,

On the wings of that Great Speckled Bird.

In the American Deep South in the Depression year of our Lord 1936, mysticism was floating in the air like the molting plumage of the Great Speckled Bird. It haunted the red dirt hollows, hovered like swamp gas in the Cajun bayous, lingered like gray ghosts of the Great Rebellion across the played-out dominion of King Cotton: mysticism and miracles and the slaying power of the Holy Ghost and all the snake-handling, poison-gulping fevers that fall, from time to time, upon the Bride.

"Great Speckled Bird" had a certain fated charm about it, as if all the dispersed rivulets of custom and tradition and poor folk religion ran together in a moment's time to speak through Roy Claxton Acuff. It's a song that echoes a convoluted saga the likes of which had never been heard before or are likely to be heard again; a tale of men's souls tried in the sanctifying fires of righteousness and judgment; a story told in music born white-hot, like tempered steel forged from true faith.

"It is a fearful thing to fall into the hands of the living God," states the tenth chapter of Hebrews, verse 31, and you'd get no argument from John Wesley, whose quest for Christlike purity was akin to a drowning man's thirst for oxygen. At age six, in his native Epworth, England, the rectory of his minister father burned to the ground. John was the last person pulled from the flames, and for the rest of his life he considered himself set apart: "a brand plucked from the burning" by the very hand of the Almighty. In 1735 Wesley sailed for the New World—destination Georgia—with the express intent of saving both the heathen Indian and his own soul. He salvaged neither but, returning to England, finally stumbled onto Damascus Road at a meeting of Moravian Christians on Aldersgate Street in London.

From the moment, at that fateful service, that he felt his "heart strangely warmed" to his finished work in founding the Methodist Church, Wesley wrestled mightily with the promise of holiness, not in some impending dispensation on the far side of the grave but here and now and for eternity. Wesley had no interest in dry ceremonial observances of Christianity or any patience with the notion that while wandering through this vale of tears, man is perpetually victim to sin and all the consequences of his fallen nature. Christianity, if it meant anything, meant living a victorious life, free from Adam's curse. Wesley was determined to walk the talk, and he neatly summed up his resolve in a 1777 tract entitled *A Plain Account of Christian Perfection as Believed and Taught by the Reverend Mr. John Wesley*. There it was, in three syllables, for all to see: "Perfection." The word haunted the earnest acolytes of the Reverend Mr. John Wesley for the next two hundred years, creating in the process a genuine American outpost religion.

By the time Wesley settled down to a career of preaching in England, Ireland, and Scotland—demonstrating a genius for founding societies and cell groups that would eventually coagulate into Methodism—he had a firm grip on his silver-lined vision of holiness. It all came down, he claimed, to a twofold encounter with the threefold Godhead. The first experience was conversion, or justification, which offered forgiveness of sin. The second, variously termed Christian perfection, sanctification, or the second blessing, endowed the believer with perfect love toward God and man.

This notion of being Born Again was pretty radical for the time. And a pretty clear reaction against what one historian termed "a prevailing creedal rigidity, liturgical strictness and 'ironclad institutionalism' that had largely depersonalized religion." The institution in question being, of course, the creaky Church of England. Wesley's double dose of grace was "a swing toward warmth, feeling, experience and morality," a "heart religion," in Wesley's own words, which, considering what was to follow, had the distinctive ring of understatement.

Wesley's concept of a Second Blessing was fine as far as it went, and the good reverend took it as far as he could. The perfection Wesley laid claim to was the result of relentless self-examination, methodical discipline, and stringent abstinence, all with the aim of driving out the devil. This method (which led to the name Methodism) didn't sit well with either the stern Calvinists, steeped in their own divine election and doctrines of man's total depravity, or the laissez-faire rank and file of the Church of England, who got along quite well, thank you, on one blessing.

The folks who took to Methodism were, at that moment, swarming all over the virgin vastness of the New World. The startling idea of attainable perfection was proving irresistible to the poor, tired, and hungry flocking to America in the late eighteenth century. Sinless perfection was an apt goal for the boundless optimism that was fueling the westward expansion. As the Church of England became the denomination of choice among respectable colonists on the Atlantic Seaboard, dissenting sects—Presbyterians, Lutherans, Baptists, and Methodists were driven further into the forested heart of the continent, particularly the Appalachian Mountains and the Deep South. There, freed of the strictures of "creedal rigidity" and prying eyes, they cut loose with a rude, rough-hewn frontier faith that set the wilderness on fire.

Take the outrageous Cane-Ridge camp meetings in Logan County, Kentucky, in 1800. The pompous fathers of proper English Christianity would've dived beneath their goose-down comforters in holy terror. The volatile, highly emotional faith of the pioneer folk, seekers of Wes-

37

ley's "double cure," exploded in a display of godly hysteria that included dropping like dead men, jerking and twitching, barking like dogs, crawling around on all fours ("treeing the devil"), falling into trances, laughing uncontrollably, and dancing for their very lives. It was the sensation of "sancitification," the fabled Second Blessing that broke loose on the frontier like nothing anyone had seen since Pentecost, when there "came from heaven a noise like a violent, rushing wind" bringing three thousand into the fold with one fell swoop. By 1801 it seemed the Holy Spirit was crackling like heat lightning all over the South—and spreading north into areas like western New York, known at the time as "the burned over district" because revival had ravaged it so often.

Sanctification was the fuse that set off a keg of repressed religious ecstasy throughout America, and Methodism, quickly consolidating into a mainline denomination, could hardly quench the fires set by Wesley and the circuit-riding preachers sent out to spread the Word. The promise of a totally sinless life gave rise to a whole new sort of hardscrabble American Christian, unswervingly committed to a standard of absolute holiness and spawning a score of thriving Holiness sects. By the 1880s, dissident Methodists formed both "come-outism" and "crush-outism" movements against the Mother Church. The National Holiness Association was founded, but even these good brethren could hardly keep up with the wild-eyed innovations out on the edge of the ever-expanding frontier. "The Fire," a third religious experience on the far side of sancitification, was proclaimed along with the "baptism of burning love." A fourth, fifth, and even sixth blessing was announced: freedom from death was part of the new dispensation; anything, it seemed, was possible in God's perfect plan.

In an attempt to quell the fervor, Methodists began sending out "anti-Holiness squads" in the mid-1890s to undo the work of renegade preachers. It was like holding a match to a monsoon. "Brother and sisters," exhorted one Holiness preacher, "this morning I intend to explain the unexplainable, find out the undefinable, ponder over the inponderable and unscrew the unscrutable."

He, and hundreds like him, did just that, as Holiness movements grew apace with the scourge of Darwinism and the lures of liberal theology. "Dogmatic, emotional, often intolerant, anti-intellectual and tribal, the thrust of the old-time religion is . . . opposed to that of the major denominations," writes author Robert Mapes Anderson. In leaving mainline churches, Holiness followers were casting a spiritual vote against everything newfangled that was crowding the American landscape. They were out to reject, not reform society. The ills of the modern world were not social or economic injustices; they were stumbling blocks to holiness such as movies, ball games, dancing, lipstick, and booze.

And the most radical of the righteous flourished in the South. By the turn of the century, hundreds of hardcore Holiness churches championed doctrines ranging from divine healing to speaking in tongues to such outlandish concepts as the "baptism of dynamite," when believers praised God "for the blood that cleans up, the Holy Ghost that fills up, the fire that burns up and the dynamite that blows up."

In 1906 the Holiness movement reached the Western edge of the continent and, with nowhere left to go, sent up an awesome pillar of fire that could be seen around the world. It began inauspiciously with a black Baptist preacher by the name of William Joseph Seymour. Born a slave in Louisiana, stocky, disheveled, and blind in one eye, Seymour was the disciple of Charles Parham, who founded an influential Holiness offshoot in the Midwest called the Apostolic Faith, given to glossolalia and the laying on of hands. After being "saved and sanctified," Seymour made his way to Los Angeles, where he was invited to preach in the living room of the home of one Richard Asbury.

On August 9, 1906, in the midst of a prayer service, Seymour and seven others fell to the floor and began speaking in tongues, a bona fide case of being "slain in the spirit." Asbury's daughter, frightened by the supine bodies on the carpet, ran to tell the neighbors, and soon a crowd had gathered in front of the small cottage on Bonnie Brae Street. A woman began playing piano and singing in what sounded like Hebrew. Occurrences of tongues began to sweep the assembly, and the crowd grew larger, jamming the street. Seymour preached from a makeshift pulpit on the front porch, extolling the virtues of the second blessing with all its attendant manifestations of the Holy Spirit. The crowd began pressing into the house until the floor collapsed. Seymour subsequently moved the operation to an abandoned Methodist church building in a rundown industrial section of Los Angeles: 312 Azusa Street.

Thus began the most astonishing outbreak of an unfettered, over-the-top, blistering spiritual fire storm in modern times. It was the mighty wind of the Book of Acts all over again but this time cranked up to gale force. A puzzled and alarmed headline in the Los Angeles *Times* for April 18, 1906, warned,

WEIRD BABEL OF TONGUES
NEW SECT OF FANATICS IS BREAKING LOOSE
WILD SCENE LAST NIGHT ON AZUSA STREET
GURGLE OF WORDLESS TALK BY A SISTER

Babbling tongues wasn't all. Seymour, for a time at the center of the monumental revival that would continue unabated for three solid years, began his preaching at Azusa Street by issuing a press release. He'd received a vision, he wrote, in which the people of Los Angeles flocked "in a mighty stream to perdition." He warned of "awful destruction to this city unless its citizens are brought to a belief in the tenets of the new faith." The next day, April 18, San Francisco was leveled by earthquake and fire. Seymour's dire prediction was off by five hundred miles, but it didn't seem to make any difference. His followers proclaimed a "hallelujah earthquake" in the City of Angels to match the fury of the ground splitter up north. Seymour's dubious authority was subsequently swept away in a tide of religious frenzy. "In the middle of it all was 'Elder' Seymour," writes Vinson Synon, "who rarely preached and much of the time kept his head covered in an empty shoe box behind the pulpit. At times he would be seen walking through the crowds with five-and-ten-dollar bills sticking out of his hip pockets which people had crammed there unnoticed by him."

As eyewitness Frank Bartleman recounts, "In the early 'Asuza' days both heaven and hell seemed to have come to town. Men were at the breaking point. Conviction was mightily on the people. They would fly to pieces even on the street, almost without provocation. A very 'dead line' seemed to be drawn around 'Azusa Mission' by the Spirit. When men came within two or three blocks of the place they were seized with conviction."

That's not all they were seized with. Shouting, dancing, uncontrolled weeping and laughing, trances, speaking and shouting in tongues; the carnival atmosphere at Azusa Street continued day and night and, predictably, not everyone joined in the party spirit. Evangelist Ruben Torry denounced the upheaval as "the last vomit of Satan," while Bible scholar W. B. Godby characterized the revelers as "Satan's preachers, jugglers, necromancers, enchanters, magicians and all sorts of mendicants." Even Seymour's mentor Charles Parham deplored "white people imitating the unintelligent, crude negroisms of the Southland, and laying it on the Holy Ghost." The Azusa Street revival was indeed a remarkably interracial phenomenon for the times. Black, whites, Chinese, and even Jews were aglow with the sanctifying power. "The color line is washed away in the blood," was how one of the faithful described it.

When the fires of Azusa Street finally cooled, a new era in indigenous American religion had been born. "Holiness" had been transfigured into the "Pentecostal" experience, a term taken directly from that same seminal second chapter of the Acts of the Apostles, shorthand for all the hair-raising, life-changing, miracle-manifesting Holy Spirit action that had followed Wesley's modest proposal for Christian perfection. Many of those who survived the Pentecostal holocaust in Los Angeles would go on to establish entire denominations: Pentecostal Assemblies of America, Canada and the World; Pentecostal Churches of Jesus Christ, the Nazarene and God; Pentecostal Rescue Mission; and the Pentecostal Church, Inc.

Glossolalia (speaking a heavenly or ecstatic language) and xenoglossy (speaking a language unknown to the speaker), along with the laying on of hands, fervency of prayer, scripture reading and the winning of souls became the cornerstones of Pentecostalism's explosive growth following the Azusa Street conflagration. Pentecostal leaders were, overwhelmingly, young; some, like Foursquare founder Aimee Semple McPherson, were reaching the apex of their ministries while still in their twenties. They cast themselves scrupulously in the mold of first-century Christians, eschewing wealth and notoriety. Many of them lived haunted by personal tragedy and private despair.

But more important to the stunning impact of Pentecostalism than its leaders were the anxious souls it caught up and carried away by the tens and hundreds of thousands. By 1910 the revival had peaked, passing into relative obscurity, with the extravagant rise and fall of Aimee Semple McPherson notwithstanding. It suddenly returned with renewed vigor during the Great Depression. The reason was simple. Like the American Methodist and Holiness movements that prefigured it, Pentecostal Christianity belonged, by and large, to the dirt poor. And the dirt that the poor belonged to was, by and large, below the Mason-Dixon line.

In 1937, the year Roy Acuff recorded "Great Speckled Bird," one of every two Pentecostals lived in the Deep South, most of them eking out a living on dying farms throughout the Appalachian and Ozark mountains. They were tenant croppers, clans of migrant farmhands, the sons and daughters of the dissenting sects originally pushed into the sticks by more respectable religions. They were malnourished, illiterate, and backward. For generations, some had never seen another soul outside the skunk hollows they had called home. "I have gone to places," reported Pentecostal evangelist Ambrose Tomlinson, "where the people were so wild that as I entered the front door the whole family ran out the back door." Another preacher allowed that those most likely to be attracted to the rigors of the new faith were "the scum of society . . . habitual drunkards, veteran gamblers and even immoral women and infidels." If they lived in the cities, they were, according to Oklahoma minister Dan Muse, "addicted to narcotics, alcohol and slovenly living . . . broken down lawyers, doctors, common prostitutes and perverts." In short, it was the faith of losers, the disinherited and dispossessed, who found, in Pentecostalism's message and methods, a sort of promise of a kind of heaven right here on earth.

Elvis

Chapter Three

THE KING AND
THE KILLER

What a friend we have in Elvis
—The Memphis Mafia,
　　　　　　　singing around the table at Graceland

I must be a sinner. If I wasn't, I'd be a Christian.
　　　　　　　　　　　　—Jerry Lee Lewis

In 1938, with Roy Acuff's apocalyptic vision still echoing over the airwaves, Vernon and Gladys Presley's little boy, Elvis, squirmed off his mother's lap at the Sunday service of the Reverend W. Frank Smith's First Assembly of God Church in East Tupelo, Mississippi. The little towheaded three-year-old toddled down the aisle, turned, and stood before the small congregation to deliver a childish but uncanny imitation of the preacher's full-spirited singing.

As the first public performance by the King of Rock 'n' Roll, it is altogether fitting that the advent of Elvis Presley should occur at the altar of a Pentecostal church. The impact of Pentecostalism on the music of Elvis, and so on the shape and substance of rock 'n' roll itself, has been the subject of more than a little speculation. Sources most often cited as shaping Elvis's sound are, to quote *The Encyclopedia of Rock*, "gospel concerts, church singing, R & B radio shows . . . and country singers of the '40s." Which is sort of like a recipe for chocolate cake that reads, "Chocolate, flour, water, and eggs. Mix and heat." Never did a total more self-evidently surpass the sum of its parts than in the musical amalgamation that Elvis instinctively achieved. It's in the crucible of character and personal history that art is alloyed, and along with the South, the fifties, Hollywood, and maternal love, Pentecostalism formed the crucible of Elvis's singularity.

But how? Had Elvis been a well-heeled Episcopalian, a dour Lutheran, or even a Jew, what would his rock 'n' roll have sounded like? Would there even have been rock 'n' roll? The prevailing and chiefly inaccurate perception is that Elvis copped his best licks from the fire-and-brimstone Pentecostal preachers of his youth, barnstorming P. T. Barnum charismatics in the Elmer Gantry mold.

By the time the little Presley boy made his adorable if not precisely decorous debut, high-stepping, sermonizing showmen were hardly in demand among poor white Assembly of God congregations. In the mid-thirties Pentecostalism had lost much of its Azusa-spawned flamboyance. The endemic racism of southern society had severed the fabric of the movement's earlier racial harmony. And while black brethren may have been making a joyful noise, white folks wanted something a little less wild, wooly, and frighteningly unpredictable. From a religion of unrestrained and inexplicible ecstasies, Pentecostal theology in the Depression expressed the hard times and uncertain fates of the flock. Outwardly the services were subdued and somber, reflecting the crushing burdens of poverty, the increasingly forlorn hope of better times, and the social stigma of white-trash religion.

"Worship in and around Tupelo," writes Van K. Brock in *Elvis, the South, and America,* "was, generally, conservative and restrained. . . . Whether the preacher talked from a text . . . or read his sermon from a written script or from the Lesson of the Day, most white people, at least, sat attentively in their pews, dressed in their best or next best and listened solemnly, responding only in hymns or choral readings or, depending perhaps on their class, with an occasional amen, or 'that's the gospel'—and reverently rather than loudly. Some women, even a man or two, might weep silently through most of the sermon— whether for themselves, a loved one, or simply the vision of the flawless, joyful kingdom none could know for sure, and occasionally their sobs or sniffles would rise to counterpoint the peaks of oratory and emotion. Clearly there were both release and relief, but not orgiastic emotion. . . . Pentecostalism was considered the frayed edge of the fabric, a religion of last resort; and generally it was."

Yet the gifts of the Spirit were still manifest, it seemed, in those desperate times—more desperate for the Presley family, perhaps, than most. The year little Elvis mimicked the Reverend Smith in song, his father was convicted of check forging and sentenced to three years in the infamous Parchman Prison. During these and other frequent absences by Vernon Presley, Elvis was virtually raised by his doting mother, a woman susceptible to the full spectrum of backwood superstitions, prone to prophetic dreams and mystical intuitions. At the age of nine, Elvis is said to have received the baptism of tongues.

But it was at the feet of Assembly of God preachers that

47

Elvis learned the magic power of individualism. A preacher's originality was, writes Brock, "a sign of grace, and the lack of conformity to denomination was an evidence of the congregation's otherworldliness and spirituality." Pentecostalism reenforced the sense of identity that comes from a closely knit, socially intertwined group, rejected by the world and seeking release in a shared moment of transcendence. Most Pentecostal congregations in the South were small neighborhood gatherings, commonly no larger than a few dozen people. Spiritual authority was bestowed not by education, office, or institutions. It was as an anointing, a gift, directly proportional to a private, intensely personal relationship with God. Pentecostalism was, finally, a transrational release, rooted in the emotions and offering the potential for an experience that blew the mind and beggared the imagination: the genuine, life-pumping "heart religion."

The musical innovations of Pentecostalism reflected the emotional mooring of the faith and the renegade nature of the denomination. They came, in time, to be exemplified in Pentecostalism's favorite son, Elvis. "The few serious attempts to trace the origins of Elvis Presley's music," comments Charles Wolfe in his essay "Presley and the Gospel Tradition," "have traditionally focused on . . . country music as exemplified by the honky-tonk and bluegrass styles . . . and blues, as represented by the early urban styles of Big Boy Crudup, Howlin' Wolf and B. B. King." Yet blues and country are only the most obvious reference points, and even these musical styles were at one time or another incorporated into Pentecostal worship, performed in church on piano, guitar, banjo, and drum kit.

Of equal importance to these secular musical styles was the influence of gospel music, both black and white. Memphis, where Elvis grew up, had been known as a thriving center for gospel stylists since the late forties, when artists such as the Delmore Brothers and Wayne Rainey mixed sacred lyrics, blues and boogie with spectacular commercial results. The town often called the City of Churches annually hosted a national gospel quartet convention.

And The Blackwood Brothers were at the top of the heap. Since the mid-thirties, the brothers Roy, James, and Doyle Blackwood, along with Roy's son R.W., had championed the smooth, syrupy tones of the white gospel sound, a harmonic blend not unlike that of a barbershop quartet and usually dished up a cappella. Appropriately, Doyle Blackwood first learned to play music on a Russian balalaika, an instrument that would've been distinctly out of place in a Baptist or Methodist service but fit right in to the cheerful cacophony of much Pentecostal worship, with its multiinstrumental freedom of expression. In '51, after several personnel changes, the Blackwood Brothers signed with RCA and scored a major hit with "The Man Upstairs," rendering them the most popular white gospel quartet in the country.

Elvis could certainly be counted among their most devoted fans. He was a familiar face in the studio audience at WMPS, a Memphis radio station that featured a live lunch-break music show often starring the Blackwoods. In '54, after a plane crash killed two of the foursome, the group recruited booming bass singer J. D. Sumner as one replacement. Sumner recalls sneaking the young Elvis into the back of Ellis Auditorium to see the group's shows, while the Blackwoods' founder, James Blackwood, recounts the time Elvis nearly joined a fledgling quartet called the Songfellows featuring James's nephew Cecil. At eighteen, Elvis auditioned for the group but was aced out by another singer. James Blackwell: "I think Elvis was disappointed, but he still sang with the boys from time to time . . . and he would often come to our all-night gospel sings at the auditorium."

After Elvis's own career began to build steam, he finally was offered a berth with the Blackwoods. J. D. Sumner remembers the young singer's dilemma: "Elvis went to his father and said, 'Daddy, what am I going to do?' His father said, 'Well, son, you're doing all right the way you're going now, so I would just keep it up." As Charles Wolfe notes, "The fact that Presley, while starting to change the face of American music with his new rock music, would even seriously consider an invitation to join a major gospel group suggests how much gospel music counted in his musical values at the time."

One of the most revealing, and oft-repeated, incidents from the early years of Elvis's career concerns the legendary Million Dollar Quartet session surreptitiously taped by Sun Records engineer Jack Clement late in 1956. Having shaken the airwaves throughout that watershed year with an unprecedented string of hits that included "Heartbreak Hotel," "Don't Be Cruel," "Hound Dog," and "Love Me Tender," Elvis had already signed with RCA and the stardom express when he dropped by Sun Records studios to pay a call on Sam Phillips, the man widely acknowledged as the first to capture the essential Elvis on record. In the studio was Jerry Lee Lewis, hot on the scent of his own fated encounter with fame, rehearsing for an upcoming recording session. Elsewhere in the confines of Sun's cramped Union Avenue studios, Carl Perkins was previewing his latest single, "Match Box Blues," for his friend Johnny Cash. The four young singers gradually grouped around Jerry Lee's piano, where Elvis sat, picking out the intro to "Blueberry Hill." The impromptu session picked up momentum as the quartet, backed by Perkins, his brothers, and W. S. Holland, began to run through a gospel music repertoire that included such standards as "Just a Little Talk with Jesus," "I Shall Not Be Moved," "I'm With the Crowd but Oh, So Alone," "Blessed Jesus Hold

My Hand," "Farther Along," "I Hear a Sweet Voice Calling," "Keeper of the Key," and dozens of others; upward
of three hours of gospel revelry, according to Clement. A
thirty-five-minute tape of the session was located in 1978
and subsequently released as *The Million Dollar Quartet.*

The fact that the four young rock and country performers would find a mutual affinity in gospel chestnuts like
"Peace in the Valley" is hardly surprising. "I dare say that
there were never any 'infidels'—or agnostics, even—that
came in my studios," says Sam Phillips. "There was a
deep-seated feeling for God, very much so, in probably
every artist I ever worked with. Whether they knew how
to express it in any way, they showed it to me in the way
they did what they did."

That historic session with Elvis, Jerry, Johnny, and Carl
is remarkable in its exposing just how solid were the gospel
underpinnings of rock 'n' roll. The call-and-response musical banter between Elvis and Jerry Lee—with the Killer
echoing and underlining the King's vocal lead—harkens
to a Holiness preaching and singing tradition that stretches
back as far as anyone would care to go. And farther. The
often-maudlin sentiments rolling out in Elvis's marbles-in-
the-mouth delivery reflected the range of Pentecostal
truisms that Southern spirituality rested on: "You've gotta
walk that lonesome valley"; "On this Rock of Ages, I will
not be moved"; "You might have doubts and fears and
your eyes be filled with tears, but Jesus is a friend who
watches day and night." Perkins's hiccuping rockabilly
guitar fills, the gut-bucket bass line, the sheer delight the
singers took in bouncing and bending rhythms and melodies—it was gospel music wrapped with a rock 'n' roll rib-
bon and delivered with exuberant abandon. Whatever
moral invectives would later be hurled against their music
by the keepers of Christian virtue, it's obvious that on that
December day in '56, the Million Dollar Quartet saw no

sin in cloaking the spirit of gospel in the flesh of rock music.

Why should they? In an age before rock concerts represented a bloated apex in the glitzy art of showmanship, gospel performers were the flashiest, snazziest, most cut-loose and free-wheeling figures in entertainment. Elvis and his ilk may not have learned the tricks of onstage charisma in the humble white Pentecostal churches of their youth, but the later scandalous antics of the white boy rockers were unquestionably affected by the moves and mannerisms of black gospel artists plying the professional concert circuit.

In the early fifties, immensely popular black gospel attractions such as the Soul Stirrers, the Harmonizing Four, the Swan Silvertones, Pilgrim Travelers, and Dixie Hummingbirds not only stood at the cusp of the creation of rhythm & blues and doo-wop, they had perfected a kind of smoothly synchronized frenzy, a highly stylized, intense, and evocative mix of religious energy and dazzling dramatics. Dressed to the nines, with every crescendo of overcoming emotion milked for its last drop of sweat, black gospel groups worked audiences into a well-mixed froth of sanctifying power and sexual attraction. What would in time burst forth in the music of Ray Charles, Sam Cooke, James Brown, and scores of others could hardly be mistaken in Elvis's earliest live performances. Outraged arbiters of taste decrying his "spastic gyrations" and "primitive jungle-beat rhythm" recognized the origins of Elvis's raw appeal. So did Sam Phillips, who, at the time Elvis walked through his office door, was reported to be looking for a 'white boy who could sing like a nigger.'

Elvis retained his connection to gospel throughout his twenty-three year career, hiring a succession of major gospel groups as backup singers, including the Jordanaires (1956–67), the Imperials (1969–71), and the Stamps Quartet with J. D. Sumner (1972–77). In 1957, shortly after the Million Dollar Quartet did its off-the-cuff rendition, Elvis released "Peace in the Valley," a version of the Thomas Dorsey classic saturated with sonorous sentimentality. Popular reaction was so strong that RCA rushed out an extended play 45 with three more gospel standards. "Little older than five was Elvis when he started singing in church in his native deep Southland," read the liner notes, and ". . . To the fortunate folks who have known Elvis, whether as a schoolboy, movie usher, delivery man, or performer, 'Peace in the Valley' will be no surprise." Three years later he cut *His Hand in Mine*, featuring a heavily airbrushed Elvis on the cover, frill-cuffed and blue-suited, reflecting all the sacred iconography of Christian purity. The album, which still holds the record for the most weeks at the number-one spot in the United Kingdom, dished up a creamy feast of the King's favorite spirituals: "Joshua Fought The Battle of Jericho," "I'm Gonna Walk Dem Golden Stairs," "Working on a Building." It was matched for Sunday morning sanctity by the 1967 *How Great Thou Art*, a million-seller highlighting songs such as "In the Garden" and "Farther Along," first popularized by Billy Graham singer George Beverly Shea. Five years later, *He Touched Me* plowed the same field with reverent treatments of "Amazing Grace" and Kris Kristofferson's "Why Me, Lord."

But Elvis's explicitly gospel output, scant enough over the course of thirty-seven albums, ultimately revealed little if anything of the spiritual energies unleashed in the best of his purely rock 'n' roll music. Sanctimonious renderings of "Where No One Stands Alone" may have helped Elvis to find peace in the very dark valley of his own fame, but the homogenized sentiment of most of these beloved gospel chestnuts only reveals how far he was from understanding the source of his own inspiration.

Singer Johnny Rivers, (as quoted by Jerry Hopkins in *Elvis: The Final Years*) recalls, "One of his idols when he was young was a man named Jake Hess, who was the lead singer for the Statesmen Quartet. If you'll listen to some of their recordings, you'll hear some of that style that is now Elvis Presley's style, especially in his ballad singing style. He was playing some of their records one day and he said, 'Now you know where I got my style from. Caught—a hundred million records too late.'"

"He was raised listening to gospel music," says J. D. Sumner, "and was raised in the Pentecostal church. . . . He got his beat from the music of the Pentecostal church. He took white gospel, black gospel, and country and that was where his music came from."

Maybe. He may certainly have cadged his style from the church and from professional gospel crooners, but it's hard to believe that an artist whose music galvanized so many millions was simply and finally the opportunistic end result of an amalgamation of genres, a young man who stole the best from Jake Hess and a dozen other unheralded innovators. Something lies far beyond all the academic autopsies of Elvis Presley's power, and it's the power of Pentecostalism on Elvis Presley's soul.

The unbearable tension of a life lived in the shadow of sinless perfection found its ecstatic release in the abandonment of rock 'n' roll, the dark, bastard offspring of all charismatic frenzy. It wasn't the style but the substance of Elvis that bore the bruises of consuming contradictions between an ideal of holiness and a life of travail. It wasn't the form so much as the content of his music that was hammered out on the stumbling block of the double cure. To the very end Elvis carried with him the simple convictions and sad suppositions of Pentecostalism.

The values of Pentecostalism, as embodied in Elvis, were freely cribbed for the resulting, and infamous, rock 'n' roll life-style. The rebel as the "true original"; the fervent following of hip cognoscenti; the certain, mercurial "something" born from the soul that defines real rock and its heroes; and, of course, the lure of frenzied liberation from the fatally ordinary—it all became, in time, codified as the World According to Rock.

But even these connections are more cosmetic than real. The actual, tingling touch points lay even deeper, beyond the apparent parallels of old-time religion and rock culture. For Elvis, the dynamic tensions and horrifying paradoxes that fueled Pentecostalism could be expressed most succinctly, evoked most clearly, through music. Van K. Brock: "[The] people . . . in his ballads usually do not overcome or transcend: they are characteristically down and out in their loves or their lives and struggling just to make it through, to the next town, a job, a woman. They are always Trying to Get to You. . . . They believe, pray, love and dream their way; and though they never get through, the belief in the power of the wish-fulfilling magic of the right emotion sustains and gives them hope in their otherwise unyielding circumstances. The assertion is persistent enough in Presley's lyrics, and perhaps in popular music generally, to be a coherent and insistent epistemology that excludes and even denies the value of rational analysis and the critical intellect."

That's saying a mouthful, especially the part about denying "rational analysis and critical intellect." Elvis had the simple, astounding ability to express, aside from sexual hunger, teenage frustrations and maudlin sentimentality, something of the horrendous, exhilarating spiritual energies unleashed in the Methodist/Holiness/Pentecostal American epic. Like no other religious endeavor, the quest for perfection brings heaven and hell into sparking, radioactive proximity. The conviction—sown by Wesley and reaped on Azusa Street—that mortal humans can Call It

Down from Above, that justification and sanctification lead to a permanent vacation of perfect sinlessness, has the proven power to drive men past distraction to madness and then, perhaps, to bliss.

Elvis never made it that far, but he never forgot where he started. Not only in his music but in his private life Pentecostalism cast its shadow. The role of preacher was one he could step into at will; he was sometimes called the evangelist by the circle of good old boys he kept in constant attendance. He returned the compliment by calling them the disciples, regaling them with religious insights that, more often than not, were strange permutations of Christian dogma. He believed, for instance, that Jesus slept with his female followers. It was all in line with the Pentecostal belief that divine revelation was an intensely personal matter, a mystical communication with the Almighty. "Each person regarded himself as the final authority between heaven and earth," writes one scholar. It's an authority, "based on ever more profound knowledge and ever more glorious experiences of salvation."

Elvis's notion of divine appointment was supported by the worship and adulation of his fans. Journalist Patsy Hammontree recounts the experience of one Maryland housewife who drove several hundred miles to an Elvis concert for the chance to press a memento into his palm. When the King received her offering, patting her hand on the way to his motel room, she burst into tears. "I have had only one other emotional experience to equal this one," she told Hammontree, "and that was when I gave birth to my children. . . . The fact is, I don't think there was any other person other than Christ himself who could bring about that reaction from a touch of the hand. The warmth was unreal. There was so much love being transmitted from him that it was actually heavenly."

With love or orgasmic abandon, Elvis's adoring millions—screaming, tearing out their hair, shaking and heaving and shuddering—were acting out the Pentecostal epiphanies that made up the substance of the singer's religious life. "I can't help it," he told one interviewer on the subject of his provocative stage antics. "I have to move around. I can't stand still. I've tried it, and I can't do it." When the Spirit moves, men are helpless to resist.

> I had played a few bars of 'Drinking Wine Spo-Dee-O-Dee' . . . when this strange feeling came over me. I was able to do runs on that piano I hadn't been able to do before. It seemed like a force beyond me had gripped and charged my body. My fingers literally flew over the keys. . . . For the first time in my life I sensed what it felt like to be anointed by the devil. I don't know any way to describe it. It was unlike anything I had experienced in my life. I knew it wasn't from God.

So writes Jimmy Lee Swaggart in his autobiography *To Cross a River*. If anyone is going to know the difference between the anointing of God and the seductive counterfeits of Beelzebub, it is Jimmy Swaggart, world-renowned evangelist, fire-breathing bolt hurler, sworn enemy of rock 'n' roll, and supporting player in the most awesome Faustian battle royale in the annals of American music. For Jimmy Lee Swaggart is kith and kin to Jerry Lee Lewis, and Jerry Lee Lewis is living proof that no one walks through the purifying flames of God's holy wrath unscathed.

If Pentecostalism was folded into the substance of Elvis's music, like eggs folded into pancake batter, then it can only be said to have been vengefully curdled by the pounding piano riffs of Jerry Lee. The double cure was sweet to the tongue and sour in the stomach of this most hounded and haunted of rock 'n' roll's early heroes. His music embodied what Jim Miller would call "the ungodly miscegenation Presley and Little Richard only hinted at," and his life and times read like the mordant schemings of a demented novelist, caring nothing for the happiness of his characters so long as they bear the weight of heavy-handed symbolism.

Jerry Lee Lewis stands proud as a genuine American archetype; a modern Ahab, Young Goodman Brown in a leopard-skin jacket, Willie Stark, Asa Hawks, and Dean Moriarty. In 1941, when Elmo and Mamie Lewis's firstborn son was only six years old, W. J. Cash wrote this idealized depiction of Southern manhood in *The Mind of the South*:

> To stand on his head in a bar, to toss down a pint of raw whiskey at a gulp, to fiddle and dance all night, to bite off the nose or gouge out the eye of a favorite enemy, to fight harder and love harder than the next man . . . to lie on his back for days and weeks, storing power as the air he breathed stores power under the sun of August, and then to explode, as that air explodes in a thunderstorm, in a violent outburst of emotion—in such a fashion he would make his life not only tolerable but infinitely sweet.

And further:

> If he was a hedonist, and however paradoxical it may sound, he was also likely to be a Puritan. The sense of sin, if obscured, continued to move darkly in him at every time. . . . The world he knew, that hot sting of the sun in his blood, the sidelong glance of the all-complaisant Negro

woman—all these impelled him irresistibly to joy. But even as he danced, and even though he sloughed off all formal religion, his thoughts were on the piper and his fee.

With a prophetic flourish, Wilbur Cash had announced the Advent of Jerry Lee Lewis.

Ferriday, Louisiana, is hard on the banks of the Mississippi in Concordia Parish. In the mid-thirties it boasted a singular citizen of substance, a man of shrewd instinct and forceful character, a landowner and patriarch of a sprawling, inbred clan, many of whom had worked, at one time or another, in his profitable bootlegging business. His name was Lee Calhoun, and in his honor two nephews, Jerry Lee and Jimmy Lee, were christened.

Among the legends that hover around Lee Calhoun is one that tells of his decisive encounter with a mother and daughter from Laurel, Mississippi, by the name of Sumrall. One day in the spring of 1936, Lee happened upon Mother Sumrall and Leona in a vacant lot on the corner of Texas Avenue and Eighth Street in Ferriday. He pulled over his pickup truck and watched awhile, his curiosity peaked as the two dusty, dour women pulled weeds from the lot. Lee wanted to know why, and Mother Sumrall, with a flinty light sparking in her eyes, told him. God had called them into the heart of Lee Calhoun's turf to plant a church, she declared, an Assembly of God church that would preach the pure doctrine espoused by that flourishing Pentecostal offshoot. The Assembly of God was founded in 1914 over in Hot Springs, Arkansas, in convocation at the old Grand Opera House on Central Avenue, and now, with 150,000 on-fire converts, was one of the largest Holiness sects in the South.

Assembly of God theology maintained the sinfulness of such things as public swimming, life insurance, and women wearing trousers and had been built around a new twist on sanctification called "the Finished Work" (asserting that Christ had supplied all that was needed for perfection by His death). But none of that really interested Lee Calhoun. The truth is, no one's really sure why Lee tarried at Texas and Eighth that fine spring day, listening to the impassioned certitudes of Mother Sumrall and Leona. Perhaps, as music scholar Stephen Tucker suggests, he sensed a kindred entrepreneurial spirit. Perhaps God told Lee something, too. Or perhaps it was when Mamie Lewis received the Call and began holding prayer meetings in Lee's living room that the old man became convinced a permanent site was needed. All anyone can say for certain is that five years later, a little white Assembly of God church stood at that corner, a church whose construction Lee Calhoun had personally financed with the money brewed in his backwood stills.

In the summer of 1943, the Lewises and the Swaggarts and the Gilleys, another branch of Lee Calhoun's sprawling extended family (with still another nephew, Mickey), attended the church to hear a traveling evangelist named J. M. Cason. It was on that occasion that Jerry Lee's mama, his aunt Minnie Bell, his uncle Willie Leon, and a number of others were seized by the Holy Spirit to begin singing, dancing, and praising God in unknown tongues. Not long afterward, Jimmy Lee Swaggart received his own gift of glossolalia. Nick Toches, in *Hellfire*, a visionary biodrama of Jerry Lee Lewis, claims that the future evangelist "spoke very little English for days after that. His mother sent him to the post office for a three-cent stamp. Jimmy Lee placed a nickel on the counter and tried to tell the man what he wanted, but it wouldn't come out in English, only the unknown tongue, and he had to go home without the stamp."

Something was sweeping over Jerry Lee Lewis as well,

but it wasn't the language of angels. When he was eight, his parents had trucked home an old upright Starck piano for their little boy, and it wasn't long before he was able to pick out his first song, "Silent Night," played, according to legend, boogie-woogie style. "He just had the knack," recalled cousin Carl Glasscock to Nick Toches. ". . . He knew the boogie." He had, in other words, what Jimmy Lee would come to call "the anointing of the devil," and it didn't seem to faze him in the least. Not then, anyway, in those precocious preteen years. Two of his favorite early numbers were raw-and-raucous boogie-woogie hits, "Down the Road Apiece" and "House of Blue Lights," as well as tuneful favorites by Jimmy Rodgers, Al Jolson, and Gene Autry that he heard on his folks' Victrola. By 1947 Elmo had bought a radio, and his blond, big-eared son spent hours listening to dance-music shows on WWL out of New Orleans, "The Grand Ole Opry" in Nashville, and, in 1948, "The Louisiana Hayride," featuring the frightful genius of Hank Williams.

Two more cornerstone influences completed Jerry Lee's musical apprenticeship. Brother Janway was, according to Jerry Lee's child bride, Myra Lewis, "the best preachin' piano player in those parts." A Pentecostal circuit rider, Janway "pounded a heavy bass line with his left hand, hammered out simple melodies with the right and flipped through the Testament at the same time." Jimmy Swaggart had, according to Myra, found his role model. Like his cousin, a prodigiously promising musician, Jimmy "prayed that the Holy Spirit would fill him with the special gift that would enable him to play like Brother Janway and move congregations to new heights of religious ecstasy. He bargained that in exchange for that ability, his talent would never be used for material gain except in service to the Lord. 'And if I ever go back on my promise, Lord, you can paralyze my fingers.'"

The Lord never did wither Jimmy's digits, even when, around the age of thirteen, he took to stealing away at night with Jerry Lee to hear the devil's music at Haney's Big House, across the tracks in the Chocolate Quarters of Ferriday. Haney's was a showcase for some of the most phenomenal fledgling black talent of the era: ivory pounders like Sunnyland Slim, Big Maceo, and Piano Red; dance bands with a booming beat like Roy Milton and His Solid Senders and such fast-emerging young stars as Ray Charles, B. B. King, Muddy Waters, and Bobby Bland. "Man," says Jerry Lee in *Hellfire*, "those old black cats come through in them old buses, feet stickin' out the windows, eatin' sardines. But I tell you, they could really play some music—that's a guaranteed fact."

Jerry Lee was starting to play some kind of music, too, hovering there between paradise and Sheol, striking people in church and at political meetings, business openings, and local talent shows with a thunderous awe over his irresistible, two-fisted style. He was quickly becoming the talk of the town, and in his early teens he was playing across the river in Natchez roadhouse dives like the Wagon Wheel and the Blue Cat and had his own fifteen-minute radio show on WNAT.

The Texas Street Assembly of God made good use of the boy's burgeoning talents as well, setting aside, for the moment, questions of divine and infernal anointings. Jimmy Lee could offer up a serviceable enough hymn, but it was Jerry Lee who packed 'em in and turned up the spiritual thermostat. Eventually he was recruited by traveling evangelists to rouse Ferriday's faithful at tent revivals.

It was clear enough that Jerry Lee didn't care much where he played, as long as he could cut loose and raise the roof. For Jimmy Lee, life was laid out differently. Shortly after feeling the awful pull of the fallen angel spurring him on to a dizzying rendition of "Drinking Wine Spo-Dee-O-Dee," Jimmy Lee made good his earnest promise to God. He stopped going to Haney's; he stopped roaming the Ferriday streets after dark, shoplifting from Vogt's Drugstore or the Ellis Five-and-Dime. And most of all he stopped playing the boogie. Or did he? Rockabilly historian Art Fein recently ventured a guess that an obscure singer named Jimmy Stringer, fronting a band named the Sabres on a one-off single for Gala Records circa '57 called "Hot Rod Kelly" was, in fact, Jimmy Swaggart, having one last fling with the ungodly sound that had transformed his cousin into an international sensation.

"The cousins," according to Myra Lewis, "reached a fundamental division over the concept of talent and its uses and applications: Jimmy claimed that God-given talents were for the glory of God; Jerry was of the opinion that God-given talents were for the glory of the talented. Jimmy played piano only in church; Jerry, for anyone standing still long enough to listen."

By 1950 more than a few folk were stopping to listen. The Killer, a nickname Jerry had acquired in school by admirers of his pumping piano style, continued to alternate between church and the shadow world of roadhouses and nightclubs. The strange, divided life plagued Jerry Lee. It was hard, after all, to shake the lessons of Pentecostalism he had learned at his mama's knee. "The more the music took hold," writes Toches, "the more he suffered, until it got to where he felt the good and the bad, the Holy Spirit and the Demon, so crowding his lungs with their battle that it was hard to breathe. . . ." Late that year Jerry Lee succumbed to good and enrolled at the Southwestern Bible Institute in Waxahachie, Texas, with the express intent of following his cousin Jimmy into the ministry.

The passion lasted for three months, with Jerry Lee

sneaking off campus at night to hitchike to Dallas thirty miles away, lingering in nightclubs, and tasting the wild life of that wide-open town. His frenzied, double-time rendering of "My God Is Real" during the school's chapel service earned him the ire of the pastor; he lit back to Ferriday, and in the summer of '51 married one Dorothy Barton.

But marriage did nothing to quell the cruel spirits picking and nudging at him. The sanctified life still called out to Jerry Lee, and he commenced preaching to the family from the pinewood mantel. Occasionally he even exhorted the congregation at the Church of God on Mississippi Avenue at the invitation of the minister, and all agreed, he spoke a fine sermon. In 1955 he toured Louisiana with yet another cousin, David Beatty, who was warming up for a career as a full-time Pentecostal evangelist.

But Jerry Lee Lewis eventually stopped revealing the gospel to his kin and to the congregation at the Church of God and to the good Christians of Louisiana. His marriage failed, and he wandered aimlessly through honky-tonk havens in Monroe and New Orleans and anywhere else with a piano, a bar and a crowd of people looking for nothing good. He trekked to Shreveport to audition for "The Louisiana Hayride," to Nashville, where he played in the Musician's Hideaway on Commerce Street until the place was busted, and then home again to his second wife, Jane, and his burning, racking guilt. "He was tortured," said Johnny Littlejohn, who played drums behind Jerry Lee. "He was torn between music and that Assembly of God. He'd get onto that thing about God and Mammon, get on that preacher kick. . . . He'd tell me he was gonna be a preacher. 'I ain't gonna play in no more clubs. I'm gonna live for the Lord,' he'd say."

Finally, in the watershed year of '57, he journeyed to Memphis, to Union Avenue, Sam Phillips, and Sun Records. There he recorded a song he'd written called "End of the Road," and later another, called "Whole Lotta Shakin' Goin' On." He cut the tune in the spring of that year, and by the summer it had sold one hundred thousand copies. He toured far and wide singing his hit and tossing his wavy blond hair and harboring his Pentecostal fury, all for a thousand dollars a night.

By 1957, and the release of his second huge hit "Great Balls of Fire," he had become a contender to Elvis's rock 'n' roll throne. But success hardly freed him from thoughts of the piper and the fee that would one day come due. An accidental recording of the historic magnitude of the Million Dollar Quartet reveals how Jerry Lee's redneck religion gnawed away at him even as fame flashed before his eyes.

The occasion was the very session that yielded "Great Balls of Fire," a song whose references to shaken nerves, rattled brains, and broken wills sounded suspiciously like a raging Holiness attack. In attendance were Jerry Lee, Sam Phillips, engineer Jack Clement, bassist Billy Lee Riley, and drummer James Van Eaton. There was drinking that night, and between one of the takes, Jerry Lee, shuddering with conviction, spelled out the abode of lost souls. Clement caught the conversation on tape.

"H-E-L-L!" Jerry Lee proclaimed.

"I don't believe this," sighed Phillips.

"It says make merry with the joy of God only," spouted Jerry Lee, convulsively. "But when it comes to worldly music, rock 'n' roll . . ."

"Pluck it out!" shouted Billy Lee Riley gleefully.

"You have done brought yourself into the world, and you're in the world, and you're still a sinner. You're a sinner and unless you be saved and borned again and made as a little child and walk before God and be holy . . . and, brother, I mean you got to be so pure! No sin shall enter there . . . no sin! For it says no sin. It doesn't say a little bit; it says no sin shall enter there. Brother, not one little bit. You got to walk and talk with God to go to heaven. You got to be so good!"

"Hallelujah," Riley snidely interjected.

"All right," Phillips responded, the voice of reason. "Now look, Jerry, religious conviction doesn't mean anything resembling extremism. All right. Do you mean to tell me that you're gonna take the Bible, that you're gonna take God's word, and that you're gonna revolutionize the whole universe?"

"Right!" Jerry Lee shouted.

The exchange continued, going nowhere fast, with the musicians periodically pleading to just get on with the session. At last, Jerry Lee was unable to endure any more of Phillip's vacillations.

"You can have a kind heart," Phillips tells the rock 'n' roll star. "You can save souls!"

"How can the devil save souls," screams Jerry Lee. "What are you talkin' about? Man, I got the devil in me. If I didn't have, I'd be a Christian!"

Jerry Lee Lewis knew who he was, and if he didn't exactly know the price he would pay to possess the things that this world laid out before him in tempting array, he knew at least that they would cost him dearly. Jimmy Lee Swaggart knew it also. At "the pinnacle of his success," writes Swaggart, Jerry Lee came to see his cousin preach in Ferriday and became "deeply affected by the Holy Spirit. . . . His face turned ashen and he gripped the pew in front of him so tightly his knuckles turned white, shaking as he wept and sobbed." Others responded to the altar call that day but not Jerry Lee. Despite the stirring Jimmy had set off in his breast, the Killer "would not yield to the Holy Spirit's bidding."

The public and private tragedies of Jerry Lee Lewis in

the years following his heady early success could only have borne out his terrifying conviction that, as he again insisted as late as 1979, he was indeed "a sinner," who would one day "reckon with the chilling hands of death." The scandal surrounding his marriage to Myra Lewis, his thirteen-year-old cousin, effectively shipwrecked his career by May of 1958. On Easter Day, 1962, the couple's first son, Steve Allen Lewis, drowned in a pool at the age of three.

"Jesus died for the sins of all mankind so that we might be saved," Jerry Lee told Sam Phillips's brother Jud at the wake. "So that we'd learn the error of our way, repent, and follow Him. Stevie died on Easter Sunday. Stevie died for my sins so that I might be saved."

"Don't it seem a mite cruel," Jud Phillips ventured, "for God to take a baby 'cause his daddy done wrong?"

"Nossir," insisted Jerry Lee, "not if you've studied the Bible like I done—'Shall I give my firstborn for my transgressions, the fruit of my body for the sin of my soul?' it says."

"You ain't gotta be a saint though," Jud responded. "An you're not a bad man."

Jerry Lee just shook his head. "You gotta be good," he said. "You gotta be so good; you gotta be so pure. I don't expect you to understand. Your brother didn't."

Good, pure, and holy. Justified, sanctified, and washed in the blood. For Jerry Lee Lewis, errant son of Pentecostalism, Christianity was not the faith of the set-free, of the sinner saved by grace, or the wretch at the Rock of Ages. It was, instead, a deep, demanding law unto itself; an implacable judge, a separator of wheat from chaff and goats from God's lambs. It was the certain doom of damnation that Jerry Lee clung to, the central tenet of his religion and the mighty engine of his music. Robert Palmer: "Jerry Lee Lewis knew from the very first that he was going to hell for playing rock and roll, and he went ahead and rocked anyway." Jim Miller: "What makes Jerry Lee Lewis great is . . . the tension in his persona between worldly sin and salvation, a battle in which sin seems destined inevitably to win."

Sin, and with it death and suffering and all the confounding tragedies that haunt those bereft of God's protection. By the mid-sixties Jerry Lee had sunk deep into his self-appointed destiny. Addicted to drugs, drowning in liquor, obsessed with guns and fast cars, he was frequently arrested, constantly in trouble with the IRS, and relentlessly pursued by the hound of hell. The substantial sums of money he earned, first as a rock pioneer, and later in a successful country career, were recklessly squandered. His marriage to Myra crumbled, and Lee Calhoun passed on to the reward reserved for a man Jimmy Swaggart would later call 'vile, vulgar and profane." In 1970, at the age of thirty-five, Jerry Lee recommitted his life to Jesus Christ. He announced he would no longer play in nightclubs. "I've made my stand for God," he said. "I went back to the church and I got myself saved, and the Lord forgave my sins and wiped 'em away. . . . I believe God will give me wisdom enough to make this decision. I'll just pray and see what happens." Jerry Lee figured he'd finally had enough.

He hadn't. "I meant it when I said it," he confessed later, "and I was going good there for a while. . . . I just couldn't keep it up." The day after Easter 1971, his mother, Mamie, died. Six months later he was sued by a woman who claimed that he physically assaulted her in a Memphis nightclub. In the same week, he married a twenty-nine-year old Memphis divorcée only to divorce her in two weeks. Two years later he buried his second son, Jerry Lee Lewis, Jr., his neck broken in a fatal crash in a jeep his father had bought for him for his nineteenth birthday. Three weeks later Jerry Lee's fourth wife filed for divorce, claiming cruel and inhuman treatment. In 1976, in a famous incident, he was arrested for brandishing a gun outside the gates of Graceland and disturbing the sleep of Elvis Presley. A year later, on the occasion of Elvis's death, he was asked for his reaction.

"I was glad," he said. "Just another one out of the way. . . . You expect me to sit here and lie about something? Look, we've only got one life to live. We don't have the promise of the next breath." In 1981 he was rushed to the hospital for massive stomach surgery and came close to dying.

He didn't. "I was raised in the Assemblies of God church and taught to believe in the church and, even more so, the Bible," Jerry Lee Lewis told journalist John Pugh in 1974. "You're supposed to believe in the worth and dignity of every human being, and look for every person's good points." Yet the one person in whose worth and dignity Jerry Lee never seemed able to believe was his own. "God is no respecter of persons," says the Bible (Acts 10:34), but it was Pentecostalism that laid the value of human worth at the altar of perfection, and it was there that a man learned to love or hate himself.

Whatever Jerry Lee Lewis, Elvis Presley, and all the other Deep Southern sons of Pentecostalism were taught to believe, the lessons of their lives would prove far more exacting and punitive. The double cure could rip a man apart as readily as heal him and set him to howling and shouting and singing like his life depended on it. Theologian John Stevens Kerr put it like this in *The Fire Flares Anew*: "Cradled in ignorance, raised in an outrageously permissive nursery, sowing its adolescent wild oats in scandalous behavior, and picking up twenty million adherents in the bargain . . ." He was referring to Pentecostalism, but it might as well have been rock 'n' roll.

Little Richard

Chapter Four

CAN I GET A WITNESS?

If you dig one ditch you better dig two.
The trap you set just may be for you.

— Black gospel song

The greatest artist was Jesus, and the rest of us can
only imitate His perfect suffering.

— Marvin Gaye

April 4, 1968: The day Martin Luther King was gunned
down on the balcony of a Memphis motel. It seemed, for
many, the beginning of the end. A country choking on
the bile of racism would now, inevitably, convulse in violence and hatred. King's assassination was the cue for
seething black masses to take to the streets. America trem-
bled on the brink of self-destruction.

For eleven days riots swept the cities, with looting and

burning and shoot-to-kill orders. In Boston, city fathers fretted anxiously about an upcoming performance at the Boston Gardens by the popularly acclaimed Godfather of Soul, James Brown. Would Brown's urgent, hypnotic rhythm & blues incite the crowd to rage and revenge? Would canceling the show bring a worse cataclysm down on their heads?

No one remembers exactly whose bright idea it was, but no one denies it was a stroke of desperate genius. Why not air James Brown—the hardest-working man in show business, Mr. "Please, Please, Please" himself—live and in person that evening over the local public television affiliate? Blacks who would otherwise be inclined to roam the streets looking for white throats to slit might just be persuaded to stay home and watch the performer who, five months later, would score with a churning anthem called "Say It Loud, I'm Black and I'm Proud."

A videotape of that evening, bootlegged and passed down through the years from hand to hand like some precious splinter of the true cross, is an astonishing musical artifact. It captures a ritual of mystical intensity, spiraling from one feverish crescendo to another as spasms of true belief surge up the spine. The Master is at work.

Shot in black and white with two cameras—positioned stage right and from deep within the hall—the film is murky and indistinct with a clandestine feel to it, as if the video crews were in hiding, fearful for their lives. The stage lights are harsh, the shadows sharp and long. The only area that is free of the crush of audience and musicians is a narrow strip along the apron of the stage. It's here that Brother James, impeccably turned out in a tight sharkskin suit and turtleneck, struts and poses and pounces. For nearly two hours he is the complete and demanding center of attention. In one incredible, twenty-minute-plus set piece built around his 1967 smash "There

Was a Time" he does the Mashed Potato, The Jerk, The Camel Walk, The Bugaloo, The James Brown, and, finally, in a jaw-dropping climax, The Monster. To the relentless groove laid down by the Famous Flames, he shudders and lurches across the stage in perfect and fluid time, a black Frankenstein hooked to a rhythm machine. "There was a day," he moans, "there was a time, when I used to dance. There was a time when I used to prance. But dig me now, don't worry 'bout later. . . . Everybody relax, and watch me work." No one in the surging crowd seemed worried about anything except the remote chance that somehow the music might come to an end.

It does in fact end late that night, the tape running out or the cameramen running away. The crowd breaks up, spreading out onto streets shuddering with retribution. Time prances on.

By the mid-fifties, currents of showmanship and sanctification in black American culture were rapidly converging. Whether the glory-bound black pentecostal preacher was an archetype for James Brown (and every other conked and sweating rhythm & blues hero), or whether it was, in fact, the other way around hardly seems to matter. They were two sides of the same Janus-faced coin.

And it was a coin minted in the same blazing heat of contradiction that had forged Jerry Lee and Elvis. If the birth of soul music seems a process less fraught with paradox than that of rock 'n' roll, it's only because, for blacks, believing was a way of life and the fulsome, exuberant expression of that belief a racial heritage. But the indivisible rift between spirit and flesh would exact the same demanding price on some of the most gifted black artists of the era.

It was an era ushered in with the twilight of Gospel's Golden Age. The years preceding the Second World War

73

saw explosive growth in the ranks of professional gospel singers and the mushroom proliferation of independent record labels to serve a robust market. The period was marked by the dominance of the "quartet," a catch-all category that defined any gospel group regardless of the number of vocalists. The Kings of Harmony, the Five Blind Boys of Mississippi, the Golden Gate Quartet, the Four Great Wonders, and dozens of other all-male aggregates had perfected a smoothly harmonic backing against which was set an overpowering lead vocal; it came to be known as "house wrecking" after its effect on a full house of on-fire believers. An extraordinary number of the most successful housewreckers hailed from Jefferson County, Alabama, in and around the towns of Birmingham, Bessemer, and Fairfield, under the tutelage of R. C. Foster, a gospel entrepreneur in the Thomas Dorsey mold. The Tidewater region of Virginia, for reasons less explicable, also yielded a number of polished quartets: among them, the Norfolk Jubilee Quartet, the Silver Leaf Quartette, and the Pearly Gates of Suffolk.

By the late forties and early fifties, legendary gospel groups such as the Dixie Hummingbirds, the Swan Silvertones (featuring falsetto master Claude Jeter) and the Sensational Nightingales (with roaring lead vocalist Julius Cheeks) both made their mark on white rockers. Their rhythm & blues counterparts were such popular mainstream acts as the Inkspots, the Robins, the Ravens, and, perhaps the best of them all, the Dominoes, a group boasting, at various times, the bombastic glory of Clyde Mc-Phatter and the keening pathos of Jackie Wilson. The sophisticated musical melodrama of the Swan Silvertones or the Spirit of Memphis Quartet was unerringly reflected in the debonair warbling of the Inkspots or the Orioles, while the housewrecking hard gospel of the Nightingales or the Five Blind Boys of Mississippi was echoed in vocal acrobatics of McPhatter, and, subsequently, in countless r & b ravers including James Brown. In 1952, for example, McPhatter and the Dominoes cut the blistering "Have Mercy, Baby," a quick-tempo pulse pounder that simply substituted the word "baby" for "Lord." It was a hit-making formula that was to be repeated countless times.

The simple, and oft-stated, fact was, r & b had become a popular and lucrative new musical form by stealing gospel's best licks. But was it really larceny? "We have a lot of rock and roll singers out in the audience," gospel thrush Inez Andrews once told the New York *Times*. "They come purposely to see what they can learn—or what they can steal. . . . Rock and roll singers steal even worse than gospel singers. Because we had something to steal from the very beginning, while they had nothing." Maybe, yet in the very beginning it was all gospel, and there was hardly a hopeful singer who hadn't dedicated his or her vocal chords to the Lord.

A quick glance backward at the roots of black music's best-known and most successful artists tells the tale. Before he laid the groundwork for rock 'n' roll lead guitar and the teen anthem, Chuck Berry learned how to sing in a Saint Louis church choir. The best-known hits of Ray Charles were wild and worldly reworkings of gospel standards, including "I Got a Woman," "Halleujah, I Love Her So," "I Want to Know," "Talkin' 'Bout You," and "Yes, Indeed." Guitar slinger Bo Diddley's earliest musical influences were the classical violin lessons he took and the Sunday afternoons he spent at the neighborhood Baptist church. Aretha Franklin was the featured soloist in her father's Detroit church. The Isley Brothers were originally a gospel trio backing their piano-playing mother. Before they formed the Impressions, Curtis Mayfield and Jerry Butler sang in a church choir led by Curtis's grandmother. Lou Rawls was a member of the Pilgrim Travelers gospel group. The first folks to hear the haunting voice of Otis Redding were members of the local congregation in Dawson, Georgia, where he regularly sang. Dionne Warwick first sang in her family gospel group, the popular Drinkard Singers. It wasn't that long ago that Stevie Wonder stopped by a church in Gary, Indiana, to harmonize with his friend Deniece Williams and share their common gospel background. Guitarist/vocalist Bobby Womack and his four brothers sang in numerous Cleveland churches as a gospel group, while the scandalous Teddy Pendergrass hailed from a deeply religious Philadelphia family and was singing in choir while still in knee pants. The Pointer Sisters jumped to a different tune in their youth. Choir singers in an Oakland church, their fundamentalist upbringing forbade any form of secular music. When Donna Summer announced her Born Again status in the early eighties, the sultry Bad Girl of disco was coming full circle. She was one of six children in a devoutly Christian Boston brood. The same is true for Al Green, one of the most influential voices in seventies' soul. His musical apprenticeship was served in yet another family gospel group, the Greene Brothers of Forest City, Arkansas. He is now an ordained preacher with his own flock, devoting only his spare time to singing, and then only for the Lord.

The list goes on. There's hardly a group in the Motown, Stax, or Philly International staples who did not have at least one member of gospel origins. Countless r & b, soul, and even funk hits were endlessly inventive reworkings of gospel riffs. In reams of liner note copy, artists thank God, Jesus, or the Church as often as their producers, arrangers, and fans. R & b and rock didn't steal from Mother Gospel. They were, rather, her kids—sprung full-blown and stamped with an indelible genetic code.

"This is a church that defends its children like a lioness," writes Viv Broughton in *Black Gospel*. "The fellowships of young people are clutched tight to the bosom of Abraham, schooled in the Baptist or Pentecostal mystique, subject to strict disciplines over dress and behavior. It's rarely brutal or unlovely though and most who grew up under its brooding tutelage turn wistful at old memories."

Perhaps it was because music, for the talented few, was historically an avenue of escape from the poverty and despair of ghetto and farm. Perhaps it was because the Christian experience in black America was more pervasive and holistic than among whites. Or perhaps there was something in the collective memory of a disenfranchised minority that found it easier to forgive the prodigal son or daughter. Whatever the case, many of those who strayed from the embrace of the black church seemed to have found a measure of peace to complement their wordly success.

If Brother Ray Charles ever spent a sleepless night tormented by translating 'Lord' to 'baby,' it was never reflected in the sheer joy of his music. If Sister Aretha Franklin ever faced the wrath of her preaching father for daring to ask not for humility or holiness but for only a little "Respect," you sure couldn't hear it in the assertive power of that song. If Brother James Brown ever felt the pangs of remorse when testifying about "Cold Sweat," "Hot Pants," or Poppa's salacious "Brand New Bag," it never affected the way he danced. Even when it lost its sanctified credentials, becoming rock and rhythm & blues, black gospel remained one of the most powerful metaphors for cultural cohesion in history. Considering the number of mainstream black artists who sprang from gospel roots, it's remarkable that so few suffered the torturing paradoxes endured by Jerry Lee and Elvis.

The few who did, however, only served to prove the rule: "That which is born of the flesh is flesh and that which is born of the spirit is spirit." Gospel and Soul would labor mightily, and in vain, to bridge that gap. Viv Brough-

77

ton: "[The] very inclusion of temporal pleasures into the religious sphere [is what] makes the black church so down to earth and full of humanity. There's no false asceticism, and worship is a thing of riotous exuberance that extends over long periods. It's a form of therapy for the soul, healing wounds inflicted on it by the heartlessness of the world."

Perhaps more than any other figure in American popular music, Sam Cooke personifies the rewards and pitfalls along the road from gospel to soul. So, too, in some awful way, his death seems to signify the fate of those who can find peace neither in sin nor in salvation. He was born in Clarksdale, Mississippi, on January 22, 1931, one of eight children of the Reverend Charles C. Cook (Sam later added the 'e' to his last name), a Baptist minister. Early in Cooke's life he and his family joined the great black migration from the rural South to the industrialized North, in this case Chicago, where his father preached at the Highway Baptist Church. It was there that Cooke began a singing career that was to make him one of the most popular black artists on either side of the gospel and racial divide, a man who sold more records for RCA at the height of his career than anyone short of Elvis, a singer whose pliant, supple tenor set a standard for the emerging art of soul.

The Singing Children, consisting of Sam, two sisters, and a brother, gave the young vocalist a chance to develop his chops on the black Baptist hymnody, but it was in his teen years that he was exposed to the major influence of both his sacred and secular careers. Another Cook family group, The Highway QC's, were apprenticed to R. B. Robinson, at that time the baritone singer of the legendary Soul Stirrers. The Texas-spawned Stirrers are largely credited with breaking the prevailing tradition of silky smooth harmonics championed by various "jubilee quartets" and opening the way for the harder-edged "Southern quartet" style popularized by the Swan Silvertones and the Sensational Nightingales. It was an innovative approach that focused on two lead voices, an effect musicologist Alan Lomax characterized as "the most incredible polyrhythmic stuff you've ever heard." The Soul Stirrers frontman was Rebert H. Harris, a singer who almost singlehandedly introduced such techniques as delayed time signatures, melismas (a string of notes sung on a single syllable), antiphony (call and response singing), and falsetto leads into the gospel mainstream. He became Sam Cooke's idol.

In time the Highway QC's became a popular attraction in their own right, touring with the Stirrers, the Blind Boys of Mississippi, Pilgrim Travelers, and others. Viv Broughton picks up the story in *Black Gospel*: "During the late 1940s, quartets had become exceptionally popular and moral laxity had subsequently infected the circuit—even to the extent of female groupies following the male groups around for casual affairs. R. H. Harris was raised to carry himself with integrity and this new thing wasn't his style at all. 'I believe there's this virtue that goes along with gospel. There's more to it than good singing. It's a beaconing thing that other folks can see without you talking it.'"

By the late forties, professional gospel was already beginning to take on the dazzling aspects of show business that would later characterize rock and soul. In 1950 Harris quit the Soul Stirrers; his replacement was a teenaged Sam Cooke.

For six years Cooke toured through North America with the premier gospel quartet of his day, sharpening both his performance and vocal skills. Svelte and doe-eyed, he was shaping up as a sort of holy heartthrob, milking more than just spiritual fervor from his audieuce. Another Stirrer, Jesse Farley, recalls, "In the old days, young people took their seats six rows from the back, the old folks stayed up front. When Sam came on the scene, it reversed itself. The young people took over." The line between gospel sanctity and showmanship was getting steadily fuzzier.

Cooke's first recordings with the Soul Stirrers, in 1951, included remakes of such standards as "Peace in the Valley" and "I'm Gonna Build on That Shore." They were followed by a string of classic gospel hits exemplified by the mellifluous "Touch the Hem of His Garment." Then, in late 1956, while appearing in Los Angeles, he was approached by Robert "Bumps" Blackwell, an arranger, producer, and talent scout with a sinister Mephistophelian touch. "Bumps told me I ought to switch to the pop field," Cooke later recounted. "Frankly, the pop field hadn't much attraction for me up until then. I was happy enough on the gospel trail and making a nice living for myself. But the more I thought about the pop field, the more interesting it became. Bumps, of course, had a good deal of influence. He was constantly prodding me to make the change whenever he got the chance."

Like a devil sitting on his shoulder, whispering in his ear, Blackwell enticed Cooke to record some pop sides for Specialty Records, the Stirrers' label. Cooke took the challenge seriously. He quit the Soul Stirrers, to be replaced by Johnnie Taylor, later a powerhouse in the Stax roster during the sixties. Cooke listened carefully to Top Ten hits, read the trade papers, and even attended drama school briefly. In 1957, with Blackwell producing, he cut "Lovable" under the pseudonym Dale Cook. It was a ploy that fooled no one, least of all his gospel fans, who responded to Cooke's secular swing by ignoring his records in droves.

Cooke must have been having second thoughts about his career when he recorded a tune called "You Send Me." Specialty Records' owner Art Rupe rejected the song, convinced that Cooke was squandering his talents, and Blackwell bought up the singer's contract. "Rupe's reservations about Cooke's style were understandable," writes Charlie Gillett in *The Sound of the City*, "since it apparently contradicted the fiery spirit of rock 'n' roll that the audience seemed to expect at the time. Cooke sang with a delicate purity that had no precedent in popular music, controlling his voice in a lyrical declaration of helplessness." In short, Sam Cooke was laying the foundations of soul music, and record buyers responded by making "You Send Me" a number-one hit in late 1957. Viv Broughton puts it into perspective: "Cooke took his place as the greatest of all black male singers in commercial music, fawned upon by the press, idolised by women for his excessive charm and looks, revered by the rising generation of young gospel singers who would soon themselves dominate the pop market. He was the very first true superstar of soul but he was forever looking over his shoulder at the church he'd left behind."

Looking back and trying in vain to make amends for worldly success. In 1960 he signed to RCA Records releasing a string of pallid and pandering pop ditties with titles like "Teenage Sonata" and "Cupid." There was no question about it; Cooke was being groomed. He was photographed in soft focus and cardigans, hyped as a wholesome supper club crooner in the Perry Como mold, playing a Purim date with comic Myron Cohen at the Copa in 1958. Cooke was also expertly molded to fit the burgeoning teenage market, just coming into its own as a consumer class. "Chain Gang," his smash hit released in October of 1960, with its provocative grunts and groans proved an exception to the rule: Cooke's forte increasingly became such bland exercises in white bread sock-hop revelry as "Having a Party," with its innocuous references to cold Coke and warm popcorn.

It all must have been painful for those who had heard

in Cooke's exquisite gospel renderings a foretaste of the divine. "Nobody put more people in stretchers than Sam Cooke, nobody," producer Jerry Wexler told writer Gerri Hirshey. "He's got to be the best singer that ever lived, bar none. . . . When I listen to Sam everything goes away. Modulation, shading, dynamics, progression, emotion, every essential quality—he had it all. I speak of his gospel work. The pop stuff never came close to making the fullest use of his talents. Most people don't realize how bad those records are."

Whether Cooke himself realized it remains uncertain. He certainly proved a pliable subject for the image molders, recording everything from "Tammy," to "The Wayward Wind" and gamely jumping on the twist bandwagon with his 1962 hit "Twistin' the Night Away." But there is also evidence of a deeply felt ache, a spirit of sorrow that hovered over songs like "Sad Mood" and "Bring It on Home to Me" like a chained ghost. More to the point, shortly after signing to RCA, Cooke formed his own label, Sar/Derby Records, specifically to record up-and-coming gospel artists. Perhaps it was to offset his investment in a beer company, Cooke's Beer, but more likely it was an attempt to come to terms with his own ambivalence and guilt. He produced demos and laid the career groundwork for Johnnie Taylor, his successor in the Soul Stirrers. He recorded a young keyboardist named Billy Preston. He cut sides for the Soul Stirrers themselves as well as a spin-off ensemble called the Paraders. He even took a boxer by the name of Cassius Clay into a New York studio to record his own album. There was some talk of Cooke himself returning to gospel.

If he doubted it, an appearance in Chicago at a Soul Stirrers' anniversary proved to Cooke that you can never go home again. With all the original members reassembled, Cooke was called out of the audience to sing once again with the quartet he had helped to make famous. The crowd turned stony, and shouts began to ring out. R. H. Harris recalls: "Folks were hollering, 'Get that blues singer down. Get that no good so-and-so down. This is a Christian program.' And it pierced my heart; it shamed me how he was rejected by the home people. He walked offstage tearin'. He was hurt badly."

Cooke eventually bought a house in California but preferred life on the road, driving from date to date in his Ferrari and living on room service. He married his childhood sweetheart, Barbara Campbell, and she bore him three children: two daughters and a son, Vincent Luncy. When the boy was eighteen months old, he accidentally drowned in a swimming pool. Unlike Jerry Lee Lewis, Cooke left no recorded words at the grave site for his son.

What is left for posterity are Cooke's own last words: "Lady, you shot me." On December 11, 1964, Cooke was shot and bludgeoned by Bertha Franklin, a meaty-faced motel clerk in Los Angeles. The circumstances of the killing remain obscure. Some say, for reasons not altogether clear, that it was a Mafia hit. Others claim Franklin was a prostitute or a jilted lover. Franklin insists she was attacked and, with a large stick and three .22-caliber bullets, had stopped Cooke from raping her. A Eurasian woman named Elisa Boyer had a different story: after offering to drive her home from a party, Cooke had forced her into the motel room from which she had escaped, taking with her some of his clothing and his wallet.

Whatever the truth, Cooke's sordid and ignominious end hardly prevented Mother Church from doing in his death what she refused to do while he lived. A 1965 *Ebony* magazine account of his funeral (one of two; the first in Los Angeles, another in Chicago) paints the picture: "At the Mount Sinai Baptist Church in Los Angeles, a crowd of 5,000 persons, some of whom arrived five hours before the scheduled last rites, over-ran facilities designed to accommodate 1,500. In an emotion-packed atmosphere, supercharged by the singing of Lou Rawls, Bobby Blue Band, and Arthur Lee Simpkins, women fainted, tears rolled down men's cheeks and onlookers shouted. Gospel singer Bessie Griffin, who was to appear on the funeral program, became so grief-stricken she had to be carried off. Blues singer Ray Charles stepped in from the audience to sing and play 'Angels Watching over Me.'

"Outside someone started a fistfight, and people paid a freelance photographer to take pictures of them on the scene of Sam Cooke's funeral posing with a celebrity. One photographer was banished from the funeral parlor after he snapped pictures of Sam Cooke's casket, then peddled them outside for 25 cents apiece."

"To most of his white audience," observes soul historian Joe McEwen, "Sam Cooke remained little more than a handsome, well-groomed black man, the quaint bearer of the cha-cha and the twist. Across the tracks, on the other hand, his stature was almost comparable to that of Malcolm X and Martin Luther King. His death, like theirs, only enhanced his standing."

Which leaves the question hanging: Why? Certainly, Cooke represented a level of success that was only occasionally reached by black Americans. In a very real sense, he had had it both ways, playing the white man's game without losing his soul. But the power of Sam Cooke's legend ultimately lay elsewhere. It was, in short, in his voice. His was an instrument of sensitivity and, yes, spirituality, articulating yearnings and hopes that most folks didn't even know they had until Cooke stirred them up. He was a gospel singer, and despite the banalities he sometimes stooped to, he remained a gospel singer his whole life, expressing fullness, riches, and unearthly joy through that special sort of anointing. It was a quality not necessarily lodged in lyrics or the melody; even when singing about Saturday night or the chain gang, Sam Cooke could embue his songs with special grace. Cooke's sad end, no less than the contradictions that defined his life, served to underscore the travails and truths his music celebrated. "Faith is sustained by the many who keep it," says Broughton, "but it's also given urgency by those who don't." Sam Cooke lived and died by that cruel irony.

As it turned out, "Lady, you shot me," was not to be Sam Cooke's epitaph. In February, 1964, RCA released what was at once a scary piece of prophecy and the finest posthumous tribute a man could bestow on himself. If anyone doubted the price Sam Cooke paid for his success, the majestic sorrows of "A Change Is Gonna Come" dispelled disbelief. Written by Cooke, and first performed on the "Tonight Show," the song has since been compared to such landmarks in black history as Martin Luther King's "I Have a Dream" speech. And rightly so. It's the singer's masterpiece, thick with yearning, shimmering with the evidence of things not seen.

> I was born by the river, in a little tent.
> And just like that river, I've been running ever
>   since.
> It's been a long time coming,
> but I know, a change is gonna come.

With "A Change Is Gonna Come," Cooke succeeded in bridging, for one shining moment, the gap between the spirit and the flesh, between gospel and soul. The pain of living and the fear of dying had been united with the hope of heaven, even as Cooke shed this mortal coil to meet a far-from-certain fate.

If it was the too-late triumph of Sam Cooke to briefly touch

85

the flame of gospel to the wick of this world, it was for Richard Penniman to melt the whole ball of wax with one mighty blast of the devil's own music. Cooke's dark night of the soul was a long and solitary vigil: Little Richard's was a careening roller coaster ride in full view of the gaping crowd. The Georgia Peach knew that no matter how rich or famous or loved you might be in this world, one day you would face the Throne of Judgment when all you said and sang and did would be weighed on the awful balance beam of Jehovah. He knew all that. And it never slowed him down. . . .

"My music is healing music," Little Richard would declare at the drop of a hat. "It makes the blind see, the lame walk; it makes the deaf hear and the dumb talk." You can almost picture him saying it, eyeballs popping, sweat leaking from beneath the thick pancake makeup, his teased, matted, and permed pompadour trembling with conviction. He'd be waving his hands like some kind of rock 'n' roll pontiff, dispensing the bountiful blessing of his own sweet self—a most beautiful and favored creature in God's glorious creation.

And it was blasphemy, every last word of it. Healing is God's business; Pentecostal P. T. Barnums would never dare to claim for themselves such powers. But Little Richard wasn't cut from such cloth; wasn't subject to the mundane frailties of mere mortals; wasn't even, it seemed, bound by the laws of sin and death. A homosexual, a drug addict, corrupter of youth, and despoiler of innocence, a Bible salesman and a minister of the gospel, hooked on repentance, drunk on regeneration, Little Richard stands as the greatest object lesson in the whole harrowing history of rock 'n' roll.

The saga of Little Richard begins with a now-familiar pattern: Deep Southern roots, poor-folk religious fervor, and the ineluctable lure of sinful music. Born and raised in Macon, Georgia, Richard Wayne Penniman was the typical product of a black family below the Mason/Dixon line circa 1935. The only thing he seemed not to share with his twelve brothers and sisters was an exotic name: he was surrounded by siblings who answered to Marquette de Lafayette, Horace Dearcy, Elnora, Peaches, and Freka Diedra. Everything else was held in common: the poverty, the stern Seventh Day Adventist upbringing, the sprawling extended family that included two preacher uncles and a bootlegging father.

Common, too, was his musical education, playing piano and singing in the local church. "The first time I got to sing in public before an audience was with a little gospel group that this old lady, Ma Sweetie, got together, called the Tiny Tots," Little Richard told his biographer Charles White in *The Life and Times of Little Richard*. "Ma Sweetie taught us all these church songs. She had a prayer meeting just for kids every Wednesday night. We would go over to her house to listen and pray and sing and learn Bible verses and stuff like that. It was really nice. . . . They didn't use no piano. When they sang they would stomp their feet. They'd be praying, be crying to God. You could hear 'em for blocks."

Audible as well were the sounds emanating from the Macon City Auditorium where Richard got a job selling soft drinks. Artists with such evocative stage names as Cootie Williams, Hot Lips Page, Lucky Millinder, and the scandalous Cab Calloway performed there regularly, as did gospel great Rosetta Tharpe, who, according to legend, invited Richard onstage one evening to sing "Two Little Fish and Five Loaves of Bread."

"I came from a family where my people didn't like rhythm & blues," Little Richard recounts. "Bing Crosby, 'Pennies from Heaven,' Ella Fitzgerald, was all I heard.

And I knew there was something that could be louder than that."

Louder and considerably more outrageous than anything offered in the somnambulant small-town atmosphere that had nurtured Richard Penniman. The boy was, in fact, something of a disgrace to his family, given to garish clothing, bizarre affectations, and a taste for the seedy sounds pulsing from roadhouse dives like Macon's Tick Tock Club. At age thirteen he was thrown out by his father, who claimed, "My father had seven sons, and I wanted seven sons. You've spoiled it, you're only half a son."

No one really knew, exactly, what the other half was. The stigma of homosexuality in the provincial backwaters of the South initially prevented Richard himself from fully understanding, or coming to terms with, his own nature. But it wasn't only his nascent sexuality that was struggling to express itself. Little Richard (after some early shows he gained the title from the time-honored black tradition of bestowing "Little" on exceptional young performers) was a natural born showman, a shameless and inventive exhibitionist who found, in the wide-open embrace of black entertainment in the late forties, a world that welcomed and rewarded the freakish and misbegotten.

Cut loose from the respectable trappings of gospel, black show business was a kaleidoscope of minstrel strutters, sideshow come-ons, growling, whiskey-cured bluesmen, flamboyant vaudevillians, and disreputable "race music." Little Richard fit right in. After being tossed out of his home, he joined a traveling medicine show operated by a quintessential snake oil salesman named Dr. Hudson. While the charlatan was making his pitch, Little Richard would sing and was shortly stolen away by an itinerant big band with whom he toured the South. From there he joined a series of minstrel shows and circuses; first Sugarfoot Sam from Alabama, where he appeared onstage in a dress under the name Princess Lavonne, then the King Brothers Circus, the Jolly Tidy Steppers, and the L. J. Heath Show of Birmingham, Alabama. Eventually he hooked up with the Broadway Follies, sharing the stage with such blues and r & b luminaries as B.B. King, Jimmy Witherspoon, and the gospel-grounded Billy Wright, a notable influence on Richard's emerging vocal antics. He was shortly to become a regular in such notorious dives as Nashville's New Era Club and the Dew Drop Inn and Club Tijuana in New Orleans.

It was around this time, back in Macon and cruising the Greyhound bus station for pickups, that he encountered a wild-eyed piano player by the name of Esquirita, who was backing a wandering holy woman named Sister Rosa who sang hymns and sold "blessed bread." Esquirita, with eight inches of frothed and Dixie-peached hair piled high, a pencil mustache, and a frantic, boogying piano style, served as the prototype for Little Richard's furious eccentricity. Like his protegé, Esquirita inhabited a shadowy world of sideshow thrills and superstition, as far-removed from the pearly robed sanctity of legitimate black gospel as it was from the squeaky-clean wonderland of postwar white America. The geeks and deviates and all-night jammers that roamed the Deep Southern circuit had their antecedents in the medieval circus troupes of Chaucer and Boccaccio, carting mangy lions and soothsaying mendicants through the plague-ravaged landscape, delighting, disgusting, and deceiving the yahoos and bumpkins.

For poor blacks, Jesus, too, could have the pallor and stench of the Middle Ages about him. Faith among the disenfranchised—in the unreconstructed backwaters of America—was a mix of relics and icons, pentecostal terror and mystic fevers. It was, in most ways, a parody of holiness, a corrupt and pagan folk religion; and the fevor of all that grotesque spiritualism worked its way into the music and mannerisms of Little Richard.

In 1951 he landed first place in an Atlanta talent contest. The prize: an RCA recording contract. Two subsequent recording sessions with the eighteen-year-old singer revealed a heavy stylistic debt to both Billy Wright and jump-blues shouter Roy Brown. The records proved a commercial failure, and a year later, after his father had been shot dead in a roadhouse brawl, Little Richard got a job washing dishes at the Macon Greyhound station.

He might have languished there, all primped and preened with nowhere to go, if it hadn't been for Bumps Blackwell, the same keen-eared Svengali who had lured Sam Cooke away from the Soul Stirrers. After another aborted attempt at local fame, this time fronting a band called the Tempo Toppers and recording a handful of singles for Texas–based Peacock Records, Little Richard sent a demo to Specialty Records in Los Angeles. The songs he chose to submit were two gospel-flavored r & b numbers called "He's My Star" and "Wonderin'." "The voice was unmistakably star material," Blackwell recalled for Charles White. "I can't tell how I knew, but I knew. . . . The songs were not out-and-out gospel, but I could tell by the tone of his voice and all those churchy turns that he was a gospel singer who could sing the blues."

Booking a studio in New Orleans, Blackwell cut a number of clearly disappointing sides before stumbling onto a lewd ditty called "Tutti Frutti," sung by Richard during a break. Almost as an afterthought, Blackwell called in a lyricist to clean up the words and cut the tune in three takes and fifteen minutes.

In that quarter hour an alchemical transmutation of historic consequence took place. As Langdon Winner writes, "Suddenly, all the restraints and vanities of imitation are gone from Richard's singing. What we hear is a kind of comic madness which requires a gleeful, bombastic voice, chaotic piano playing and hard charging drums, guitars and saxophones." In other words, Little Richard had suddenly, wonderfully, discovered how to rock. All the elements of his checkered musical history—gospel, jump, r & b, crooners, big bands, and blues—had rushed together to occupy one moment of utter abandon. It's one of those rare times that mark a distinct and emphatic beginning, the rock 'n' roll equivalent of "Eureka!"

"Tutti Frutti" was an instant, monstrous hit and led immediately to a two-year run of chart-topping classics including "Long Tall Sally," "Rip It Up," "Lucille," "Good Golly, Miss Molly," and "The Girl Can't Help It," the latter the title song to a torrid rock flick, featuring Little Richard at the height of his otherworldly prowess. In the film's central scene, Richard sings "She's Got It," shining with sweat and grinning with salacious glee as Jayne Mansfield performs an eye-popping bump and grind. The effect is riveting, the more so in light of the moral taboo attached to interracial sexuality at the time.

Virtually overnight, Little Richard became a major American music figure, flaunting his dazzling oddness and overamped charisma with one hit after another on a nonstop round of barnstorming personal appearances. It was twenty-four months the likes of which popular music and the media mill had never seen, a kind of glorious comeuppance to normalcy, an outbreak of originality and chutzpah in a wasteland of smug Anglo-Saxon conformity.

And when it came to a sudden, screeching halt . . . well, even that had a certain nose-thumbing unpredictability about it. According to the prevailing musical myth, the moment of truth came early in 1957 when Richard answered a knock at the front door of his Los Angeles mansion. Brother Wilbur Gulley, missionary of the Church of God of the Ten Commandments, was making the rounds through the movie-and-music-star districts, seeking out influential, spirit-starved converts. He found, in Little Richard, an eager disciple.

"Richard was ready, both spiritually and economically, to make a break with the world of show business," writes Charles White. "Misused, ripped off, and cheated by racists, promoters, and record companies, he was also being hassled by the Internal Revenue Service for an accounting of his huge earnings. He was becoming tired of the heavy traveling schedules and of the business of being a star in general. The spiritual pressures were such that he needed only a sign that he could interpret as divine to clinch the decision."

It all sounds perfectly rational. The problem is, Little Richard was hardly a pillar of rationality. Racist promoters and the IRS notwithstanding, Richard was at the time the most flamboyant, energetic, and outrageous performer before the public eye. The notion that he was ready to get out of fame's kitchen because he couldn't stand the heat seems distinctly out of character.

So, for that matter, does a guilty conscience and a sin-burdened soul. It's true enough that as a redeemed backslider, Richard would denounce the evils of his former life and music in no uncertain terms. What he never quite got around to giving up was showmanship. Rock and religion were, for him, simply variations on the same themes of emotional abandon and charismatic annointing. Homosexuality, wordly acclaim, and throbbing music were certainly from the devil. But where's it written that making a spectacle of yourself is a sin?

Brother Gulley put Richard in touch with Joe Lutcher, a saxophonist who had worked with Nat "King" Cole and Sammy Davis, Jr., in the forties before giving it all up for the Lord and becoming an evangelist. The pair's proselytizing of the willing Richard was cut short by a two-week tour of Australia, where events took a further bizarre twist.

Or twists, depending on which of the several accounts from Little Richard himself you want to believe. As nearly as can be determined, the singer, on his way Down Under, had a lurid, apocalyptic dream detailing his imminent demise. Shortly afterward, on a plane that he imagined was on fire, he prayed to the Almighty to send angels to keep the craft aloft. He was evidently recalling, in that moment, a picture of hovering, yellow-haired angels he had once seen in a religious tract called *The Great Controversy*. A few days later, in a sold-out concert in Sydney, he saw the Russian Sputnik blinking its way across the skies. It looked, he recalls in *The Life and Times of Little Richard*, "as though the big ball of fire came directly over the stadium about two or three hundred feet above our heads. It shook my mind. It really shook my mind. I got up from the piano and said, 'This is it. I am through. I am leaving show business to go back to God.'"

The next day, to prove the point to his disbelieving band, he threw some jewelry into the bay and canceled the rest of the tour. "I wanted to work for Jehovah and find that peace of mind," he avowed. "I had always wanted to be a preacher and dedicate my life to God. I knew I had a message to say to the world outside show business. I was not sure what it was 'til I met Joe and Brother Gulley. When I knew I came to God." Before arriving, however, there was time to play a farewell concert before an ogling crowd at New York's Apollo Theater amid rumors that he was about to enter a monastery.

What followed was a mix of holy intentions and bad habits. A picture from the period tells the story. Little Richard, Man of God, sits propped on a satin quilted bedspread inside his flocked and flounced boudoir. His hair is immaculately coiffed, and he wears a silk bathrobe and a large cross that somehow survived Sydney bay. He studies four Bibles laid out in front of him, apparently contrasting translations. It's a study of intense, if somewhat lavish, devotion.

His new life revolved for a time around the Little Richard Evangelistic Team, a traveling tent revival he organized with Joe Lutcher. "I served at the tent meetings," he recalls, "doing all the menial tasks like ushering, tightening the ropes, showing slides, and collecting questions from the audience. I shared in the ordinance of humility by washing the feet of other members before taking communion." He also enrolled in the Voice of Prophesy correspondence Bible course and, eventually, at Oakwood College, "a commandment-keeping college in Huntsville, Alabama, on a three-year course aimed at my becoming ordained as an elder of the church." Along the way he married Ernestine Cambell, a girl he had met at a Washington, D.C., revival.

The redeemed rocker plainly gave holiness a fair shake. Yet disturbing signs began to surface—indications that perhaps the cure hadn't touched Richard's kinesthetic core after all. He would often show up for classes in one of his fleet of outlandishly equipped Caddys. He was called up before the Board of Elders and warned to keep his hands off a young student, the deacon's son. And eventually, he was busted in a queer-bashing police raid of a Trailways bus station bathroom in Long Beach, California—a scandal that led to divorce proceedings in which Ernestine cited "grievous mental suffering."

Yet, through all these dark intimations of Falling Away, Richard continued gamely to try to use his gifts for God. He recorded a number of gospel sides—"Joy, Joy, Joy," "Why Don't You Change Your Ways," "He's Not Just a Soldier"—even as he was secretly cutting second-rate rock 'n' roll under an assumed name. The 1962 galvanizing rave-up, "He Got What He Wanted (But He Lost What He Had)," featured his old band the Upsetters and came across more like a preconversion rocker than a gospel caution.

Finally, he could stand it no longer. Shedding the cloak of sanctity, he agreed to tour England as an opener for Sam Cooke. Richard was later to claim that he was booked under false pretenses and that he thought the show was a strictly gospel package. Whatever the case, he ended up delivering neither sweet comfort nor fire and brimstone but pure, blazing rock 'n' roll, releasing what had been pent up and bubbling under for almost five years.

By 1964 there was no turning back, even in the face of studied indifference from rock audiences who had moved on and could barely remember what the excitement was all about. He cut "Bama Lama Bama Loo" for Specialty, a slice of joyous gibberish in the "Tutti Frutti" mold. The tune's lukewarm reception told the tale: while Richard was basking in the glow of godliness, his moment had passed. What had seemed wild and dangerous and incandescent only a few years before, now seemed simply indulgent and slightly dotty. Little Richard returned to the shadowy fringes of show business from which he had emerged, making mediocre records laced with occasional flashes of brilliance, touring doggedly, descending into self-parody and unchecked drug abuse. He was arrested for tax evasion and jeered offstage for his alternately chaotic, bleary, and belligerent performances.

In 1976 Little Richard appealed to the court of last resort and returned once again to the fold of faith. The cycle, and the cycles within cycles, were complete. Shorn and repentant, he began a career as a door-to-door salesman, selling editions of the *Black Heritage Bible*, which purported to show that many heroes of Scripture had been black. He renounced homosexuality and rock music, exhorting audiences, "If God can save me, he can save anybody!" He joined the Universal Remnant Church of God and cut a gospel album called *God's Beautiful City*. Victimized by fame, his prodigious energies depleted, staring mortality in the face, Little Richard had run a hard, scary, high-stakes race. Whether he won or lost is strictly a matter of perspective.

"When I listen to my old music," he says today, "it's like a dream. In my dream I was famous all over the universe. It all seems so unreal to me, but it's a good dream because I woke up." Little Richard seems unlikely to tumble back into revery. "I walk in victory," he insists. "I have no desire for the old things. God has made me a minister, ordained and anointed me. I used to give it all to rock, but now I'm giving it all to the Rock of Ages." The cause of a car wreck in late 1985, in which the singer came within a hairsbreadth of death, seems, in fact, to be just what he insists. Not drugs, not booze, not a top-speed race with the devil. "I was tired," he says. "I fell asleep at the wheel."

The history of rock and soul music, and of the gospel artists who were there at the creation, is hardly littered with the wrecks of ruined lives and gutted careers. "[E]veryone who sang gospel believed that if you switched to popular music, something bad would happen to you," observes Sam Cooke's former guitarist Bobby Womack. But it isn't true. Ray Charles sings at baseball season openers and superstar sessions to aid starving Africans. Aretha Franklin rides the freeway of love "in a pink Cadillac," while Teddy Pendergrass still weakens female knees even after the terrible auto accident that left him in a wheelchair. Al Green and Johnny Otis set aside successful careers to take up the calling and put on the collar, and they did it without first reaching the end of their ropes. For every tragedy and torn-up life there are a dozen certified successes—men and women who have squared the circle, laying to rest the paradox of rhythm versus religion or, better still, making it work for them.

What's the rule, then, that's proved by the glaring exceptions, by the ones who couldn't find balance in the blunt oppositions that ruled their lives? The easy answer is, none: Little Richard and Sam Cooke were hair-trigger anomalies, artistic temperaments tattered and frayed by a spiritual battle that most of us neatly sidestep.

Or maybe there's something in the nature of faith, a glitch in the relationship of creature to Creator, some fatal flaw of heart or mind. "It was for freedom that Christ set us free," is Saint Paul's confident assertion, but, if anything, the lives of men like Sam Cooke and Little Richard were marked by bondage to an overpowering, unending conflict. It was for the Church to rub salt in those wounds. Doctrines that rammed home the implacable enmity of spirit and flesh would find their outworkings in the creative process. Music, not allowed to exist for its own sake, was sacrificed on the altars of piety or profanity. It's useless to speculate on what such men might have accomplished had they not spent half their lives rebelling against religious strictures and the other half trying guiltily to make amends. The substance of their music may well have been formed out of that tension. Suffice it to say, the age-old debate over music's inherent ability to inspire good or evil wasn't settled by the course of their careers.

What remains is a record, not simply of music made but of lives lived. The songs just don't make sense outside the context of those who wrote and sang them. In the same way, the deep divisions that ran through those lives aren't confined solely to the sounds that made them famous. These are men split apart in all sorts of ways. They are spiritual schizophrenics.

•   •   •

A man's image of God, it's said, is built from the image of his earthly father. If it's true, then Marvin Pentz Gaye imagined the Almighty with deeply shaded ambivalence—as an implacable, unforgiving, and remote object of love and loathing. It was a relationship touched on the deepest levels by an inarticulate, beseeching pain, a grim Greek tragedy that took as its text Freudian imperatives and the stern tenets of old-time religion.

As one of the most original and expressive talents of soul music's gilded age—the Motown era—Marvin Gaye's stylistically diverse musical catalog reflects a supple, mercurial gift. Ranging from the jiving, gospel-gleaned pleasures of "Can I Get a Witness" and "You're a Wonderful One" to the sophisticated syncopation of "I'll Be Doggone" and "Ain't That Peculiar"; from the dangerous mysteries of "I Heard It Through the Grapevine" to the operatic pronouncements of love divine with Tammi Terrell on "Ain't No Mountain High Enough" and "You're All I Need to Get By," Gaye's biggest hits offer a startingly clear insight into his influences. And the ever-changing fortunes of his career. But it's his later work that reveals with painful clarity the shifts and ripples of his spiritual temperature, charting a torturous—and torturously self-indulgent—odyssey.

Make no mistake: Marvin Gaye was a man seeped and saturated in the supernatural. His father, Marvin Pentz Gay (like Sam Cooke before him, Marvin, Jr., added the *e* as a bit of show business flash), was an elder in the House of God, the Holy Church of the Living God, the Pillar and Ground of the Truth, the House of Prayer for All People, a long-winded Pentecostal sect with a strong Orthodox Jewish overlay. Gay's Washington, D.C. congregation, for example, required head covering for women, decorated its sanctuary with the star of David, maintained strict Jewish dietary laws, and celebrated only Old Testament religious holidays—no Christmas or Easter. More important, perhaps, were the habits of worship in the House of God; died-in-the-wool Pentecostal roof raising utilizing any instrument that could fit through the door along with repetitive praise chants, glossalalia, and ecstatic emotional outbursts. Ordination was by the Spirit of God.

It was against this background of strict, set-apart religiosity that Marvin, Jr., was raised. "Living with father was something like living with a king," he told David Ritz for that writer's extraordinary and insightful biography *Divided Soul: The Life of Marvin Gaye*, "a very peculiar, changeable, cruel and all-powerful king. . . . Even though winning his love was the ultimate goal of my childhood, I defied him. . . . I thought I could win his love through singing, so I sang my heart out. But the better I became, the greater his demands. I could never please him."

Gay, Senior, was, in fact, less a king than a tyrant, a cruel overseer who mercilessly beat all his children but most particularly the rebellious Marvin. An effeminate man, the elder Gay was given to wearing his wife's silk blouses, panties, and even, on occasion, her nylons. His son was cruelly teased by friends about his father's dandified affectations. The preacher rarely worked and, after a falling-out with the sect over a piece of doctrinal minutiae, began to drink heavily.

It's remarkable that with such a role model, Marvin, Jr., retained any love for the Church or the things of faith. "I could see the truth," he told Ritz, "not in my father's example, but in the words he preached. . . . [H]e offered me Jesus. He made Jesus come alive for me, and that's reason to be grateful to him for the rest of my life." He was, in fact, an extraordinarily attuned youth to begin with, as sensitive to the Spirit as he was to his own blossoming sexuality. He expressed them both through music. "Mother kept me singing," he wrote on the liner notes to his *Anthology* album. "She would say, 'Get up and sing "Journey to the Sky."' The ladies in the church, they would hug me and bring me to them. Psychologically, sensually, I liked this." As a youngster, Gaye indeed exhibited a glorious vocal prowess, appearing at the age of five at a Kentucky church convention and, as a teenager, on Washington, D.C., streetcorners, lending his ethereal tenor to neighborhood doo-wop groups. "I wanted to be a pop singer," he told Ritz, "like Nat Cole or Sinatra or Tony Bennett. I wanted to be a pop singer like Sam Cooke, proving that our kind of music and our kind of feeling could work in the context of pop ballads."

Gaye, in fact, felt himself to be divinely appointed. In childhood dreams, he saw himself onstage, "while all the world watched and waited for me to sing something so stupendous that life as we know it would be forever altered. I was brought here to make a change." By his early teens, however, destiny was opening up whole new vistas. "I still felt the call," he insisted. "I still believed in Jesus, but by then so many sorts of music were buzzing in my ear. Other musical voices were stronger."

In 1957, after a discharge from the Air Force, he returned to Washington to form his first professional singing group, a doo-wop aggregate called the Marquees. They were, in turn, recruited by Harvey Fuqua, when his popular vocal group, the Moonglows, broke up. By 1959 Gaye had left both the Moonglows and the East Coast, heading for Detroit and fame. It was in the Motor City that he met Berry Gordy, a former boxer and record-store proprietor who was in the process of creating a musical empire of mythic proportions with help from his extended family. That family would eventually include Gaye himself when, in 1961, he married Gordy's sister Anna.

A canny songwriting talent, Gordy was capitalizing on the emerging fusion of gospel, blues, and r & b with tunes like "Reet Petite," for Jackie Wilson, and a string of modest successes with a local singer named Marv Johnson. By the time Gaye arrived, Gordy had his bustling enterprise up to speed, landing hits with the Miracles, featuring Smokey Robinson.

Gaye began his twenty-year-plus tenure at Motown as a backing singer and session drummer. By the early sixties he had launched a solo career and shortly scored with "Stubborn Kind of Fellow," the first in a string of quintessential Motown soul standards, "Hitch Hike," "Pride and Joy," "Can I Get a Witness," and "You're a Wonderful One." In '64 he began a singing partnership with Mary Wells, the first of several hit-making matchups that was to include Kim Weston and Tammi Terrell and spanned such landmarks as "It Takes Two," "What Good Am I Without You," and "Ain't Nothing Like the Real Thing." Throughout this period, his solo career continued to skyrocket as well, with a succession of luminous chart toppers led by "Ain't That Peculiar" and "Too Busy Thinking About My Baby."

So much for Gaye's soul dossier—one of the more purely joyous chapters in pop's annals. By the late sixties, however, the star-crossed subcurrents of Gaye's life were beginning to surface. In 1967, at age twenty-two, Tammi Terrell collapsed in his arms onstage. The victim of crippling headaches, she was said to have a brain tumor; darker rumors suggested she had been beaten in the head by a jealous boyfriend. After eight operations, she died in 1970, leaving Gaye grief-stricken. "Tammi was a victim of the violent side of love," Gaye remarked for his biography, "at least that's how I felt. . . . [I]t was a deep vibe, as though she were dying for everyone who couldn't find love."

The statement was typical of Gaye. The thunderous cultural dislocations of the sixties were having their effect on his hypersensitive psyche. Spirituality and sexuality, as twin poles of overpowering attraction, became increasingly intermingled, even interchangeable. Sex was salvation; carnality was in the mind of the beholder; Jesus was love, and love believes all things, suffers all things, and ultimately permits all things.

"A fundamentalist Christian view of Marvin Gaye would see him as a fallen preacher," writes David Ritz, a confidant and friend of the singer. "Born with the sacred power to transmit Jesus' love through heavenly song, his religious responsibility was, at least in Marvin's own mind, clear. According to his own testimony, he'd felt the calling as a small child. But Marvin's electricity . . . generated two sorts of reactions, sexual or spiritual, depending on which switch Gaye chose to pull."

In the early seventies, on two landmark albums that together represent a stunning creative coup, he chose to pull both. The 1971 *What's Going On*, an LP written, produced, arranged, and performed by Gaye, was initially met with puzzled frowns at Motown. Little wonder. A *Time* magazine review of the album tells the tale: "The LP laments war, pollution, heroin and the miseries of ghetto life. It also praises God and Jesus, blesses peace, love, children and the poor. Musically it is a far cry from the gospel or blues a black singer-composer might normally apply to such subjects. Instead Gaye weaves a vast, melodically deft symphonic pop suite in which Latin beats, soft soul and white pop, and occasionally scat and Hollywood schmaltz, yield effortlessly to each other."

That wasn't all Gaye was weaving. The same review quotes him as saying, "'God and I travel together with righteousness and goodness. If people want to follow along, they can.'" Mr. Wonderful One, Motown's pride and joy, had suddenly, with a single audacious stroke, elevated himself to the status of God's own traveling com-

102

panion. The public responded with fascination, turning *What's Going On* into a major hit.

The album's success gave Gaye the confidence to delve deeply into his metaphysical conceits, which, in turn, brought him in touch with darker, more depraved facets of his complex nature. It was a textbook case of raging messianic complex. His publicly validated prophetic credentials provided a license for licentiousness familiar to anyone who has tasted adoration and acclaim. But Gaye was not simply indulging his vices; he was on a search for Truth, a road of excess that led to the palace of wisdom.

Whether he was, at the same time, rebelling against the puritanical strictures of church and family is a matter of speculation. Yet one wonders what the faithful at the House of God would have made of such statements as the following: "I respect the Eastern religions," Gaye pontificated. "Their philosophies are beautiful and wise. . . . I also believe in reincarnation. We're destined to return to repeat our mistakes if we don't grow towards God in this form." So much for scrupulous adherence to biblical Christianity.

What his fundamentalist brethren would certainly have called idolatry was, in fact, springing up everywhere in the soul superstar's life. It comes as no surprise that a man as sexually charged as Gaye could elevate his passions to sacramental status. What is surprising is his slavish devotion to his gonads. For Gaye, sex was not only spiritual transcendence; it was fast becoming the universal principal of human existence.

Let's Get It On proved the point. Released in 1973, it was dubbed by critic Don Waller "the most seductive, sensual record in all popular music." It is, if anything, an understatement. The album came at a time when Gaye was tasting fully the fruits of success. His marriage to Anna Gordy had been faltering for some time, and when he met the impossibly beautiful Janis Hunter, daughter of legendary jazzman Slim Galliard, he found a suitable object for his blossoming obsessions.

Hailed as a "carnal feast" and "a brilliant celebration of the joys of sex," *Let's Get It On* spotlighted such original tunes as "Come Get to This," "You Sure Love to Ball," and the title track, a manifesto of seduction that took up the LP's entire first side. The liner notes included the T. S. Eliot aphorism: "Birth, and copulation, and death./ That's all the facts when you come to brass tacks," as well as Gaye's own ruminations of his favorite subject. "I don't believe in overly moralistic philosophies," he intoned. "Have your sex; it can be very exciting if you're lucky. I hope the music that I present here makes you lucky."

It certainly made Gaye lucky. *Let's Get It On* was his biggest seller to date, a multiplatinum smash that saturated the singer's bank account with record royalties.

It also marked the beginning of a long and hideous decline. A lavish 1974 tour in support of the LP saw a rapid escalation in his use of drugs, particularly cocaine. According to Ritz, Gaye also found comfort in the company of prostitutes. "Marvin not only sympathized with ladies of the night," he writes, "but given his attitude about sexy music—in his heart, he always felt he should be singing holy hymns—Gaye closely identified with prostitutes."

Maybe, but Gaye was losing touch with his heart. And his head. Following the birth of a daughter to Janis Hunter, Gaye recorded and released *I Want You*, another sexual marathon that didn't sell nearly as well as its predecessor and was roundly scorned by the critics; writer Don Waller called it "one of the most twisted expressions of desire this side of the Velvet Underground." He was now living full-time with Janis, and in 1975 the couple had a second child, a son. When the time came to settle accounts with Anna, his wife of fourteen years, Gaye played a cruel, bizarre, dirty trick. By arrangement with his lawyers, he agreed to hand over $600,000 in royalties on his next album as part of the divorce settlement. The LP, released in 1978, was titled *Here, My Dear*, a gory, pathetic, blow-by-blow account of their marriage and its dissolution. The song titles tell it all: "I Met a Little Girl," "When Did You Stop Loving Me, When Did I Stop Loving You," "Is That Enough?" "You Can Leave, but It's Going to Cost You."

The humiliation he visited on his former in-laws—Berry Gordy was forced to release and promote an album that publicly aired his sister's very dirty laundry—was topped only by Gaye's astounding presumption. The whole notion that the sordid details of his private life made art revealed the true depths of megalomania to which he had sunk. The album's cover was a mire of recriminating symbolism. Gaye, dressed in a toga, raises a self-righteous hand of innocence; fire burns from the marble loins of a statue; the LP's gatefold reveals a Monopoly board across which is written Judgment. The scales of justice sit on a mantel. *Here, My Dear* is the work of a man in the full flush of self-deception and overweening egotism. "Pretentious is too good a word for this clutter," wrote one critic. "Banal meandering," chimed another.

But Gaye was hardly meandering. He was, rather, heading relentlessly toward self-destruction. Having squandered a fortune, he was being hounded by the IRS for millions in back taxes. He moved to Hawaii, where he lived for a time in a converted bread truck. He married Janis Hunter only to see her stolen away by Teddy Pendergrass, his arch rival in the sexual soul sweepstakes. Rumor had it that after she filed for divorce, he attempted suicide by snorting an ounce of pure cocaine. The man who had taken to wearing a thick rubber band around his wrist to remind him of the transitory nature of the material world evinced an increasing dependence on pornography, in video cassette, magazine, and even postcard form. The lusts he had awakened became more and more explicit in his music. Toward the end of his career, Gaye wrote a song called "Sanctified Pussy," bearing witness to the near-complete corruption of his essential Christian impulses. In numerous interviews, he referred to the tune as "religious" and "spiritual."

Finally, in 1980, with the tax men hot on his trail, he left the country and moved to Belgium, ending, at the same time, his long tenure at Motown. It was there, at the tag end of his career, that Gaye seemed to take a deep breath, stand back, and try to make sense of a life gone badly wrong. He signed a recording contract with Columbia for a hefty sum and recorded his twenty-seventh and final album. Titled *Midnight Love*, it contained one song among the rote recitations of kinky sex and cocaine orgies that came as close to achieving Gaye's sacred synthesis of sex and spirituality as anything he ever recorded.

The title itself attested to the deeply rent spirit that even then was in its death throes. "Sexual Healing" was, at first listening, yet another salvation-through-orgasm opus. "Baby, I'm hot just like an oven," he crooned. But it was in the performance itself—one of his sweetest and most affecting—that the truth could be heard. It wasn't the sex that Gaye seemed to be crying out for, so much as for the healing. In a moment of naked need, he reveals between the lines an ache that nothing soothing could touch. The brilliance of "Sexual Healing" lies somewhere beyond what is being sung, the trite come-on that fades out on the line "if you procrastinate, I'll have to masturbate." A quality that magically cloaks Marvin Gaye in innocence, that does indeed render desire as a metaphor for spiritual longing, pulses, radiates, and fades. Musical sermons of sexual transcendence would be heard again, most particularly in the work of another influential black artist, Prince.

But it would never again be sung with such heartbreaking conviction.

"Sexual Healing" was a hit of major proportions, restoring to a large degree his tattered reputation and resulting in a 1983 tour that featured, as a finale, a performance of the song with Gaye dressed only in black bikini briefs. His cocaine habit had long since spiraled out of control. In the throes of convulsive paranoia, he was convinced he was about to be murdered. He moved back home with his mother and his father. On April 1, 1984, after a violent argument, Marvin Gay, Sr., shot Marvin Gaye, Jr., through the heart, then again at point-blank range, killing him.

In the end, Bishop Simon Peter Rawlings, elder of the House of God, the Holy Church of the Living God, the Pillar and Ground of the Truth, the House of Prayer for All People, came from Lexington, Kentucky, to speak the eulogy. As with all parting words spoken from the graveside, they carried the hope of restoration and forgiveness, better late than never at all.

Pat Boone

Chapter Five

WHITE BUCKS
AND RED NECKS

Louie, Louie, oh, baby, yeah,
we gotta go now, yeah, yeah, yeah, yeah.
—The Kingsmen

Elvis Presley isn't obscene or lewd. He's just
different.
—Janet Winn, *The New Republic*, December 1956

In the fall of 1956, the hottest rivalry in show business was featured on the front cover of *Collier's* magazine in an exposé titled "Rock 'n' Roll Battle: Boone vs. Presley." For months previously, the national media had been struggling to come to terms with the phenomenology of Presleymania. Tabloids referred to him as a "Howling Hillbilly Success," a "twitching Caruso," a "Sexhibitionist," and "the apotheosis of immature, a too-sensuous adolescent."

He was, in short, a too-puzzling prototype of a threatening new role model for teen America. And while taste makers and scene watchers were expending reams of newsprint trying to put it all in perspective, Elvis was industriously dominating the pop culture landscape, thanks largely to the efforts of one Henry J. Saperstein. Saperstein, a marketing wizard, had cut a deal with Elvis's manager, Col. Tom Parker, to handle over twenty-six million dollars' worth of Presley merchandise: everything from pillows, blue jeans, and lipstick to statuettes and lunch pails. Both Saperstein and Parker were out for a quick killing, under the assumption that all the brouhaha would be over before they knew it. The merchandiser estimated for *Newsweek* magazine that Elvis's shelf life would be about two years. "He's too hot," Saperstein said. "He can't be maintained at the maximum level." In the meantime, however, the effect on the taste mavin establishment must have been unsettling. His face, his lips, his hips were everywhere.

But Elvis's charismatic secret couldn't be cracked by just anyone; it all had to do with being young and troubled and rebellious and . . . well, shook up. And if you weren't any of those things, then it was kind of hard to see what the fuss was all about. Moreover, it was hard not to feel vaguely threatened, or repulsed by the spectacle of such flagrant hormonal defiance.

Enter Pat Boone, like an amiable, cardigan-clad knight to the rescue. While it is unfair to suggest, as many have, that Boone's early success was due entirely to his role as a palatable alternative to Elvis, there *is* a suspicious hint of contrivance to his rapid emergence as a teen idol.

If the spooked establishment had indeed chosen Boone to do battle against the Powers of Presley, they couldn't have chosen a nobler champion. Boone, in his way, was as genuine as Elvis in his. There was nothing, initially, that smacked of cynical pandering in either singer, nothing to suggest that what you saw wasn't exactly what you got.

And what you got depended on what you wanted. Pat Boone, a genuine descendant of trail blazer Daniel Boone, had been quietly building a career for himself since the early fifties as a clean-cut, clean-living singer, earning early on the moniker of "the next Bing Crosby." Television appearances on Ted Mack's and Arthur Godfrey's amateur talent shows had brought him to the attention of Randy Wood, a scout for Dot Records. Under Woods' guidance, Boone cut "Two Hearts, Two Kisses," a lightweight showcase for his crooning skills that reached the Top Ten. Then, a full four months before Elvis cut "Heartbreak Hotel," five months before Little Richard's "Tutti Frutti," and a year before Jerry Lee Lewis's "Whole Lot of Shakin' Going On," Woods suggested that Boone record a cover of an r & b hit called "Ain't That a Shame," as performed by a black New Orleans piano player named Fats Domino. Boone, in his autobiography *Together*, takes up the story:

"It may be hard to remember back before there was rock 'n' roll, but for me it was quite a transition to make. I was a ballad singer. . . . I was aghast when Randy played ["Ain't That a Shame"] for me: as an English major I didn't want to sing 'ain't'. . . . When the song was a hit a lot of disc jockeys and record fans around the country thought I was black because of the songs I sang and the way I sounded. I took that as quite a compliment. Soon enough they found out that not only was I white, but so were my shoes."

Although it would be hard to mistake his version of "Ain't That a Shame" with the barrelhouse boom of the original, Boone's account, more than a little disingenuous, is nonetheless revealing. If anything, disc jockeys and records fans probably heaved an audible sigh of relief to dis-

111

cover that Boone was not black. And that, of course, was the crux of the matter.

Elvis wasn't black, but his body language was and his music had the same libido-liberating effect as the best blues and r & b. There was, in short, something unsavory about this sneering Memphis boy, and that was the none-too-subtle slant of *Collier's* cover story. A pair of pictures told the tale. The first captured Elvis reclining on a motel room bed, leering at a dewy-eyed fan who'd won a date with the star. It was contrasted with a shot of Boone, exuding wholesomeness as he romped in his modest living room with his infant daughter, Debby, one of four button-cute Boonettes.

Pat Boone: "I had only a six-or-eight month head start on him, and we rode into the national limelight together. We were both from Tennessee; we were both from lower middle-class economic backgrounds; we both grew up in church. But there the similarities stopped. I was salt, and he was pepper. I was a conformist and he was a rebel.

"We seesawed up and down the record charts, bumping each other out of the number one spot time and again, launching our movie careers at just about the same time, and our fan clubs reached mammoth proportions simultaneously. As a result, every fan magazine in America ran contests: 'Who's your favorite? Elvis or Pat?' The circulation of all the magazines soared. . . . Sometimes I'd win, but usually Elvis did. I have no doubt that my being in sharp contrast to Elvis actually helped my career."

No doubt. But the contrast ran deeper than sideburns and sex appeal. As quaintly anachronistic as a popularity contest between Pat Boone and Elvis Presley may seem today, in early 1956 it was fraught with serious social implications. In the rose-colored Era of Ike, even the frivolous pursuits of pop fans were discolored by dark undertones of racism, paranoia, and moral hypocrisy.

Which is not to suggest, God forbid, a conspiracy. There was really no need for the forces allied against rock 'n' roll's pernicious influence to gather in back rooms for plot-hatching sessions. Those who equated normalcy with decency and morality with conformity knew who they were. And who their friends were.

And they were everywhere. The coalitions of PTA watchdogs, law-and-order tub thumpers, Red-baiting demagogues, and purebred zealots simply coalesced out of the prevailing prejudices and half-baked presumptions of the time. America—victorious in war, vigorous in economic expansion—was plagued with a sense of its own incipient vulnerability. Enemies assailed from within and without, and by the mid-fifties they seemed to come together in a jury-rigged grand conspiracy all their own: pinkos, degenerates, intellectuals, beatniks, and those with certain suspicious and exotic tastes. America was defined by what it was not, partaking in an exclusionary ritual that reached a kind of cracked-brain frenzy in its battle with rock 'n' roll.

And like warrior-priests leading the troops into battle, churchmen stood front and center in the fray. "Hot rods, Reefers and Rock 'n' Roll" was the subject of one thunderous sermon delivered by a Methodist minister in the summer of '56. "A new low in spiritual degeneracy," was how a Baptist preacher described the advent of Elvis. "A wave of smut," is the way another excoriated rock 'n' roll's growing popularity. A May 1956 article in the New York *Times* reported on the efforts of several Southern church groups to suppress rock 'n' roll. The music, they revealed, was part of a plot by the NAACP to destroy the moral fiber of white youth. Record burnings became as much a part of the fifties' cultural landscape as golf and big cars. The church not only led the charge, it lent legitimacy to the witch-hunt and a veneer of righteousness to a ruthless, vindictive campaign.

It was a matter of vested interests. The vitality of American Christianity had been previously expressed, in large measure, through its diversity. Regional and socioeconomic expressions of faith had taken root and flourished as genuine grass-roots movements with relatively little cross-pollination. World War II and television changed all that. In the fifties America became less an aggregate of distinct regions and classes than a nation united by the quest of a common utopia and tied by an expanding electronic network. The change included the homogenized church. Early in the decade the National Council of Churches was formed, an umbrella organization protecting the interests of the majority of Protestant and Orthodox denominations and representing over two-thirds of the nation's churchgoing population in an attempt to homogenize the Protestant church.

Reality, of course, superseded such grandiose ambitions. Classes still existed, as did regional interests and denominational factions, but what really mattered was perception. "The family that prays together stays together." "Worship at the church of your choice this Sunday." These and other wholesome homilies pointed up the new mission of the church. Saving souls and offering succor were one thing: public relations and image molding was what filled the pews. Even more significantly: Americanism had been deftly tied to a churchgoing theme, and the church, as a result, was firmly ensconced in the power-and-privilege elite. The responsibility for sticking up for the poor, despised and disenfranchised, had been bumped off the agenda. The American megachurch instead became the mouthpiece for established values, promulgating a strict code of civic, moral, and aesthetic rectitude.

In the process, the church willingly forfeited its mission,

forging a religious consensus that came very close to a state-sponsored faith. Plastic crèches, Easter bonnets, and an airbrushed Savior signified a faith of no offense. Christianity was employed as a tool to enforce the status quo, revealing the arrogance at the heart of America's self-image. The implications were clear: citizens of the most powerful nation on earth, at the height of their prowess, had singlehandedly constructed a culture as close to paradise as any that history had been privileged to witness. The function of religion, ergo, was not to remind the culture of its shortcomings and sins but simply to add its voice to the chorus of praise. Anyone or anything that stood in the way of this glorious progression to national perfection would be ruthlessly swept aside, with the blessing of the church.

It didn't, of course, turn out that way; the church, with a wrongheadedness that was becoming chronic, had chosen the losing side. It was the kids who, in time, would be called upon to fill the pews, and the kids, in time, would want no part of an institution that had so stubbornly re fused to understand what it meant to be young, troubled, rebellious, and . . . shook up. It seems unlikely that the church, engaged in the shrill and endless secular/sacred musical debate, would ever have lent wholehearted support to a hip-shaking Elvis. Yet its influence could doubtless have mitigated the rancor that would arise as the rock 'n' roll controversy heated up.

Nor could the kids count on the music industry to champion the cause of rock 'n' roll. This was the business, after all, that rolled over and played dead when the NBC radio network banned Cole Porter's "Love for Sale" in 1940. Nor could a spokesman be found to defend Duke Ellington and his tune "The Mooche," which was blamed for a national rise in the rape statistics. Hank Ballard and the Midnighters' "Work with Me, Annie" and Georgia Gibbs's "Dance with Me, Henry" were two more early r & b classics to fall under the censor's vengeful axe. This sort of manic smut-hunting reached an extreme in the early sixties. After persistent attempts by watchdogs to ban the Kingsmen's adenoidal anthem "Louie, Louie," the Federal Communications Commission concluded that the song could not possibly corrupt youthful morals because the lyrics were virtually indecipherable.

The fact was, mini-moguls making a profit from "race music" were positively panic stricken at the prospect of incurring the ire of the Wonder Bread moralists. This was at least partially because the music they peddled *was*, more often than not, ladened with risqué double entrendre. That was part of the appeal, and not an argument that would have convinced the guardians of public decency. The rock 'n' roll merchants took a decidedly low profile; they knew better than to tangle with a preacher or politician with God on his side.

The payola scandals of the late fifties proved the point. The music industry had only itself to blame when the merciless glare of public scrutiny was turned on the practice of record labels paying cash or gifts for radio airplay. A nasty feud between the two giants of music publishing—the American Society of Composers, Authors & Publishers (ASCAP) and Broadcast Music, Inc. (BMI)—had ended up as part of a House subcommittee investigation into corrupt broadcast practices. ASCAP, the more respectable and established of the two companies, lobbied for the government to look into payola, rampant at the time among rock 'n' roll disc jockeys. BMI had cornered the market on rock, r & b, and country music; a blow to the already dubious credibility of rock 'n' roll would, ASCAP reasoned, be a blow to its competitor.

It wasn't the first time ASCAP had tried to sabotage BMI's rock 'n' roll hegemony. It had successfully gotten

Johnny Ray's "Such a Night" banned for lewdness. The lyrics, in part, ran,

> Just the thought of her kiss,
> sets me on fire.
> I reminisce
> and I'm filled with desire.

"Not only are most of the BMI songs junk," remarked Billy Rose, an ASCAP spokesman, "but in many cases they are obscene junk, pretty much on the level with dirty comic magazines." So much for the spirit of friendly competition.

This interindustry scheming fell right into the hands of pop music's sworn enemies, who were only looking for an excuse to outlaw the backbeat entirely. "It was commonly believed," writes critic John Morthland, "the music was so terrible that teenagers listened to it only because they had been tricked into doing so by greedy DJ's who pocketed payola and then played the record so often it was imprinted on listeners' impressionable young minds. Many considered rock 'n' roll a passing fad that would soon die out; the payola hearings were in part an attempt to insure this, and thus it was perfectly appropriate to hold these hearings in the election year of 1960."

In the end, the payola uproar ruined the career of at least one tireless champion of teen-age music. Alan Freed, a man who claimed to have invented the term "rock 'n' roll" (he later tried to copyright it) was indicted on twenty-six charges of receiving illegal gratuities and eventually pled guilty to a pair of commercial bribery charges. Freed, a legendary New York-based DJ and dance/concert promoter, refused "on principle" to sign an affidavit denying any involvement in payola. He paid the price for his defiance, becoming the principle scapegoat in the payola hearings.

Another pop music impresario embroiled in the scandal was Dick Clark. Clark had no compunction about signing affidavits, and in the end—after divesting himself of thirty-three music-related businesses and admitting that he had personal interest in 27 percent of the songs heard over a two-year period on his hit TV music show "American Bandstand"—Clark walked away smelling like a rose. It comes as no surprise that he emerged shortly afterward at the forefront of a whole new, safe, and sanitized trend in popular music.

But that would come later. "You know how long we fought to keep [rock 'n' roll] music alive?" Clark was quoted as asking in *The History of American Bandstand*. "How hard we fought? I mean, so many assassins . . . they wanted to kill rock 'n' roll. In 1959 there were the Congressional payola hearings, which were a huge trumped-up witch-hunt, an excuse to try and kill this thing. The old licensing organizations, Congress and the whole adult generation, they all despised rock 'n' roll. Hated the music. Hated the kids . . . You know, the reason I wore a coat and tie and had the dress code for the kids was not because I'm such a big fan of coats and ties and dress codes. It helped us pass the music through as legitimate."

Clark had the right idea. "Passing music through" became the primary concern of the industry in the wake of the payola uproar. The business was caught between the horns of a very sticky dilemma. Rock 'n' rollers were proving their commercial appeal to a whole new, and immensely promising, consumer class: teenagers. They were also proving themselves unruly, unsavory, and, worst of all, controversial. By the close of the decade, pop music, in the words of pop historian Greg Shaw, "fell into the hands of those same old men of the music industry—promoters, radio programmers, A&R men, record executives—who had long sought a means to remove the un-

118

predictability originally inherent in rock and roll, and bring the phenomenon (or fad as they considered it) more into line with their own standards and marketing expertise." The problem was to keep the golden goose laying without arousing the indignation of righteous, upstanding citizens. The way the cigar-chomping tune peddlers accomplished their goal was a triumph of style over substance.

No one peddled harder or smoked a bigger cigar than Colonel Tom Parker. From almost the beginning, Elvis's mysterious, all-powerful manager seemed to have a single goal: to transform his client from a symbol of youthful rebellion into a neutered inoffensive Entertainment Institution. He used Elvis's army stint to set the stage, heaping on the patriotic hokum and rendering the lurid pelvis thruster an aw-shucks G.I. It was almost as if Elvis, shorn and uniformed, was doing penance for his hell-raising. After his discharge he appeared on a Frank Sinatra television special, offering humble deference to "Mr. Sinatra." "No further notice of Elvis's acceptance into the mainstream of show business was necessary," writes Stephen Tucker, "once viewers glimpsed him standing stiffly in a pseudo-army uniform while surrounded by the beaming countenances of Sinatra, Joey Bishop [and] Sammy Davis, Jr."

Further notice may not have been necessary, but Colonel Tom was taking no chances. To greet the new decade, Elvis recorded "It's Now or Never," a bit of mock opera that would have made Mario Lanza envious and, with one stroke, made Presley safe for grandmothers. He was, according to *Newsweek*, "no longer the sneering, hip-twitching symbol of the untamed beast that resides in 17-year-old breasts. . . . he has come back from the Army easygoing, unassuming, fatherly." Fatherly. It was Colonel Tom's finest moment. No longer would Elvis be unfavorably compared to Pat Boone. Elvis had *become* Pat Boone.

The lesson wasn't lost on all the others in Colonel Tom's footsteps hustling for a piece of the pop music pie. The early sixties, the era of the Teen Idol, saw a grim proliferation of dimly talented artists in the safe-and-sane Elvis mold—numberless Fabians, Rydells, Avalons, and Ankas—supported by saturation-marketing campaigns, oceans of swelling strings, and the throbbing puppy love of numberless nymphettes.

The center of this syrupy storm was Philadelphia, home of Clark's "American Bandstand," the staging area for the short, profitable careers of dozens of teen idols. The consummate pragmatist, Clark had seemingly abandoned his quest to "get the music through," concentrating instead on catering to the pubescent whims of the largely female audience who flocked around these interchangeable dreamboats. "[W]hile it's true that teen idols were all clean-cut and white and good-looking and all-together less threatening than those who preceded them," writes Clark biographer Michael Shore, "there was something fascinating about their appeal. . . . The teen idols *were* white, but they were also heavily ethnic . . . specifically Italian. Thus, while ostensibly 'safe' they also had a particularly exotic appeal to Middle America."

Maybe, but exotic hardly equals dangerous or arrogant or all shook up. The rise of the teen idols is not surprising in a culture as monolithically vapid as America in the early sixties. In a society so smug, under an establishment so ruthlessly self-righteous, low common denominators inevitably prevail. What is surprising is that the kids seemed perfectly willing to be told what was good for them. The myth of the sensitive, mumbling "juvie," lashing out against parents and authority figures, wanting only to be left alone, was a Hollywood creation that did less to dramatize a reality than to present an appealing image for teen audiences. Kids, like everyone else, inhabited a wasteland

120

of prosperity. Rebellion, risk, and originality all seemed pointless. How do you lash out against a marshmallow? How do you make a stand in quicksand? What's the option to cooption? The will to resist it, even just for the thrill of it, was drained away by enervating, sanctimonious complacency.

It's no wonder change came as such a rude and traumatizing shock.

The Beatles in a Hollywood Museum Wax Display

Chapter Six

ZEITGEIST!

It would take me six months to explain all the
things I believe in.
> —George Harrison

I know what it's like to be dead.
> —Peter Fonda, as told to John Lennon

In 1966 it was a weird year for the Beatles and, by extension, for the whole wide-eyed, fibrillating world of Western
civ. For twenty-four ear-piercing, flash-popping, gravity-
defying months, the Fab Four had held it all in thrall, putting a new spin on terra firma, sending it hurling round
faster and faster until all the bolts and battens came loose
and the concrete started to crack and some people swore
the sky was a different color.

They were right. Up there in the heavens Someone seemed to be smiling sardonically, and the gleaming grin was burning off the mists of a long and dreamless sleep. Life was once again sparking and sputtering with a thousand contradictions. The light and noise and pennywhistle shrieking signaled the end of the interminable intermission.

The curtain had finally risen on the sixties. Blacks marched around acting like the chosen folks of Moses himself. Gun muzzle flashes lit Indochinese backwaters and the back room of a Dallas schoolbook depository. Artists played Pop Goes the Context in fifteen-minute flings with fame. Crew-cut golden boys made ellipitical orbits in flaming tin cans. Deviate, folksinging poets took a stand for "every hung-up person in the whole wide universe." Neighbors and strangers pointed to each other and laughed and shouted, "Hey! You're one, too!"

Question: Do you believe in lunacy?
Answer: Yeah; it's healthy.
Question: What do you think of the criticism that you're not very good?
Answer: We're not.
Question: You've admitted to being agnostics. Are you also irreverent?
Answer: We are agnostics, so there is no point in being irreverent.
Question: Do you date much?
Answer: What are you doing tonight?
Question: How did you find America?
Answer: We went to Greenland and made a left.
Question: What excuse do you have for your collar-length hair?
Answer: Well, it just grows out your head.
Question: Do you have any advice for teenagers?

124

Answer: Don't get pimples.
Question: Why aren't you wearing a hat?
Answer: Why aren't you wearing a tie?
Question: Who in the world would you like to meet
more than anyone else?
Answer: The real Santa Claus.
Question: What do you think you've contributed to
the musical field?
Answer: A laugh and a smile.
Question: How does it feel putting on the whole
world?
Answer: How does it feel to be put on?

It felt pretty good, truth be told; like a slap and a tickle and a sly wink that whispered with a Liverpudlian lilt, "You're part of it, too, you know." The wit and charm and gregarious good humor that John, Paul, George, and Ringo splattered all over newsmen at the airport press conference that launched their first American tour in February 1964 was a tart sample of a whole new kind of rebellion. It was so audaciously unexpected—the brittle, jangling sound of their music, the hair and suits, the Limey accents, the spicy hint of mockery, and the self-effacing aura of innocence; the whole nudging conspiratorial circus act— it all worked to disarm and dispel and delight.

Meet the Beatles and you were introduced to a whole new code of hip, nothing at all like the sullen, hot-rodding good-kids-gone-bad syndrome occupying the attention of sociologists and shrinks back there in the fifties. "The Presleyian gyrations and caterwauling were but lukewarm dandelion tea compared to the 100-proof elixir served up by the Beatles," crowed the New York *Daily News* on the occasion of the lads' '64 arrival. Evangelist Billy Graham broke Sabbath to join 73 million Americans who tuned in for the foursome's Ed Sullivan appearance. "They're a passing phase," he avowed. "All are symptoms of the uncertainty of the times and the confusion about us."

Could be, but the Beatles didn't *seem* confused or uncertain. When the righteousness regulators, who had previously been able to fuel rock 'n' roll bonfires with just a hint of will-sapping Commie plots, tried the same tactic on the Fab Four, it sounded sort of silly. If the boys were a threat, it was a hard one to put your finger on, particularly in the midst of a full-court jubilee of fascinated adulation. Something like the Beatles had just never happened before, and if you couldn't get enough of George's big ears or Ringo's big nose or Paul's big eyes or John's big mouth . . . well, welcome to the world's biggest fan club.

Musically, the Beatles *weren't* much of a threat. Despite their insistence that the music they liked best was "colored American groups," their early string of hit singles—"I Want to Hold Your Hand," "Please, Please Me," "She Loves You," "Love Me Do"—bore less resemblance to race music than a sort of revved-up teen idol fare. A punchy rhythm section and a spirited, guitar-driven bounce—components of some definitive pop music advances by the British—gave the sound a pleasing edge, but the prevailing commercial appeal lay in those falsetto harmonies, the musical counterpart to the cute head shakes and frothy mum-pleasing charm.

Before too long, however, it was becoming plainly evident that Lennon & McCartney were retooling rock 'n' roll, tapping into potentials long dormant and even brand-new. *Beatles '65*, released in December '64, was an impressive leap forward in the pure pop craftsmanship, bristling with sharp, funny, infectious tunes and increasingly assured performances. The best Beatle music worked from various points of view: "No Reply," "I'm a Loser," "She's a Woman," and later that year with "Eight Days a Week,"

126

"I Don't Want to Spoil the Party," "The Night Before," "Help!" "Another Girl"—these were songs not so much about love as about people in love, different kinds of people with different attitudes—wry, ironic, pathetic, hopeful, mad. It was music that neatly sidestepped the crude moral scrutiny that rock 'n' roll had suffered since Presley and payola. "She's Got a Ticket to Ride"—what did that mean, exactly? It was innocent and suggestive, concealing and revealing at the same time. The Beatles made music for a new corps of cognoscenti. Their emerging fans were no longer just weak-kneed teenettes. They were precocious young adults, canny, cynical, and slightly spoiled.

And nobody's fool. Unlike many of their musical idols, the Beatles owed no debt and paid no homage to any religious tradition. The reason is simple: they *had* no religious tradition. Beatles biographies are conspicuously silent on the subject of early spiritual training* and it would be hard to imagine a collection of gospel standards or Church of England hymns, a la Elvis's *His Hand in Mine*, with the Fab Four posing devotedly in frilled shirts with folded hands. The group spoke for an entire, disdainful generation when they simply ignored the church and all its archaic admonitory credos. In its long, unrelenting battle against rock 'n' roll teen culture, the church had rendered itself utterly superfluous to anything youthful and new.

Another factor contributed heavily to the studied indifference of the Beatles toward religion. Postwar British Socialism had transformed the Isles into a secular utopian laboratory. Public housing, public schooling, National Health, cradle-to-grave government care—it was perhaps the grandest attempt by a society to pull itself up by its own bootstraps outside the Iron Curtain. To the degree

---

* Save some vague references by Lennon's Aunt Mimi concerning the boy's early attraction to Christianity.

that it succeeded, it guaranteed every citizen the right to an education, a job, and medical attention. To the degree that it failed, it enforced a grim and grimy low common denominator for life that reached its apex in the New Towns of the industrial north.

And to the degree that it embodied a political and religious philosophy, British Socialism had set its citizens on the slow, spiral path of secularized perfectibility. The church was left to minister rites of birth and death, attending to the stubborn, superstitious hopes and fears of the old. Like the Crown, the church was a musky reminder of an age when Britannia ruled the waves and the Almighty ruled Albion's destiny. Both were subject to the ridicule of Britain's brave and cheeky new children. "On this next number I want you all to join in," quipped John Lennon on the occasion of the Beatles' Royal Command Variety Performance at the Prince of Wales Theatre in Piccadilly Circus with the Queen Mother and Princess Margaret in attendance. "Would those in the cheap seats clap their hands? The rest of you can rattle your jewelry."

It was funny and quick and fashionable, and it was one more reminder that the Queen of England, Protector of the Faith, was inspiring something more than love and devotion in her subjects.

As Lennonisms go, however, it wasn't nearly as revealing as another remark he let slip at a press conference a few months later. "What will you do when Beatlemania subsides?" was the question to which Paul McCartney first replied, "It's disturbing that people should go about blowing us up, but if an atom bomb should explode I'd say, 'Oh well' . . . I know the bomb is ethically wrong . . . but it's something like religion that I don't think about. It doesn't fit into my life." Lennon picked up the cue. "I don't suppose I think much about the future. I don't really give a damn. Though now we've made it, it would be a pity to get bombed. It's selfish, but I don't care too much about humanity—I'm an escapist. Everybody's always drumming on about the future but I'm not letting it interfere with my laughs, if you see what I mean. Perhaps I was worried more when I was working it out about God."

There it was, in among all that trendy nihilism—the offhanded admission that God was a problem that had been "worked out." For Paul, God simply didn't compute. He was arcane, imponderable, ultimately as inexplicable as the idea of people dropping A-bombs on each other. For John, on the other hand, God, who could potentially interfere with the laughs, needed resolution. He was something to worry about. The statements were, of course, expressions of personality traits that in time would become as famous as the music of Lennon and McCartney. But at the moment they were simply part of the provocative patchwork of Beatleology—controversy undercut by unfailing charm.

It wasn't until that watershed year of '66 that things started to come unraveled and the seamless charisma of the Beatles began to feel the strain of an increasingly sharp generational conflict. On March 4 of that year, a lengthy profile of Lennon ran in the London *Evening Standard*. It was written by Maureen Cleave, a friend of the Beatles who had been allowed extensive access to each of the foursome the previous spring. It seemed Lennon had finally worked out his problem about the Almighty. "Christianity will go," he said. "It will vanish and shrink. I needn't argue about that, I'm right and will be proved right. We're more popular than Jesus Christ right now. I don't know which will go first—rock 'n' roll or Christianity. Jesus was all right but his disciples were thick and ordinary. It's them twisting it that ruins it for me."

"We're more popular than Jesus." It remains one of Lennon's most enduring slogans, right up there with "All you need is love" and "I don't believe in Beatles." Given his smug, slightly belligerent tone, it's easy to imagine that Lennon, as was his habit, was simply mouthing off, engaging in a bit of Fleet Street grandstanding. He'd done it before and gotten away with it, but not this time. The remark went largely unnoticed in the British press, but when an American teen magazine called *Datebook* picked it up, on the eve of the Beatles' second American tour, it set off a bonfire. In at least six Southern states, churches collected Beatles albums and memorabilia from house to house and then organized mass torchings. Record stores in the south refused delivery on Beatles products, and in the first week after the story broke, thirty-five radio stations completely banned the group's music, largely at the howling demands of religious groups.

Things quickly degenerated. Brian Epstein, the group's manager, first considered canceling the tour and returning millions to promoters. He quickly got a better idea and suggested to his client that an apology was in order. Lennon refused on the grounds that he had only told the truth: the Beatles *were* more popular than Jesus. Stateside the frenzied outrage was reaching levels not seen since the fifties heyday of rock hysteria. Thurman Babbs, pastor of the New Haven Baptist Church in Cleveland, promised to excommunicate any member of his congregation who attended a Beatles concert. The Grand Dragon of the South Carolina chapter of the Ku Klux Klan nailed copies of *Meet the Beatles* and *Something New* to a burning cross and muttered death threats against the godless mop tops. In South Africa, all Beatles sales and airplay was banned. As of this writing, John Lennon's records are still not allowed in the country. Even the Vatican got into the act, observing indignantly if not entirely accurately that "some subjects must not be dealt with profanely, even in the world of beatniks."

By this time Lennon was a penitent beatnik. Agreeing at last to hold a press conference "explaining" what he'd said, he met with a horde of newsmen at O'Hare Airport on August 11. What followed was a meandering, equivocating disavowal that reveals, with naked clarity, a deep-seated ambivalence toward organized religion. Unwittingly perhaps, he was speaking the minds of millions of his contemporaries. Even as he stonewalled and backpedaled, it was obvious that Lennon had, indeed, "worked out God."

"I'm not anti-God or anti-Christ or anti-religion," he pleaded. "I was not saying we are greater or better. I believe in God, but not as one thing, not as an old man in the sky. I believe that what people call God is something in all of us. I believe that what Jesus and Mohammed and Buddha and all the rest said was right. It's just the translations that have gone wrong. I wasn't saying the Beatles are better than God or Jesus. I used the Beatles because it's easy for me to talk about Beatles. I could have said TV or the cinema or anything popular and I would have gotten away with it . . . I wasn't saying whatever they're saying I was saying. . . . I'm sorry I said it, really. I never meant it to be a lousy anti-religious thing. From what I've read, or observed, Christianity seems to me to be shrinking, to be losing contact. . . ."

The crow-eating session continued with Lennon claiming that his views on Christianity were formed from a popular book called *The Passover Plot* by Hugh Schonfield. The premise, according to Lennon, was that Jesus' simple message of love and brotherhood had been garbled by the apostles for a variety of self-serving reasons. Consequently, the message had lost validity for "many in the modern age," he insisted. When asked what his own religious background was, Lennon offered this deadpan reply: "Normal Church of England, Sunday School and

Sunday Church. But there was nothing actually going on in the church I went to. Nothing really touched us. . . . By the time I was 19, I was cynical about religion and never even considered the goings-on in Christianity. It's only in the last two years that I—all the Beatles—have started looking for something else. We live in a moving hothouse. We've been mushroom-grown, forced to grow up a bit quick, like having 30-to-40-year-old heads in 20-year-old bodies. We had to develop more sides, more attitudes. . . . we had to sort of be more than four mopheads up on a stage. We had to grow up or we'd have been swamped."

In the end, the "Jesus" controversy came to nothing. Perhaps Lennon's chagrin helped; more likely the Beatlemania juggernaut was simply unstoppable. In any case, the group's third American tour was duly launched, and in August, in San Francisco's Cow Palace, the group played onstage together for the last time, marking the end of their three-year stint in the "moving hothouse."

It's surprising that more wasn't made of Lennon's imperious put-down of all things Christian. That talk about old men in the sky, Jesus and his competition being the same . . . there was even heresy in his humility. But what's more surprising is that some vigilant newshound didn't catch the veritable catalog of thinly veiled references that peppered the follow-up news conference. Those strange allusions to old heads on young bodies, the seemingly casual use of "mushroom" . . . and was "mophead" the word John Lennon really meant to use? The Beatles were developing more attitudes, all right, more attitudes exuded, enhanced, and enforced by a wonder pill called LSD-25.

The sixties, and the Beatles' place in it, can be viewed as an escalating series in increasingly improbable accidents. The Beatles just happened to get together, just happened to decide to let their hair grow, just happened to revive rock 'n' roll, and just happened—on August 28, 1964, at the Delmonico Hotel in New York City—to get their ticket punched for a ride down the rabbit hole.

Yet there is a fated inevitability to it all. If the Beatles hadn't existed, someone would have had to invent them. Once invented, someone *else* would have had to introduce them to psychedelic drugs. Destiny lay in the quixotic fancies of the Zeitgeist, popping up here, sprinkling magic dust there, spinning coincidence into fabulous yarns. The sixties was a collision waiting to happen. What remains to be explained is how all those vehicles—those buses and bikes and trollies—ended up at the same intersection at the same moment.

According to Peter Brown and Steven Gaines in *The Love You Make: An Insider's Story of the Beatles*, Bob Dylan was a little surprised to learn that the Fab Four had never smoked marijuana. "But what about your song?" he asked. "The one about getting high?" They hadn't a clue to what he meant until he started singing, "And when I touch you, I get high, I get high, I get high." The melody was "I Want to Hold Your Hand," but the words, the lads explained, were "I can't hide, I can't hide, I can't hide."

"I'm thinking for the first time," McCartney was alleged to have said after Dylan rolled a fistful of joints and passed them around. "Really *thinking*." That wasn't all he was doing. The Beatles' introduction into the wonderful world of reefer initiated them into an old and venerable musical fraternity, peopled by jazzbos and blues men and mantra-wailing beats and a myriad of red-eyed, smoke-cured denizens of the deeply cool.

Marijuana went back as far as you'd care to go, as a potion in all manner of ecstatic cults and incantatory shamanistic rituals from American Indians to Persian dervishes. It's a drug tied closely to music for good reason. Down there in the vibrating, biochemical spheres, cannabis fumes comingle with sensory synapses to set up whole new dimensions of resonance and rhythm, unveiling hitherto unimagined realms of audio texture. Music, any kind of music, gets deep and shimmery and flecked with highlights. Space opens up between the notes, and dizzying geometric spectrums of sound crystallize—whole colonies of melody, bustling cities of syncopation. Grass blew out the limits of what could be imagined, and once that happened, you were only a threshold away from *creating* the sounds that spun and fizzed and cascaded through your frontal lobes.

LSD-25 pushed past that threshold; demolished, in fact, any flimsy differentiation between the real and the imagined. For the group it was the greatest karmic gift that fate, or the gods, could bestow. Much has been made since of the connection between the use of mind-expanding drugs in the sixties and various psychotropic sacraments in primitive religions, particularly by those anxious to promote the quasi-mystical properties of the drug experience. But the question is one of degree, not kind. "It's true that quite commonly drugs like hashish and mescaline have been used in the context of . . . ecstatic religious rituals," remarks anthropologist I. M. Lewis, "but very often the drugs that are used are not fantastically powerful. They may be, for instance, simply alcohol or tobacco."

LSD-25, on the other hand, *is* fantastically powerful, and to compare its effect with those of its primitive counterparts is like pitting a pushcart against a fuel-injected, turbocharged dragster. Whatever passing resemblance acid has to certain essences of magic mushroom or sacred cactus is more than offset by its awesome potency. In the sixties, LSD was the ground zero of chemically induced revelation. It was not only immediate, it was utterly modern, a product of space age technology synthesized in sterilized Swiss labs. Its effects on the spiritual expectations of a generation would be incalculable.

And its role in the unfolding saga of religion and rock would prove monumental. The parallels between loud electric music and instant acidic enlightenment can be charted in the same transrational sphere where Pentecostalism and tribal drums are linked. The amplified four-piece rock combo—no less than the chopped and channeled street rod, the jukebox, the boob tube, or the A-bomb—was a distillation of all the furious, chaotic energies of the epoch. Rock 'n' roll was built on the maxim that if you couldn't say it in three minutes, it wasn't worth saying. LSD was tantalizing for the same reason: it was a cheap, glitzy, mind-boggling thrill, a quick ride around a sharp corner. The future-shocked frustrations of life on an open-throttled merry-go-round relegated the Meaning of Existence to nerve-ending tingles. A tactile, kinetic urgency began to fuse pop music with chemical epiphanies. There was an overpowering conviction that if it was short and sweet and made your brain cells rattle, well then, you had your finger in the socket.

"Roll over, Beethoven," crowed Chuck Berry, and the Beatles picked up the taunt. "Dear Sir or Madam, will you read my book," they sang on "Paperback Writer," a brilliant send-up of literary aspirations in the later half of the twentieth century. "It took me years to write, will you take a look? . . . A thousand pages give or take a few, I'll be writing more in a week or two. I can make it longer if you like the style. I can change it round and I want to be a paperback writer."

Get it? It was over for all that earnest laboring in the vineyard of art. Over for all those movements and opuses and creaky symphonies. Over for all that "enduring masterpiece of literature" jazz. Life was too short, fragmenting into splinter scenes waiting to be sampled. . . .

135

Similarly, LSD reduced the religious impulse to a dissolving sugar cube on the tip of your tongue. Faith might well be the substance of things not seen, but why bother with the invisible when acid could ram the cosmos right up the cerebral cortex in livid color? What had earlier been the domain of mystics, ascetics, and droning monks was suddenly gloriously available to anyone hankering for a glimpse of God's face. Spirituality was no longer defined by devotion, discipline, and self-deprivation; it was a trip, maybe more accurately a holiday, eighteen hours long, embarking anytime, night or day. Whole centuries of incense-permeated tradition was simply shrugged off, and religion, that painful, uncertain path to saving truth, was suddenly a movie, a slide show, a state-of-the-art sound system. An experience.

What *was* the LSD-25 experience? The short answer, the one offered by the grinning true believers, remains the best. Acid was a sacrament, the Eucharist of a new faith, part church, part theater. Consistently, and amazingly, it transformed the natural into the supernatural and the ordinary into the extraordinary. Flowers really did grow from walls and horns from people's heads. Your life really did unravel before your eyes, and death really was a doorway to another reality. And people really, actually, *did* see God. Or they thought they did. Which was the same thing. Or seemed to be.

The Beatles first swallowed truth-soaked sugar cubes in the spring of '65, when their dentist surreptitiously slipped the drug into their after-dinner coffee. The next recorded trip occurred in Hollywood that summer, at the tail end of their last tour, when Peter Fonda supposedly regaled them with the hair-raising tale of a near-fatal operation he'd undergone. "I know what it's like to be dead," he kept insisting. His refrain was to end up in the distinctly skewered love song, "She Said, She Said."

The anecdote is a quick glimpse into creative processes already beginning to overheat from the friction of mutating brain cells. Awash with dazzling new potentials, the Beatles set about reinventing their music, stringing together influences, stacking nuances like building blocks, harnessing studio technology to their prancing imaginations. In December they released *Rubber Soul*, an album that neatly delineated the end of rock 'n' roll's long, unselfconscious childhood. Beatles scholar Nicholas Schaffner describes it as the moment in the *Wizard of Oz* when Dorothy's black-and-white world is suddenly turned to stunning technicolor.

"Here," write Brown and Gaines, "the simplistic love songs began to wane, replaced with a dazzling spectrum of subjects and curios, from the banal to the ephemeral. The very sound of music was strikingly different; richer, more melodious, haunting. Now, instead of producing an album that was just a hodge-podge of hit sings . . . the albums had a sense of collective identity, a mood and a sound linking them."

The Beatles, now heavily into grass and beginning a regular regimen of using acid, delivered on their early promise. Suddenly, the band's unprecedented popularity began to take on a new significance. They were writing deep, double-entendred tunes, imagistic and sophisticated with lots of nods and winks to the big, complex world of adulthood. Rock 'n' roll was now Rock, and Rock had come of age. *Rubber Soul* included urbane observations on the battle of the sexes ("Norwegian Wood," "It's Only Love"), drollery in love-song drag ("You Won't See Me," "Think for Yourself," "I'm Looking Through You"), thickly sliced irony ("Run for Your Life"), a lot of richly crafted pop work in the Gershwin/Porter vein ("In My

Life," "I've Just Seen a Face"), and even a Top 40 hit in a foreign language ("Michelle"). It also contained what Lennon claimed was a bit of religious commentary. "'Girl' I liked," he said, "because I was, in a way, trying to say something or other about Christianity which I was opposed to at the time."

"She promises the earth to me and I believe her," read the lyrics in part, "after all this time I don't know why."

Rubber Soul, in fact, foreshadowed what would ultimately become the Beatles' grand theological credo. "Say the word and you'll be free," they sang on "The Word," "say the word and be like me. . . ." The word, of course, was love, four letters that, when all was said and done, were the golden key to the giant, cosmic Rubik's Cube of existence.

> In the beginning I misunderstood,
> but now I've got it, the word is good.
> Spread the word and you'll be free,
> spread the word and be like me,
> spread the word I'm thinking of,
> have you heard, the word is love.

Rubber Soul was followed in America by *Yesterday . . . and Today*, a collection of assorted singles and extra cuts that hadn't made it on previous LP's. Aside from some druggy in-jokes ("Dr. Roberts") and further forays into rock experimentation (including an early use of tape run backward in the background of the dreamy "I'm Only Sleeping"), *Yesterday . . . and Today* demonstrated a nascent social conscience. The LP's renowned "butchered babies" cover was quickly suppressed by the record company after retailers refused to stock the gory in-joke. The artwork, quickly pasted over with an innocuous publicity shot, was dubbed by Lennon "as relevant as Vietnam."

Apparently all that talk about not letting reality interfere with the laughs was a bit of preacidic bantering unworthy of their status as enlightened prophets.

The Beatles' view of themselves was changing along with everyone else's. The shift in perception was to have seismic effects on modern music. The group's sudden and unprecedented rise to fame seemed capricious, almost frivolous. As their career continued to unfold, the question became whether or not they would make an impact commensurate with their newfound importance.

To be fair, the band really *was* important, with people hanging on their every word—spoken or sung—and dutifully recording their every move as if posterity would be immeasurably impoverished with anything less than a complete accounting of the days of their lives. A subtle but significant change was occurring. Elvis earned his adulation by tapping into hormonal yearnings. The Beatles, by '66, had other things on their expanded minds. The public's rapt attention, the great gasp of silence every time they opened their mouths: it was an invitation to profundity too tempting to resist.

Neither the music of *Rubber Soul* nor the artwork on *Yesterday . . . and Today* could, however, have prepared fans for the group's next move. Released in August of that pivotal year of 1966, *Revolver* was a refracted glimpse through the prism of psychedelia, a convoluted, sometimes queasy, astonishingly original statement of intent that scraped off the last of rock 'n' roll's good-time veneer. The LP had the feel of a watch wound too tightly, full of wails and yodels, off-kilter bumps and thuds, piercing birdcalls. Harrison's guitar work, the heart of *Revolver*, had undergone a strange metamorphosis. It kept disappearing up trebly tunnels only to come screaming out of nowhere like a vapor-sucking bat. Melodies played as elaborate pranks on the conventional idea of melody, rattling around

the brain like marbles on plate glass. McCartney's ballads—"Here, There, and Everywhere," "For No One"—
were at once sublimely wistful and isolated in their her-
mitic perfection. Lyrics acquired new meanings and levels
of meanings, all encoded with acid-drenched etching
tools. "Eleanor Rigby," even "Yellow Submarine"
sounded like emanations from some kind of hyperreality,
where pathos and colors were keyed to a glaring pitch.
Revolver, in short, was loaded.

More importantly, it rolled back the stone on what
would, in time, become a spiritual influence in rock 'n' roll
second only to Pentecostalism: the pull of Eastern religion.
"Tomorrow Never Knows" may well have begun as a bit
of fanciful conjuring by John Lennon, but in the supercharged atmosphere of 1966, artistic license had a way of
becoming divine mandate. Originally titled "The Void,"
the cut was inspired by Lennon's drug-addled readings of
the Tibetan *Book of the Dead*. LSD advance man Timothy
Leary was constantly touting the ancient volume as an
indispensible pyschedelic tour guide, a kind of *Nirvana on
500 Micrograms a Day*, which is undoubtedly why Lennon
became interested in the abstruse tome. Lennon's original
idea for his musical treatment of the *Book of the Dead* was
to cut a chorus of thousands of chanting Hindu monks.
Reason prevailed, and "Tomorrow Never Knows" is instead constructed from onion-thin layers of spliced and
overdubbed sound, kiting along on Harrison's sitar drone
and anchored to the heartbeat thud of drums.

But even more hair-and-consciousness–raising than the
music were the song's lyrics. Lennon had deftly captured
the spirit, if not the secret teachings, of the Hindu/Buddh-
ist religious axis. "Tomorrow Never Knows" evoked the
spooky karmic wheel of reincarnation, the illusory dream
state of the material world, the vast, swirling pool of the

life force and the infinite love vibe humming through time and space, all in three minutes flat.

> Turn off your mind relax and float downstream.
> It is not dying. It is not dying.
> Lay down all thoughts, surrender to the void.
> It is shining. It is shining.
> That you may see the meaning of within.
> It is being. It is being.

The lyrics faded into the ether with an endless chanting finale: "Play the game existence to the end. Of the beginning. Of the beginning. Of the beginning. . . ." LSD-25 of course, was inspiring this Cyclical Paradox version of existence, dovetailing neatly with the essential tenets of Eastern religious philosophy. Any drug that enabled the individual to see God in a flower petal, to experience death in orgasm and eternity in a drop of water, was hardly destined to bolster the claims of the Judeo/Christian tradition. Rapt gazing into life's endlessly spinning wheel rendered the concepts of heaven and hell both simplistic and vindictive. Acid blurred all sorts of formerly clear distinctions, not the least of which was the one between creature and Creator. The notion that the individual could ultimately attain the Godhead must have had a heady appeal for the Beatles, who, through their creative effort, had already reached the status of verging deities. A status enhanced by the pathogenic magic they exuded on two smash films, *A Hard Day's Night* (1964) and *Help* (1965).

What was implied by drug revelation was shortly to be made explicit in front of the entire captivated world. In late 1966, finally freed from the touring grind, the Beatles took a breather from the world and from each other. McCartney went to Africa, Lennon returned to his Ken-wood digs and his disintegrating marriage, and Ringo tooled around London in expensive sports cars.

George Harrison, meanwhile, was on a quest. After hearing the sitar for the first time on the set of the film *Help!* from Hindu musicians hired for the score, the guitarist took up an earnest study of the twenty-one stringed instrument. In the fall of '66, at a London party, he was introduced to Indian sitar star Ravi Shankar, who subsequently invited Harrison for a two-month study program at his Kashmir retreat. "Having all these material things I wanted something more," Harrison recounted. "And it happened that just at the time I wanted it, it came to me in the form of Ravi Shankar, Indian music and the whole Indian philosophy."

There was, of course, nothing whole about the philosophy of India, a country sundered by all manner of bitter sectarian quarreling. But everyone knew what George meant: it was a vibe, a feeling, a trip. "I went partly to learn music and partly to see and learn as much about India as I could," he explained. "I'd always heard stories about men in caves in the Himalayas, hundreds of years old, and people who can levitate and people who get buried under the ground for six weeks and lots of what the West would call mysticism. But when you get there you find that all this is happening all over the place, with people materializing left, right and center."

It is doubtful that Harrison was making a subtle comment on the subcontinent's chronic overpopulation. There can be no doubt, however, about what he and his wife Patti learned on a two-month Indian tour following their stint with Shankar. "Here," Harrison asserts, referring to the West, "everybody is vibrating on a material level which is nowhere. Over there, they have this great feeling of something else that's just spiritual going on. . . . I know everybody has a different interpretation of God, but whatever God is, by becoming one with that, you naturally discover every sort of law that governs. That's why people like Jesus can make these sort of miracles."

Steeped in such incense-drenched insights, Harrison returned to England just in time to begin what would prove to be the Beatles' most influential and definitive work. In the oft-quoted words of critic Langdon Winner, *Sgt. Pepper's Lonely Heart's Club Band* was "the closest . . . Western civilization has come to unity since the Congress of Vienna. . . . For a brief while, the irreparably fragmented consciousness of the West was unified, at least in the minds of the young." Yet even aside from such grandiose claims, the LP *did* represent a kind of consensus: the burgeoning drug culture, rock technology, self-conscious eclecticism and formalized nonconformity combined to create the first and perhaps greatest of all concept albums. Concept rock in itself, would have been a completely alien idea not five years before.

The message of *Sgt. Pepper's* was both simple and admirably suited to the times: "trippiness", more than a point of view, was a way of life. If you grokked properly, everything was a trip, tinged with unreality. The album's cutesy circus premise underscored the metaphor. The whole production was suffused in a surreal haze with the emphasis on color and touch and perfectly rendered little scenes like shake–up snow globe landscapes.

In an album that has become lushly unlistenable over the years, "A Day in the Life" remains a staggering summation of psychotropic transcendence. In its brilliant contrast of normalcy against sudden, overwhelming bursts of vast insight, the song encapsulates the central conviction spawned by LSD: behind everything lurks the eternal, unknowable, and mind-blowing. A lucky man who "made the grade" blew his mind out in a car." "The English army

143

. . . won the war." Or was it only in a film? You get up, "get out of bed" and "run a comb across" your head. Everything can be as it always was then, on the bus, smoking a cigarette, "someone" speaks and you "fall into a dream."

And what a dream. The legendary cacophony at the song's finale, the full Sturm und Drang of a forty-two piece symphony orchestra, is the closest approximation of acid rapture ever recorded, capturing with frightful intensity the power of the psychedelic experience. And the helplessness of all who fall under its influence. The album's 45-second final note fades on a 20,000-hertz hum audible only to dogs and, one assumes, the silent witnesses beyond the stars.

Sgt. Pepper's also codified George Harrison's increasing fascination with all things Eastern. The LP's second side opens on "Within You and Without You," a sitarized drone fest that sealed the musician's pact with Hinduism.

Ross Michaels, in his biography *George Harrison, Yesterday & Today* comments on the song; "This was not only a soundtrack for the counterculture ethos—which divided people by age (the breaking point was 30), dress, values and other abstract factors of hipness and political thought and action—but for something more profound. For Harrison went beyond and extended his vision all the way through the galaxies, dividing the spiritually graceful and the spiritually lame."

There was no question on which side of that divide the Beatles fell, but by the spring of 1967, events indicated that even the most popular band in the history of music had a thing or two to learn about true spirituality.

Despite McCartney's announcement to the press that LSD had made him "a better, more honest, more tolerant member of society"—while his songwriter partners had, by this time, taken hundreds of trips—an unsavory stigma was still attached to the drug. It was not, however, the illegality of acid that bothered the band. It was rather the unsettling notion that enlightenment could be bought and ingested like breakfast cereal. LSD's synthetic origins didn't sit well with countercultural preferences for the natural, the organic, and the holistic. No one wanted chemical companies like Sandoz or Du Pont as their gurus. Lennon's unrestrained drug use deeply disturbed his wife, Cynthia. More important, George Harrison swore off drugs after a hair-raising visit to San Francisco's hippie ghetto, the Haight-Ashbury, where he was mobbed by barefooted, saucer-eyed Aquarian kids, demanding he perform a street corner concert. "This was an important turning point for George," write Brown and Gaines, "the recognition that LSD was not the key, that there was a higher, purer form of contentment waiting for him somewhere."

That somewhere was London's Park Lane Hilton Hotel, where on the night of August 24, John, Paul, and George attended a lecture by a small brown man with an innocent smile, a high-pitched voice, and an unruly mane of graying hair.

It was Harrison's wife, Patti, who had first called the Beatles' attention to the Maharishi Mahesh Yogi, an Indian holy man with a degree in physics. Since the early sixties, the maharishi—an Indian title loosely translated as "saint" and apparently self-bestowed—had toured the world extolling the virtues of Transcendental Meditation under the auspices of his Spiritual Regeneration Movement. Transcendental Meditation, a sort of easily digestible, Occidentalized version of some ancient and highly esoteric Hindu mystical disciplines was touted as a means of shutting off the material world and hooking up to the eternal, believed to be lurking within. Patti Harrison had first caught wind of the quasiscientific technique when she toured India with George, subsequently visiting the London branch of the Spiritual Regeneration Movement (SRM). When the maharishi wandered to town, she induced her husband and his mates to attend the lecture. The results were startling.

George Harrison in many ways exemplifies the typical spiritual seeker of the sixties. Affable, impressionable, and sincere, he was genuine in his search for truth. There is little doubt that what he sought was keyed to a naïve and guileless temperament. "I don't really enjoy being a Beatle anymore," he confided to biographer Hunter Davies. "It's trivial, it's unimportant. I'm fed up with all this me, us, I stuff and all the meaningless things we do. I'm trying to work out solutions to more important things in life. . . . It's basically a cosmic vision in which life on earth is but a fleeting illusion edged between lives past and future, beyond physical, mortal reality. . . . You go on being reincarnated until you reach the actual truth. Heaven and Hell are just a state of mind. . . . The actual world is an illusion. I'm beginning to know that all I know is that I know nothing."

It's the kind of mellifluous doubletalk that passed for profundity at the height of the sixties, and Harrison really believed it. So, for that matter, did the rest of the Beatles. On arrival that night at the Hilton they were given front row seats for the maharishi's squeaky, sing-song performance. "He spoke . . . of Jesus, of Buddha, of God;" write Brown and Gaines, "of eternal happiness and peace; of the inner self and of sublime consciousness; about reaching a state of nirvana—all without the use of messy and illegal drugs." Satori lay in TM, he assured them, and to prove the point, he went into a deep trance, snapping out of it ten minutes later and inviting the lads to his hotel room for a one-on-one spiritual workout. "You have created a magic air through your names," he told them. "You have got to use the magic influence."

"I'm still in a daze," Lennon later told reporters, revealing that the Beatles, their wives, and some select friends (including Mick Jagger and Marianne Faithfull) had enrolled in a ten-day meditation course that the holy man was conducting in Wales. Not long afterward they held a press conference to announce that they had given up drugs.

Brian Epstein had also given up drugs, along with everything else. Two days after the Beatles began chanting their mantras, Epstein died of an overdose, leaving the band without the dedicated, pragmatic guidance that had helped push them over the top. Circumstances remain unclear as to Epstein's death, but it certainly wasn't from LSD. Most likely he OD'd on barbiturates. The maharishi rushed in to fill the authority-figure vacuum. "This [sic] is no such thing as death," said Harrison to reporters after some cosmic coaching from the guru. "Only in the physical sense."

The Maharishi Mahesh Yogi may well have possessed genuine Hindu religious credentials. After all, he had studied holy writ under the Indian master Guru Dev. He may well also have been one in a long line of beatific snake oil salesmen fleecing gullible Westerners. The two aspects are not necessarily mutually exclusive. Millions have since attested to the benefits of his meditation program, only too happy to invest hefty sums to attain the harmony he promises. But the Beatles were hardly the guru's usual clientele. They were, in fact, a first-class ticket to the kind of international spiritual superstardom that most avatars only dream about. The maharishi wasted no time; he urged the quartet to finish their meditation studies at Rishekesh, his remote Himalayan ashram, where they would spend three months of intensive, undistracted, and drug-free chanting.

The Beatles, on the verge of launching their ambitious multimedia corporation Apple, hoped the maharishi's ministrations would give them the wisdom to run the company. They were already, in fact, spending lots of time in the guru's London flat, gathering pearls of wisdom. Plans were afoot to produce a feature film about the holy man with proceeds going toward the founding of a Transcendental Meditation University in London. Lennon and Harrison swore off meat, although after his initial fervor, John returned to profligate acid eating.

Meanwhile, the maharishi was busy behind the scenes trying to capitalize on his new disciples. His negotiations with ABC for a Maharishi Mahesh Yogi TV special featuring the Beatles were quashed when the group caught wind of the scheme. "He's not a modern man," George insisted. "He just doesn't understand these things."

Maybe not, but it didn't take a marketing genius to figure the angle in having the Fab Four as your house guests for three uninterrupted months. News of the group's retreat was greeted with a fascinated anticipation not seen since Moses' trek up the mountain. The Beatles were ascending to the abode of the gods to bring Truth to a waiting world. The group, with a large entourage in tow, left for the Roof of the World in February, eventually reaching Rishekesh—in symbolism reminiscent of scripture—on the backs of donkeys.

What awaited them was a Himalayan soap opera, a farcical comedy of errors with the maharishi alternately playing the roles of jester, sly dog, and charlatan. The ashram, hardly an otherworldly hole-in-the wall, resembled a lushly appointed resort, replete with a full kitchen and a staff of obsequious servants. The Beatles were joined by a full complement of trendy truth seekers, including Donovan, Beach Boy Mike Love, Mia Farrow and her sister Tia, assorted well-heeled hippies, and frumpy Swedish matrons. The regimen began at dawn each morning and included lengthy lectures by the sainted Yogi and afternoon meditation marthons. Everyone dressed in the loose flowing native garb, and according to Brown and Gaines, "A friendly competition started among them to see who could meditate the longest, and there were heated debates at dinner every night about 'who was getting it' and who was not. John seemed really into it, others thought he was faking it and that George was the most readily spiritual of the group." At night the band would gather with guitars to write songs together. It was, in many ways, a restorative idyll, a long-overdue respite from the glare of fame.

It was a respite not everyone seemed to appreciate. Ringo and his wife, Maureen, stuck it out for ten days; Paul and his girlfriend, Jane Asher, six weeks. John and George hung on, determined to "get it." But the Maharishi was after something else. He wanted the band to turn over 25 percent of its income to him as a kind of tithe. He also turned out to be a hard-nosed negotiator with Beatles' associates on the subject of the proposed film project, haggling over deal points and often consulting with his full-time accountant.

Money wasn't the only thing on the genial guru's mind. Rumors began flying that the maharishi was secretly eating chicken with his vegetarian fare and, worse yet, making sexual advances toward some of his more nubile devotees. One of Lennon's associates, Alex Mardis, aka "Magic Alex," laid a trap for the master. An attractive, blond California nurse was sent to the maharishi's bungalow while Alex and several witnesses hid in the bushes outside. The girl was to scream at the first sign of unseemly behavior, a signal for the others to rush in to catch the holy man *flagrante delicto*. The plan went awry when the bait succumbed without a whimper to the maharishi. Alex crept up to the window, spied out the scene, and reported back to Lennon and Harrison.

The decision was made to leave first thing the next morning. Lennon, elected spokesman, confronted the maharishi, who could only ask why with an unaccustomed look of pain on his face. "You're the cosmic one," was Lennon's curt reply. "You should know."

The return trip to Delhi was a nightmare. The hired cars broke down, stranding the group by the side of the road in the blistering sun for over three hours. It seemed like a curse sent winging after them by a wrathful guru.

Lennon, in the bitter, vengeful style that would come to characterize much of his later music, wrote a song about the Beatles' encounter with the Maharishi Mahesh Yogi titled "Sexy Sadie":

> Sexy Sadie, what have you done?
> You've made a fool of everyone . . .
> One sunny day the world was waiting for a lover.
> She came along to turn on everyone.
> Sexy Sadie, the greatest of them all.
> Sexy Sadie, you'll get yours yet.
> However big you think you are . . .
> We gave her everything we owned just to sit at her
>   table.
> Just a smile would lighten everything.
> Sexy Sadie, she's the latest and the greatest of
>   them all.

Fair enough. The Indian had taken the Englishmen for a ride, ripped them off, and worse, made them look like fools. But Lennon's indictment had something of a hollow ring considering his willingness, even eagerness, to be led down the garden path. The maharishi's indiscretions may have been inexcusable for a holy man, but did that mean the tenets of Transcendental Meditation were also a crock?

It didn't for George Harrison. The guitarist continued to turn inward and Eastward on a path of remarkable consistency, especially in contrast to John Lennon's subsequent wild oscillations. By the close of the decade, he began frequenting the London Krishna Temple, producing several recorded chants with the Hindu sect. He became a sort of honorary member of the Hare Krishna movement, lending influence, expertise, and money while gaining frequent audience with His Divine Grace A. C. Bhaktivedanta Prabhupada, founder of the International Society for Krishna Consciousness. Prabhupada, a man directly descended from Lord Krishna himself, would have a tremendous influence on Harrison's spiritual search. Harrison eventually bought the temple, a sprawling twenty-acre estate outside London and financed the publication of their slick house organ, *KRSNA: The Supreme Personality of Godhead*. "George was finding a way to cut through all the elitism, suspiciousness and aloofness that so many of his professional colleagues foster at the top of their careers," writes biographer Ross Michaels. "Best of all, he found beyond it, a sense of divine indivisible Oneness with all being." One report has Harrison chanting for fourteen straight hours, achieving total bliss.

It was, perhaps, the sort of effort required to free him of the Beatles' accumulated karma. By late 1968 it was painfully evident that no escape clause had been written into their contract as the counterculture's spiritual heroes. The release of *The Beatles*, the double white album, signaled the fragmentation of the band even as it memorialized their epic talents. The very breadth and diffuseness of the huge work lent it a shadowed melancholy. The music was, by turns, indulgent and incandescent, trite and timeless, all things to all people, and jealously personal. Subtle hints of boredom and disaffection with their own abilities were setting in. Each was reduced to playing backup on the other's original songs. Lennon's increasing obsession with Japanese avant-garde performance artist Yoko Ono was the fatal wedge driven between him and the rest of the band. The effervescent chimera of a swinging utopia, where nothing was real and there was nothing to get hung about, had vanished as quickly as it appeared. Inertia settled over Strawberry Fields. The Beatles no longer aspired to lead the children to the Promised Land.

But no one told the children. If troubled was the brow upon which rested the crown, more troubling still was the terrible momentum that carried events to their dark, post-logical conclusions.

"Leaders is what we *don't* need," Lennon would say years later and shortly before his death, at the hand of a crazed fan. "We can have figureheads and we . . . can have examples. . . . But leaders is what we don't need. . . . The idea of leadership is a false god. If you want to use the Beatles or . . . whoever, people are expecting them to *do* something for them. That's not what's going to happen. But they are the ones who didn't understand any message that came before anyway. And they are the ones that will follow Hitler or follow Reverend Moon or whoever. . . ."

By 1969 it was already too late for that kind of talk. The inescapable fact for the Beatles was that their popularity, the unparalleled reach of their music, had elevated them to a more exalted status than any mere entertainer, politician, or religious figure could hope to attain. Like it or not, the Beatles had, it seemed, *become* a religion, and around that religion sprang up all sorts of dangerous and dedicated heretics.

What finally curdled the sixties and, with it, the Beatles,

was the counterculture's own incestuous love. It was a world unto itself, unbalanced in its tightly sealed hipness, prey to all manner of damp passions. The same spirit that lingered lovingly over the Beatles' every inflection, savoring each nuance real or imagined in their music and lives; the same conviction that music bore the meaning of life and that musicians could speak to only those with ears to hear; that same subtle warping found substance in the lunacy of Charles Manson. That Manson believed the Beatles' White Album was bristling with secret messages for his ears only was, of course, the delusion of a madman. That a ragged band of followers—the dregs of a long and narcissistic dream—would believe him and do his bidding was a sign of sick times.

Vincent Bugliosi, in *Helter Skelter*—a book named after Manson's apocalypse, named, in turn, after the Beatles' edgy rock workout—describes how, in a search for motives in the Tate/LaBianca murders, he uncovered Manson's obsession for the White Album. "Honey Pie," according to the former Los Angeles district attorney, was interpreted as a clue that the Beatles would soon join Manson and his family in the desert. "Rocky Raccoon" was a metaphor for the black man and his imminent uprising. "Piggies" was a death sentence for the Establishment, while "Revolution #9" referred to the ninth chapter of the Book of Revelation, suggesting Manson's at least passing knowledge of the New Testament. "Helter Skelter" of course was the coded go-ahead for the seven brutal murders. It was all a horrific, house-of-mirrors distortion of the loving idolatry lavished on the Beatles for so long. All the clever word play, the studio magic, the wonderful conjuring power of the band had turned ugly and malicious. In some way no one wanted to understand, the piper was being paid.

It's little wonder that Lennon, after the demise of the

Beatles, went to such lengths to deny his coronation as priest/king of the Aquarian Age. Throughout the seventies, with Yoko at his side, he alternately promoted world peace, delved primally into his dim past, excoriated his former songwriting partner, Paul McCartney, unearthed his rock 'n' roll past, celebrated endlessly the intricacies of his second marriage, and, at length, settled into a grumpy, self-imposed exile.

The seventies were also a time marked by some deliberate, often ungenerous, attempts to demystify, sum up, and lay to rest. "Imagine there's no heaven," he intoned. "It's easy if you try." "I don't believe in Beatles," he wanted us to know, insisting that, "the dream is over. What can I say?"

He was right. There wasn't much left to say. John Lennon was a man who, after a once-in-a-lifetime brush with the powers of adulation and devotion, walked away bitter and blown. "What happens is somebody comes along with a good piece of truth," he told *Playboy* magazine. "Instead of the truth being looked at, the person who bought it is looked at. It's like when bad news comes, they shoot the messenger. When good news comes, they worship the messenger and they don't listen to the message. Have you ever met a Christian who behaves like a Christian? . . . Well, nobody's perfect right? . . . [E]xcept for all those people who are *named* as being perfect."

John Lennon and the Beatles were assumed to be perfect, or at least too good to be quite true. No one, Lennon seemed to be saying, should have to carry the burden of immortality, even if once, when they were young and didn't know any better, they'd panted after fame. Ringo in time became a faded celebrity, soaking up the good life in sunny California. Paul measured himself and cleverly repackaged what he found. George made an album called *All Things Must Pass* and proved himself right. John became a house husband, withdrew into a life of studied normalcy, and treasured it.

But there are forces that, once set in motion, can't simply be shut down or diverted or ignored. It's tempting to say that the crowning irony of John Lennon's life was his death, gunned down by a deranged clone (Mark Chapman modeled himself after Lennon, even marrying a Japanese woman). But irony that cruel belongs in another category altogether. . . .

The Rolling Stones

Chapter Seven
TRAPS FOR
TROUBADOURS

The whole difficulty of understanding Hell is that
the thing to be understood is so nearly Nothing.
> —C. S. Lewis

Welcome to the super-private world of the Rolling
Stones.
> —*16* Magazine, circa 1966

In 1968 an independent filmmaker named George Romero assembled an underpaid cast and crew in the bucolic Pennsylvania farmlands outside Pittsburgh to begin work on a low-budget horror movie, the sort destined to fill bottom halves of drive-in double bills. The premise of the film, or rather the trigger for the carnage, revolved around the effects of some vaguely defined cosmic radiation on the corpses of human beings. The malevolent rays brought the dead back to a semblance of life, animated by an insatiable appetite for the flesh of the living. The only way to stop this dazed-but-determined army of hungry ghouls was to smash in their skulls, rendering them, presumably, brain dead, their autonomic systems sputtering out in paroxyms of frustrated gluttony.

There was nothing particularly original in Romero's plot for *Night of the Living Dead*. It was one more variation on a mordant beyond-the-grave convention in horror movies that stretches from *Nosferatu* to teen-age space invaders. Zombies questing for the vital essences of duly terrified humans had peopled a universe of B-grade epics—the 1959 *Invisible Invaders*, for example, sported a cast of stiff-jointed stiffs that bore an uncanny resemblance to Romero's creations.

But what *Night of the Living Dead* lacked in originality, it more than made up for in a bloody-minded singleness of purpose that has since made it the grandaddy of cult classics. The film's relentlessly terrifying quality wasn't conjured up in the grainy, vérité–style black-and-white photography or the claustrophobic jitters induced by the cramped farmhouse setting. Nor was it a function, certainly, of feeble plotting, marginal acting, or even the ghastly denouement. In fact, the whole fable of fixated cadavers out for a warm meal faded into insignificance in light of the single quality that *really* rendered *Night of the Living Dead* a kind of benchmark of horror. The real and omnipresent threat was that the filmmakers would persist in showing us things we hadn't bargained for, would never have believed could be shown, and most decidedly had never wanted to see.

Romero's trick was *explicitness*, shortly to become a watchword for every conceivable form of contemporary artistic expression. His film was a nose-rubbing exercise in the power of celluloid. Previously the inviolate cinematic assumption had been that whatever you left to an audience's imagination was far more effective than anything you could project on the screen. Romero, taking precious few cues from anyone, proved that what could be explicitly depicted was far worse than anything anyone wanted to believe they could ever imagine in their wildest nightmares.

At one point in the film's seemingly endless crescendo of gore, a little girl, previously bitten by a zombie, falls into a feverish trance. Her mother, desperately seeking safety from the horde of goners literally pounding down the farmhouse, takes her child into the basement. There, the girl dies, then comes back to life as an "undead" and then, before the maddeningly dispassionate eye of the camera, repeatedly plunges a garden trowel into her mother's chest. Measured against the charnel house excesses that were to follow, largely spawned by *Night of the Living Dead*, such scenes might seem mild. But in 1968 the artistic gross-out license had only just been validated. The scene, in show biz parlance, was a shocker.

But then, 1968 was that kind of year; a hometown roost for all sorts of historical chickens. The season opened with the Tet Offensive and an American death toll in Vietnam of nearly twenty thousand, all for a war that now nearly half the country felt was a horrible mistake. Martin Luther King and Bobby Kennedy were gunned down, Biafra was starving, France was in a state of revolutionary siege, and the Soviets stolidly recapped Hungary in Czechoslovakia. It was the year the whole world was watching the bloody streets of Chicago, the year scientists linked XYY chromosomes with chronic criminal behavior, the year of *Rosemary's Baby*, Resurrection City, *Armies of the Night*, and *Cancer Ward*. In short, 1968 was *explicit*, a bunch of bad omens piled precipitously on top of each other, steaming with all the vapors that had once made up the

Aquarian Age mirage. No wonder *Night of the Living Dead* took on positively prophetic significance.

So, also, did *Beggar's Banquet*. He "looked not like a model but like an insane advertisement for a dangerous carefree Death—black ragged hair, dead-green skin, a cougar tooth hanging from his right earlobe, his lips snarled back from a marijuana cigarette between his rotting fangs, his gums blue, the world's only bluegum white man, poisonous as a rattlesnake." In *Dance with the Devil* author Stanley Booth describes not a flesh-seeking extra from *Night of the Living Dead* but a circa '68 Keith Richards, guitarist, co-composer, and icon of chic decay in a group that had brought a whole new meaning to the term *noblesse oblige*: by popular acclamation, the Greatest Rock 'n' Roll Band in the World—ladies and gentlemen, the Rolling Stones.

Yet while resemblances between the poisonous Richards and Romero's cadavers might have been only passing, the aesthetic link between the Living Dead and the Rolling Stones was all too real. Both signaled the end of long-standing conventions in popular art that separated the spoken from the unspoken. Here was the breeching of ironclad divisions between the over- and underworlds, the expiration of civilizing restraints that for so long had, quietly but firmly, insisted for the good of society that some things can be allowed to exist only in the mind's eye. New kinds of art eviscerated standards of public morality that, however hypocritically, had tightly clamped a Pandora's box of seething evils. Once released, these evils could consume a culture. It was the voiding of a covenant between man's darkest impulses and his own best interests—interests on which rested church, government, and the rule of law—interests that the liberating spirits of the sixties most violently refuted.

Romero, Richards, and their respective co-conspirators

represented nothing new. From DeSade to the flourishing porno trade of Victorian England; from Artaud, Baudelaire, and Rimbaud to the howling mantras of beat poets they were in direct line of succession of an artistic credo responsible for some of the most brilliant, influential, and reprehensible works in the twentieth century. The music of the Stones, like Romero's low-budget epic, gave sound and substance to the creepy, clandestine urges of the human animal with the same celebratory glee that had always enraged and befuddled smug bourgeois sensibilities. But there was one important difference: these were mass media phenomenons. What before had been peddled and pandered to in back alleys and boudoirs had suddenly gone over-the-counter, a radical moral reordering disguised as pop fodder. "Do your own thing" had been one of the sixties' more facile rallying cries. But no one could have expected so horrific a harvest from so small a seed. The gauntlet was down: this was freedom of expression with a vengeance.

After extensive hassling with their record company over the public-toilet cover art of their new album, the Rolling Stones finally released *Beggar's Banquet* in December of '68. From the moment millions of stereo styluses around the world touched down on the opening track, it became hair-raisingly apparent that something powerful and supremely confident had breathed the cold, Faustian breath of genius onto this music. The Rolling Stones had found a junk-pile oil lamp—found it and rubbed it, and out came this genie whose very first words were "Please allow me to introduce myself . . ."

Like a field recording of some Congolese snake-handling cult, "Sympathy for the Devil," the curtain raiser of *Beggar's Banquet*, opens with smoke-smudged drum beats, gourd rattles, evil anticipatory yelps and moans. Then, in one resounding grand piano chord, Mick Jagger steps from the tangled jungle shadows and suddenly it's center stage in the Music Hall of the Mind—just in time for the incantatory monologue. Out there beyond the guttering footlights are the muted masses, the whole grungy assembly of human history, bearing silent witness as the source of their suffering, the Author of Pain and Father of Lies struts and frets his hour upon the stage.

Jagger takes to the role with the relish of a harlot slithering into black silk or a once-cowardly man accepting, at last, destiny's terms. His ironies are exquisite, his mincing enunciation arrogant and chilling, his sudden shrieks of rage deliciously vindictive. The singer's own narcissistic charisma has been distilled and amplified: it's Jagger up there prancing and preening all right, but it's Jagger magnified and ascendant, full of spit and venom and able to lay your soul to waste. "[A] figure nearly seven feet tall seems to rise up out of the crowd of people, as if he has been kneeling in prayer among them and has stood up," writes Russell Banks in his novel of voodoo and vengeance, *Continental Drift*. "This is the loa himself, with his awesome, intricate powers over death. . . . No other loa is at once so powerful and so tricky, so strong and so scheming, so kind and so cruel. . . . taller than a man, made even taller by the battered top hat on his head, and cadaverous, with a head and face like a skull, his eyes hidden behind black, wire-rimmed glasses, his teeth large and glittering with gold. He's wearing a mourning coat with no shirt beneath it, and his boney brown chest is slick with sweat. His striped gray trousers are held up by a thickly braided gold rope knotted over his crotch, and on his feet he wears white shoes with pointed toes. . . . In his high, whining, nasal voice, he says, *Mine?*"

Pleased to meet you, hope you guess my name.

162

But what's troubling you is the nature of my game.

The song has now lurched into its pounding groove, a furiously fretted samba, fighting to restrain itself. Session pianist Nicky Hopkins is the unsung hero of these six incendiary minutes. Tentative chording rushes to resolution in a great rolling progression, hurling the verses headlong toward the abyss of the chorus, falling weightless until the melody is snapped back with the neat crack of breaking bone.

> What's confusing you is just the nature of my
> game.

A chorus of voices pulses like a train whistle in a sleet storm as bass and piano push and jostle and feed off each other: "Woo woo, woo woo, woo woo." "People . . . join in the chant," writes Banks, "and commence shuffling their feet in the same, crablike, side-to-side step. Ghede's face has turned to black stone, obsidian, shiny and opaque, and he dances faster and faster, over and back, from side to side, like a pendulum increasing its velocity with each new arc."

> Just as every cop's a criminal, and all the sinners
> saints.
> As heads is tails just call me Lucifer.

Just then, as the whole howling assemblage threatens to implode, Keith Richards's cougar-toothed guitar, hemorrhaging treble sparks, begins to scream. It snarls and claws and rends bone from sinew, slashing the air with razors and broken glass. All this talk of stinking bodies, of blitzkrieg and sealed fates—it's all summed up in the jagged notes Richards unleashes.

So if you meet me have some courtesy,
have some sympathy, and some taste.
Use all your well-learned politesse,
or I'll lay your soul to waste.

The song spirals off into a long, agonized fade, full of
foaming gibberish and falsetto taunts, and, always, Keith's
nasty licks, like tongues of tormenting flame, like the final
triumph of ash and rust and wormwood.

"Sympathy for the Devil" stands as a milestone in rock 'n'
roll history, a signpost, signaling the border of a strange,
unexplored wilderness. *Beggar's Banquet*, the Rolling
Stones' tenth album, was the first foray into that territory,
a collection that restated the theme and reflected the astonishing power of its centerpiece track. From the deep-
seated sorrow evoked by Brian Jones's ethereal slide guitar
on "No Expectations" to the shattered symbolism of "Jig-
saw Puzzle," from the epic sweep of "Street Fighting Man"
to the hard-core sleaze of "Stray Cat Blues" and the liturgical solemnity of "Salt of the Earth"—each was a facet
in rock's stunning new dimensionality, unmatched in
authority, skill, and arrogance. The galvanizing effects of
that *Beggar's Banquet* and its portents for the future were,
at least in part, a function of the times from which it
sprang—voracious and full-blown.

The Stones saga conceals more than it will ever reveal.
All that can be known for certain is a circumstantial string
of coincidence, tricks of timing and temperament, offering
up a tale of Dickensian moral symmetry in which lust,
pride, and popularity are their own absurdly self-evident
rewards. What happened to the Rolling Stones was extraordinary primarily in the very ordinary way in which
it happened, a tale locked in the prosaic grip of cause and
effect. It's also a textbook case of the utter banality of evil.

If the boys had made a pact with Satan, as more than a few would come to suggest, they had ended up with the short end of the stick.

"They were people who shunned preachers as hypocrites and called churchgoers fools, preferring to put their faith in the conjure men and root doctors who were keeping the old African religions alive. And since they'd been branded evil by the proper folk around them, the blues people began to wonder: What *is* evil, anyway? Is it nothing more than the reverse image, the flip side, of good? And if good means the hypocritical values of the proper folk, their tremulous faith and Protestant work ethic and all the rest of the bourgeois baggage handed down by the slave masters—if *that's* all good is, the blues people reasoned, then evil might just be worth investigating."

So writes Robert Palmer in *The Rolling Stones*, describing not the band but the blues legends from which they drew their inspiration. It's a neatly traced line across nearly a half century, from seminal, heroic figures like Robert Johnson, Leadbelly, and Mississippi John Hurt all the way to Mick and Keith and Brian, for whom "evil as society defined it would begin to seem rich, mysterious and ever so alluring."

It's a case commonly made for the evolution of the Stones' mystique, but it's not much help. Evil, according to the hypothesis, is a contagion; and music—the blues—the carrier. The Stones, soaking up dark, voodoo vibrations of the Delta devils, were infected with feverish rhythms, consumed by hallucinogenic badness.

Could be; the blues was a potent brew, especially as concocted by juju men like Robert Johnson, who, in his day, was also suspected of striking a deal with Old Ned and who was reportedly poisoned by one of the many sharecroppers he had cuckolded. Which is just the point— evil, as it was practiced by black Americans in the twenties and thirties, was hardly a philosophical abstraction, a studied reaction against the paltry aspirations of "good niggers." Evil was a way of life and a pretty nasty one at that, full of pain and suffering and every other wage of sin. Leadbelly wrote "Goodnight Irene" when serving a prison term for murder. At the age of seven, he had kept his father from killing his mother by threatening him with a shotgun. In 1930 Blind Lemon Jefferson, one of the most influential and gifted of all early blues guitarists, was struck down by a heart attack. He was left to die of exposure on the Christmastime streets of Chicago. Lightnin' Hopkins picked up elements of his distinctive blues style while working on a chain gang in Houston County, Texas. Oppression, poverty, alcoholism, venereal afflictions, violent death—they were all part of the malignant legacy of the bluesmen: outlaws in America's most disenfranchised caste.

Mick Jagger, Keith Richards, and Brian Jones could, of course, lay no such claim to a pedigree of evil. Along with bassist Bill Wyman and drummer Charlie Watts, they were products of the dull respectability and narrowed aspirations that defined the British postwar proletariat. Boyhood friends, Jagger and Richards were raised in the lower-middle-class environs of Dartford, a colorless London suburb sprouting semidetached, subsidized housing like mushrooms. Jones hailed from Cheltenham, a faded resort town, and was expected to validate his parents' upwardly mobile aspirations by becoming a doctor or lawyer. In due course, all three would fall under the spell of black American music, in particular the raw, electrified exoticism of Chicago blues and early rock 'n' roll as championed by artists like Elmore James, Chuck Berry, and Muddy Waters. They haunted London clubs catering to the small, self-conscious clique of British blues revivalists and in 1962

166

joined forces under the leadership of Jones, the most musically accomplished, if not the most ambitious, of the trio.

Brian Jones, in fact, was the only one who could lay even nominal claim to emulating the rough-and-tumble life-style of his blues mentors. By the age of sixteen he was the father of two illegitimate children, had bummed around the Continent, and was learning to play a mean slide guitar. Keith Richards's credentials as a juvenile delinquent—street fights and school expulsions—were fairly impressive. Yet the only thing distinguishing him in the horde of Britain's troubled youth was his ability to play Chuck Berry riffs with a revved-up, adenoidal energy. Jagger was the most cautious, conventional, and calculating of the three. The son of a physical education instructor, he was attending the London School of Economics when he first began singing. "I wanted to do arts," he recalled, reflecting the concerns of a niche filler on the creaky scaffold of British society, "but I thought I ought to do science. Economics seemed about halfway in between."

As practiced by the Stones, the blues was hardly an outburst of brazen defiance, flung in the face of smug Christian sanctity. Nor was it the cry of young men who had suffered too-cruel fates. The color of their skin, their incomplete and unoffending lives made it impossible for them to drink those dregs, even if they'd wanted to. In Britain's meek bohemian underground, blues, like jazz, bebop, or folk, was the affectation of callow youth, desperate for some badge of distinction in an egalitarian wasteland. "We were blues purists who liked ever-so-commercial things but never did them onstage because we were so horrible and so aware of being blues purists," Mick Jagger told Jonathan Cott. In short, black American music was a means to an end. What could hardly have been foreseen was that the Rolling Stones, in reaching that end, would entirely transcend the evil they had so earnestly sought to emulate.

"[T]hey *chose* to be vulgar," writes Robert Christgau in his Stones essay, "—aggressively, as a stance, to counteract the dreary rigidity of their suburban middle-class mess of pottage."

Youth culture in England, circa spring 1963, was reeling with the implications of Beatlemania. Working-class yobs with guitars and pointy boots had become the toast of Western civilization; talent scouts in sharkskin suits and Baloramas scoured docksides and pubs in search of new sensations. America was suddenly, incredibly, enthralled with this poor-relations version of the music it had invented. Anything was possible.

Even the Rolling Stones. Nothing as original as the Stones—or as unlikely—could have been fabricated whole cloth. But what Andrew Loog Oldham was able to pull off was almost as impressive. A pink-faced, nineteen-year-old former PR flack, Loog Oldham was a quintessential Sammy Glick in limey drag; a canny, amoral hustler whose boundless ambition was matched by a cynical skill for media manipulation—the first requirement for any successful rock 'n' roll entrepreneur. He had worked as gofer for Chelsea fashion maven Mary Quant and had even peddled himself as a crooner under the unlikely aliases of Chancery Laine and Sandy Beach. A stint as publicist for Beatle manager Brian Epstein provided a swift and thorough education in pop music promotion as he dreamed up publicity stunts for Epstein's stable of Merseybeat hopefuls, Gerry and the Pacemakers and Billy J. Kramer and the Dakotas. Avaricious and street smart, Loog Oldham understood that underneath the blues purity and studied indifference of the Rolling Stones lurked hearts as hungry for fame and fortune as his own. "I knew what I was looking at," he says, recalling the first time he saw the band perform, during their successful eight-month run at Richmond's Crawdaddy Club in '62–'63. "It was sex. And I was just ahead of the pack."

"[I]nsofar as they wanted to be rich-and-famous," writes Christgau, "—and they did, especially Mick, who had always been into money, and Brian, a notoriety junkie—they were neither heroic nor naïve, just ambitious." It was that ambition Loog Oldham would play off, matching it with his own, convincing the band that by virtue of his age, he was one of them and by virtue of his show business savvy, he could make them stars.

He quickly delivered on his promise, employing a tried-and-true promotional strategy with the finesse of a master. It was a neat if obvious trick that couldn't have worked if the Stones hadn't been so especially unappealing from a conventional vantage. The group was hardly the exemplar of the wholesome airbrushed sex appeal that had helped catapult the Beatles to the top. The band's visual focus was, of course, Jagger's thick swollen lips, and the rest of the lads only served to underscore the point: Jones's debauched-angel blondness, Richards's delayed-adolescent smirk, and the golem visages of Watts and Wyman—they were, well, ugly; the stuff of parental nightmares.

Which was, of course, the whole attraction. By positioning the band as the anti-Beatles, emphasizing the unsavory menacing leers and mismatched mannerisms, Loog Oldham was running the oldest number in the book, illustrating, at the same time, the rock 'n' roll axiom: what is reprehensible and repulsive to the parents of the target audience is, if handled properly, a license to print money. What was remarkable was Oldham's precocious ability to realize that now was the time to maximize the axiom. In the process, he and the Stones created a role model for rock stars that would endure for the next twenty years.

Consider this: the fundamental r & b and blues that the Stones so artfully recycled for mass consumption had been, for the most part, relegated to eclectic footnotes in pop music history. More important, the image of the sullen, trouble-making rock 'n' roll hepcat had fallen into disrepute the day Elvis joined the Army. By resurrecting such a potent teen talisman and tying it to the nastiest, most antisocial music the white middle class could imagine, the Stones and their boy wonder manager had stumbled onto a combination that couldn't miss.

For all the band's vaunted bluesness, their early output proved clever, fresh, and decidedly commercial. "Come On," their first single, released in June of '63, was a sprightly, toe-tapping update of a Chuck Berry standard. A '64 debut album, *Rolling Stones*, opened with one of the most appealing pop pastiches of the period. Buddy Holly's "Not Fade Away" in the hands of the Stones was a semiprecious gem, a driving acoustic-guitar-and-maracas workout less than two minutes long. The rest of the LP, and the three that followed (*12 × 5*, *Rolling Stones Now*, and their r & b watershed *Out of Our Heads*—all released in '65) underscored the band's deft handling of roots music. Their treatments of classics by Holly, Berry, Slim Harpo, Sam Cooke, Otis Redding, Solomon Burke, Willie Dixon, Marvin Gaye, and others selected from an impeccable catalog of influences managed to meet the quota for raunch and energy even as they jostled their way onto pop charts and jukeboxes. The Stones *sounded* authentic—at least to the unpracticed ears who had never heard the original music from which the band so freely drew—but more important they sounded tough and taunting and a lot of other things missing from rock 'n' roll for too long. Who cared where the songs came from? They were plugging rock back into the socket of sexual energy and fractious teen angst, and the result was pandemonium.

170

"I was shocked when I saw them," said Ed Sullivan after presenting the band to American audiences in October of '64. "Now, the Dave Clark Five are nice fellows. They are gentlemen and they perform well. It took me seventeen years to build this show. I'm not going to have it destroyed in a matter of weeks."

It wasn't only Sullivan's variety hour that was threatened with real or imagined destruction by the advent of the Rolling Stones. After being pent up for so long, rock 'n' roll rode in on the crest of the sixties youthquake to sweep aside a status quo too stunned and enfeebled to resist. The Stones were a rude reminder of all that had been successfully suppressed less than ten years before. It was a measure of the enormous infusion of power in rock music at the time that this band could stick out their tongues and thrust out their hips and shake their shaggy heads at the Establishment with gleeful impunity.

"Satisfaction" pretty much summed it up. As the band gained a surer footing on their booster stage rocket to the big time, their studio and songwriting skills took similar quantum leaps. In April of '65 they scored with "The Last Time," a cage-rattling diatribe anchored to a bludgeoning refrain—a telltale sign of impending stokes of genius. Two months later they came roaring back with "(I Can't Get No) Satisfaction." The American debut of the song was on the television pop music showcase "Shindig!". The art director who designed the stage set remains one of the unsung heroes of rock symbolism. There they stood, bad boy superstars seeping disdain, each mounted on his own cubist pedestal—remote, impassive, hammering out a thundering slab of pig-iron rock 'n' roll, drenched with . . . not innuendo, not smirking entendre . . . but up-front sexual frustration as a metaphor for the whole appalling specter of a bite-the-hand-that-feeds-'em youth revolt. What *would* satisfy the Rolling Stones was a question no one had the

171

nerve to ask, and the song leaped to number one with the authority of a line drawn in the dust. "The Beatles want to hold your hand," quipped Tom Wolfe in a review, "but the Stones want to burn down your town."

"Satisfaction" was followed by a string of hits and near misses, strengthening the impression that the glassy stares with which the band greeted the world were due to something more than well-cultivated ennui. The Beatles had introduced their friends and arch rivals to marijuana shortly after their own initiation under Dylan's tutelage. The Stones seized the drug with unseemly relish, especially Brian Jones, who was already well acquainted with the vertiginous pleasures of pills and alcohol. If the Beatles' music took on sharp, ironic angles under psychotropic influences, the Stones' music, already sharp and ironic, simply went over the top. "Most artists believe they ought to be rich-and-famous on their own very idiosyncratic terms," writes Christgau, "—the Stones just happened to be right." Enthusiastic drug dabbling turned the band's music both idiosyncratic and innovative almost overnight. They were not only dictating terms, they were rewriting rock 'n' roll's mandate.

Four months after "Satisfaction" they released a petulant variation on the theme, the jangled, paranoid "Get Off My Cloud," featuring lyrical lighter-than-air surrealism. In "As Tears Go By," Jagger indulged in the dandyism that would become an oft-recurring persona, and in the early months of 1966, the Stones released back-to-back chart toppers, dazzling proof of rock's rapidly expanding potentials. "Nineteenth Nervous Breakdown," a savage attack on upper-class airheads, pushed social commentary into the realm of character assassination and opened the way for similar below-the-belt blows by the Kinks and others. "Paint It Black" was an extraordinary piece of work. Its modal Middle Eastern motif and dark-hued tones of doom made it one of the clearest advances on pop's exploding thematic front. Jagger portrayed himself, in the words of Stones biographer Philip Norman, "as a palpitant wreck, turning his head away from pretty girls, like Joyce's Stephen Dedalus, 'until my darkness goes. . . .'"

Originally titled *Could You Walk on The Water?*, the 1966 *Aftermath* codified the themes and eclectic preoccupations that increasingly defined the band's music. Like *Rubber Soul* before and *Revolver* after it, *Aftermath* simply blew out the boundaries, replacing them with frontier flags stuck in all sorts of far-flung aesthetic corners. The sound was spacious, leisurely, and bristling with fascinating detail. It is perhaps Jones's most complete contribution to the band's music, for while Jagger and Richards wrote all the songs, it was Brian who gave them their shimmery musical settings, playing on sitar, dulcimer, marimba, African xylophone, and anything else he could lay hands on. Despite its themes of misogyny, icy disdain, and unrequited longing, *Aftermath* had a generous and open feel. The Stones, it seemed, knew that all this clever new music was high flying by the seat of their pants. The sheer diversity of what they were concocting was a cause for celebration.

By this time the band was indeed flying high. A 1965 tour of the States ended in a tumultuous concert at the Los Angeles Sports Arena, and afterward the group members were honored guests at the second Acid Test conceived by Merry Prankster Ken Kesey. There, Richards and Jones were first introduced to LSD, and by the time the group began work on *Aftermath*, Jones had been eating cubes regularly for months. Philip Norman: "For Brian—as some snapshots taken in a Soho basement show—a good trip meant grinning and cavorting like a little blond leprechaun. A bad trip brought hallucinations that left him crumpled up and whimpering with fear. . . . At one Stones album session, he refused to go into the studio

173

where the others were working. In his dazzled, terrified mind, the whole room was alive with black beetles."

Psychedelics, in the hands of the Rolling Stones, were indeed a two-edged sword. While the rest of the counterculture found paisley proof of universal love vibes, Mick, Keith, and company were starting to stray down dingier paths. Acid served to distill, for the Stones, their essential artistic aims: dominance, power, chaos, decadence. Less a sacrament than a Jekyll-and-Hyde draught, LSD psychedelicized the Stones by turning them in on themselves. They were closer now, much closer, to the ideals of wickedness to which they had always aspired. The baneful essence of the blues had been transfigured into even more fatal blossoms.

The first real sign of the Stones' descent past the jaws of their own predilections was the October 1966 release of "Have You Seen Your Mother, Baby (Standing in the Shadows)". The song is simply one of the most astonishing moments in commercial music, if only because, by sheer chutzpah, it actually reached the British and American Top Ten Charts. Opening full-bore on a guitar droning like a hive of angry bees, it rapidly plummets into a bewildering cacophony of strife and incoherent rage. Tin trumpets blare, pianos are pounded to splinters, the air is full of snarls and wheezes and demented caterwauling. Jagger vents his spleen on a woman whose neurotic condition is more than he can bear. For reasons not entirely clear, he wants to crush her, and the weapon he uses is his withering scorn.

Tell me a story about how you adore me,
How we live in the shadow,
How we glimpse through the shadow,
How we tear at the shadow,

174

How we hate in the shadow
and love in your shadowy life.

"Have You Seen Your Mother, Baby (Standing in the Shadows)," recorded on a cheap tape deck for maximum distortion, introduced a form of music that would not dare to be attempted again until the advent of Punk: Seizure Rock. Topping their own incredible gall, the band's picture sleeve for the single featured them in hideous drag, like nightmarish maiden aunts. "The Stones needed slowing down," insisted a fellow London musician on the subject of the "Mother" cover. "I think they've been going too fast."

The police did their best to oblige. In February 1967 a series of raids, in which small amounts of marijuana, cocaine, and Methedrine were uncovered, resulted in widely publicized show trials and a night in the slammer for Mick and Keith. "We're not worried about petty morals," Jagger said at his sentencing, and to underscore their contempt, the band, with the help of Lennon and McCartney, cut "We Love You," an answer to the Beatles' "All You Need Is Love," and a spiteful curdling of countercultural naiveté. Shortly afterward, Jones, suffering from nervous collapse, was hospitalized for the first time. "Offer him a handful of pills," wrote one friend, "uppers and downers, acid, whatever, and he'd just swallow them all."

Rock 'n' roll stars were, at the time, engaging in an experiment unique to human history. Drug addiction before the sixties had been necessarily limited by the gradual advances in the pharmacologist's art. Chemical achievements during that decade released incredibly potent new agents in startling array: LSD, MDA, STP, DMT; these and other supercharged distillations were added to the potpourri of already well-abused substances: everything from cocaine and heroin to alcohol and reefer. The Stones, leaders in rock's new monied aristocracy, had the resources, the time, and, certainly, the inclination for indulgence on the grand scale, in quantities and combinations hitherto unimagined. Famous drug fiends in the past, intrepid consumers like William Burroughs, had to spend much of their time hunting down their next fix. Absinthe drinkers, opium eaters, peyote priests; they'd all been limited to their drug of choice. The Stones had at their disposal a groaning smorgasbord of enhancers, ecstacizers, and obliterators. Little wonder an observer remarked that Brian Jones, for one, "simply transcended addiction as we know it."

Drug use was the klieg, light illumination, throwing up the shadows of the Stones evermore grotesque obsessions. An unmistakable Point of No Return was reached on the 1967 *Between the Buttons*, a landmark in rock 'n' roll's quest for its own Absolute, and one of the most terrifying and brilliant works of the era. "I don't like it much," Jagger told Jonathan Cott in 1968, speaking of *Between the Buttons*. "I don't know, it just isn't any good." That was saying a mouthful. Far from being "any good," the twelve-song collection was a malevolent masterpiece, twisted and gristled and unbelievably compelling.

It's a wonder Jagger remembers the album at all. Gered Mankowitz's cover photo captured the quintet at what appeared to be the end of a week-long amphetamine jag. Huddled in overcoats in a freezing park somewhere, the band confronted the camera in ghastly defiance, used up beyond pretense or calculation. It was the apex of antiglamour, a postlogical extension of the image that had made the boys famous four long years before. Jagger's famous lips were parched and cracked; Watts and Wyman looked as if they had just been roused from a sodden sleep, and Jones . . . Brian Jones was a husk, staring from slitted eyes sunken into bruised magenta bags, his face broken by a leering smile so dazed it looked like a smudge on a city sidewalk.

If indeed the Stones had struck a deal with the devil, it was on *Between the Buttons* that the covenant was sealed. Alternately limp-wristed and rabid, dementedly droll and obscenely explicit, the animating spirit of the album was a convulsive contempt, targeted at women but generally applicable to the whole human condition. A cynical certainty of betrayal, a petulant disgust with love and lust, sinister suggestions of murderous comeuppances, *Between the Buttons* was a sort of Final Solution of human emotions.

This virtuoso vituperation was not embodied in the LP's best-known songs. "Let's Spend the Night Together" and "Ruby Tuesday," each lascivious in its way, were both hit singles, the closest thing to love songs the Stones could offer. The really hideous treasures of the album lay elsewhere: in the salivating rancor of "Complicated" and "She Smiled Sweetly," in painstaking depictions of loathing like "Who's Been Sleepin' Here?" and "Miss Amanda Jones" (concerning, it was rumored, Brian's overweening vanity), in the elaborated cruelties of "Cool, Calm & Collected" and "Yesterday's Papers." But the dark heart of the matter was revealed on a two-minute, fifteen-second excoriation called "All Sold Out." Here, not even Jagger's sarcastic rage—over the presumed infidelity of yet another treacherous bitch goddess—can overwhelm the malice in the music itself. Richards' goading guitar makes vile noises, like a cat with a hair ball stuck in its throat. The song jerks and flails in a frenzy, spitting bile, rattling the skull like a dentist's drill.

"All Sold Out" and *Between the Buttons* represented, fittingly, a kind of artistic cul-de-sac for the Rolling Stones. Backed into the corner of their own arrogance, they had simply run out of ways to express their boundless scorn. At the same time, the creative center of the group was beginning to crumble. Jones, whose decline was gathering frightening momentum, increasingly distanced himself and his talents from the Jagger/Richards axis. During a long sojourn in Morocco, following a second nervous collapse, he discovered the trance music of Moroccan dervish brotherhoods who were reported to heal sickness and soothe troubled minds with their hypnotic drumming, singsong drone, and bluesy lute playing. Jones trekked into the Rif foothills south of Tangier to capture the ancient music, offered to the goat deity Pan, and for the next several months lost himself in producing what would eventually become the posthumously released *Brian Jones Presents the Pipes of Pan at Jajouka*. He talked vaguely, according to Robert Palmer, of "revamping the Stones music, using . . . Jajouka trance rhythms as a new foundation and combining Arabic prayer-call melodies with blues and gospel shadings." It all sounds like what it was; abstracted musings of an artist who had lost touch with his creative drives.

More significant to the band's crisis of direction was the hippie ethic, reaching a fever pitch by 1967. *Sgt. Pepper's* pipes were coaxing millions down the Aquarian trail, and the Stones' aura of ill-concealed cynicism didn't sit well with the gamboling daydreams of the sunshine super-race. Gamely trying to get into the spirit of things, Jagger and his girlfriend Marianne Faithfull lit out for Wales to sit briefly with the Beatles at the feet of the maharishi. Late in '67 the Stones released their next major album.

Their Satanic Majesties Request is remembered, rightly, as a thinly disguised *Sgt. Pepper* ripoff; a jury-rigged, improvisational dither, and an ill-considered commercial calculation. Uncomfortably festooned in flowers and beads, the band seemed unlikely candidates for the peace and love ticket, yet the album occasionally achieved a kind of benign wistfulness unlike their previous work and a long way from the horrific excursions of *Between the Buttons*.

The LP's most notable contribution to the Stones myth was its title, a clever play on the line from every British passport "Their Britannic Majesties Request." It was a portent of less jovial in-jokes to come.

In the spring of 1968 they began work on what would become the greatest album of their career, the last true work of the real Rolling Stones, and the crowning touch to their legend. And it is with *Beggar's Banquet* that legend waxes most powerfully, where Faustian whispers rustle and lingering questions are answered with a shrug and a wink. Yet once past the spell of suggestion and half-truth, what is known seems only prosaic and trite; the dabblings of pampered dilettantes, halfheartedly seeking a new thrill. It's true of almost all the elements that comprise the myth of the Rolling Stones. What gave them power and an ineluctable mystique was their aloofness. Inside the camp, the emperors wore no clothes. When Jagger began reading books like the Taoist tract *Secret of the Golden Flower* and the '67 underground best-seller the Tibetan *Book of the Dead*, along with Atlantis and fairy lore and various other pulp theologies, he was simply following the same primrose path that beckoned every other psychedelic pioneer. His search for enlightenment took on a distracted self-absorption befitting his station.

Under the circumstances, it's little wonder he was ultimately attracted to more formal embodiments of evil as a spiritual principle. For years he'd been flirting with what would now become personified in a brilliant stroke of image manipulation. Robert Palmer: "[T]here was beginning to be more behind the Stones evil image than abstract ideas and clever wordplay. Mick's ambition and his upwardly-spiraling success were subtly warping him; associates noticed that he was becoming more and more wrapped up in his own thoughts and image. . . . Mick was so caught up in the personas he had developed, he

179

couldn't tell with any certainty where roles ended and his 'real' personality began."

Around this bedazzled egotist had assembled a dramatis personae worthy of a medieval allegory. Among the leading players was Anita Pallenberg, a Swedish model with a leonine body and an inscrutable vixen's smile. Pallenberg had moved in with Brian Jones back in '65 only to drop him in favor of Keith Richards when Brian was already well into his savage decline. It was rumored that she was a genuine witch, with one Stones' associate claiming to have seen her store of dried human parts for use in sundry curses and spells. Sorcery is an allegation she insists she only "wishes" were true. It is true, however, that around the time of *Beggar's Banquet*, she and Richards were pursuing an active interest in the black arts even to the point of planning a pagan marriage ritual, officiated by the notorious avant-garde filmmaker Kenneth Anger.

Anger made no bones about his occult credentials. A devoted follower of the late British warlock Aleister Crowley, Anger's slavish fascination for the Rolling Stones hinged on his conviction that they were chosen instruments of Lucifer. He announced his intent to cast Mick and Keith in his projected film epic *Lucifer Rising*, and Jagger was plainly fascinated. He volunteered to pen the score to still another Anger project, *Invocation of My Demon Brother*. In Satan, it seems, Jagger had finally discovered a character big enough and bad enough to do justice to his performing skills.

C. S. Lewis, in describing how he created the devil "Screwtape" for *The Screwtape Letters* writes that, of all literary demons, "Those of Dante are best . . . Milton's devils, by their grandeur and high poetry, have done great harm. . . . But the really pernicious image is Goethe's Mephistopheles. . . . The humorous, civilized, sensible, adaptable Mephistopheles has helped to strengthen the

180

illusion that evil is liberating." It was Marianne Faithfull, Philip Norman recounts in *Symphony for the Devil*, who first suggested just this version of Lucifer to Jagger. "Marianne had just read Mikhail Bulgakov's *The Master and Margarita*, a surrealist Russian novel of the thirties, in which Satan pays a visit to contemporary Moscow to survey the effects of the revolution. Bulgakov's is the smooth-talking Satan later epitomized by George Sanders: a figure in immacuate evening dress, with a long cigarette holder, bowing low and purring, 'Permit me to introduce myself.'"

Ultimately, the notion that the Stones, muttering chants in the middle of a candle-lit pentagram, had petitioned the dark powers for fame and genius, gives too much credit to the band and too little to the devil. To suggest a formal compact with the prince of darkness is misleading, if not absurd. But the suggestion has been made, and more than once. It's a tantalizing conjecture; that the greatest rock 'n' roll band in the world had actually negotiated their destinies, that they knew what they were doing all along, and further, that they'd had the temerity and courage to give spiritual substance to their artistic conceits.

In fact, their art had had spiritual substance all along. The devil would have had no need to get it down in writing: the Rolling Stones were rushing toward their own inevitable conclusions. The stunning authority of *Beggar's Banquet* resulted from a man and his band finally discovering what they had been seeking all along. The lure of the blues, the habits of rebellion, the intoxicating dislocations of drugs and stardom had finally jelled into this one astonishing self-revelation. The Stones had got religion.

And in 1968 their moment of truth had the solid ring of prophecy. With the hippie utopia going up in flames, the time seemed ripe not only for "violent revolution" but for the elevation of new antiheroic icons. The Stones had been right all along: peace and love was a crock; the cosmos seethed with baneful energies. The year 1968 had proved it, and in an unsettling way, the death of Brian Jones, in July of the following year, underscored the point. The first great rock casualty of the sixties, Jones drowned in his swimming pool, succumbing, according to the coroner's report, to "alcohol, drugs and severe liver degeneration." It was Death by Misadventure, a sardonic understatement. "I don't think he had enough love or understanding," George Harrison glibly ventured, a remark whose unintended irony delineated the new rules of the impending decade. The world was no longer divided into hip and square, Us or Them. Now that the long reverie had come to an end, there were only those who survived and those who didn't. Love and understanding had been supplanted by Darwinian selectivity. "Peace, peace!" Jagger intoned, quoting Shelley three days after his bandmate's death, at a free-concert-turned-memorial in London's Hyde Park. "He is not dead, he doth not sleep—"

But, of course, he was dead—stone cold—and one more shallow pretense of immortality had fallen like scales from the eyes of the new youth. As a parting gesture, the Stones had arranged to have hundreds of white butterflies released into Hyde Park after Jagger's recitation. When the cardboard boxes in which they were stored were opened, most of the insects lay suffocated and inert.

The band, with new member Mick Taylor in tow, launched into their latest hit, "Honky Tonk Woman." The Stones rolled on.

But not for long. What is finally so surprising about Mick Jagger's tenure as Lucifer-in-the-flesh is how quickly it was over. The lessons of Altamont were so obvious and heavy-handed they read like a chapter in a bad novel, yet another leaden object lesson peppering rock's spiritual saga. The most thuddingly direct aspect of the tale of the ill-fated free concert at Altamont, California, is the one reflecting on the Stones themselves. Conceiving a thank-you gesture to their American fans at the end of their wildly successful 1969 tour, the band announced their intent to restage Woodstock on a barren stretch of parched scrub outside San Francisco—Altamont Motor Speedway. The group was at the absolute apex of their power and prestige; *Beggar's Banquet* had been followed by *Let It Bleed*, and Jagger's demonic persona was in full flower. The album sported some of the band's most deliberate and gleeful incitements to destruction and rapine—the title track, the apocalyptic anthem "Gimmie Shelter," and, at the LP's center, two tracks—a perversely beautiful rumination on addiction of every description titled, "You Can't Always Get What You Want," and the reprehensible "Midnight Rambler," a loping paean to Boston Strangler Albert De Salvo. The music was diamond-hard and dangerous as a barbed wire fist, with a chilling clarity of intent. "Welcome Rolling Stones!" shrieked a radical broadside distributed on the streets of San Francisco on the eve of Altamont— "our comrades in the desperate battle against the lunatics who hold power. The revolutionary youth of the world hears your music and is inspired to even more deadly acts. We will play your music . . . as we tattoo 'burn, baby, burn' on the bellies of the wardens and generals and create a new society from the ashes of our fires."

"It seems incredible now," writes Philip Norman, "that people so addicted to signs and portents—people for whom 'vibes' were so important a consideration—could not see or feel the force already propelling them toward catastrophe." Perhaps . . . but only if the force impelling them had been anything other than the one they themselves had set in motion. Their self-willed blindness—an affliction quickly becoming endemic in the world of rock 'n' roll—hid from them the consequences of their art. Evil, for the Stones, was an artistic stance from the beginning, an attention-getting device. At Altamont, the reality of evil intruded, and the Rolling Stones, facing the grinning visage, cowered and collapsed.

Hired as security guards for the concert at the suggestion of the Grateful Dead, the Hell's Angels, blitzed on LSD, Budweiser and speed, ringed the stage, savagely enforcing "order." The dazed crowd, crushed and asphyxiated with dread and cheap acid, was sadistically beaten with pool cues by the motorcycle gang. Naked drug casualties were the target of frenzied assaults, and when the Stones finally hit the stage just after dark, the air was choked with violence and the smoke from hundreds of campfires burning across the hellish landscape.

But the most perversely fascinating sight of a night that saw the death of five people, including one fallen beneath the snickering knife blade of an Angel, the most ghastly and pathetic spectacle, was that of the devil departing Mick Jagger. It was as if, having lent his power and authority to this willing vessel, Satan had snatched it back in a jealous fit, delivering up the pawn to a terrible reward. "People," Jagger pleaded, like a schoolteacher who'd lost control of the class, "who's fighting and what for?" After the opening chords of "Sympathy for the Devil" had unleashed a new frenzy of thrashings, the singer could only implore, "Brothers and sisters . . . come on now . . . Just cool out. We can cool out, everybody." It was the last time they would play the song in concert for almost six years. Richards almost threatened to stop playing until he realized what might happen if the ravaging mob were not satisfied. The band ripped through their repertoire with, says Norman, "the lucid brilliance that terror so often inspires." From the wings a film crew captured the whole chaotic, humiliating nightmare for posterity. The Rolling Stones had OD'd on a massive dose of their own medicine.

Altamont is popularly cited as the end of the sixties, the death rattle of Aquarianism. It also marked the demise of the Rolling Stones. The band would continue to make music and hits, some even echoing the glory of their former incarnation. But outside the rarefied context of their time, the band just didn't matter anymore. After that gruesome December's eve, the facade had finally and irretrievably fallen away, revealing the paltry burlesque beneath. The face of evil would settle elsewhere in time, on men who could handle the searing heat: politicians, mass murderers . . . the same host Jagger had presumed to speak for in "Sympathy for the Devil." Eventually, in light of all that would come to pass, the Rolling Stones' lurid legend would fade and soften, a relic of innocent times or a clumsy skit on a poster paint set.

As the years wore on, Jagger and Richards played out the interminable middle acts of their own private dramas. By the late seventies Keith had grown hopelessly addicted to heroin. There were dark rumors of Swiss clinics where the rock star's blood was drained away and replaced with untainted pints. After innumerable scuffles with the law, he was finally brought to the ground in Canada in 1977, when Mounties uncovered an ounce of high-quality smack. It was the beginning of a long climb out of a decade-deep pit of abuse. Jagger, seeking a sort of legitimacy that would free him from the prison of his clownish rock 'n' roll persona, took up a desperate courtship of the international jet set, who, in turn, offered tolerant, if bemused, acceptance. Turntables turned; gossip mills churned; the enterprise ground on.

Eventually Jagger, Richards, and the Rolling Stones would be afforded the respect reserved for celebrity survivors. Their faces, once so fraught with menace and distance and mystery, have become measures by which we mark the passage of time.

Grateful Dead

Chapter Eight

PROPHETS ON THE BURNING SHORE

[T]he adepts, considered together as the citizens of
an invisible empire of the philosophic elect,
constitute the heroic elder brothers, the custodians
and protectors of humanity. As the interpreters of
the Mysteries, they are the true educators and
illuminators.

> —Henry L. Drake, vice president,
> the Philosophical Research Society

And I'll call down thunder and speak the same.
And my word fills the sky with flame.
And might and glory are gonna be my name.
And men are gonna light my way.

> —The Grateful Dead

It was everywhere that summer; propped up in the window of the Psychedelic Shop; stacked at Cody's out on the
jingle jangle streets of Berkeley; up for sale at the Phoenix
or Middle Earth or the Magic Theater for Madmen Only
or downstairs in the brick basement of City Lights. You
could find it next to the *I Ching* or the *Book of the Dead* or
Howl or *The Joyous Cosmology*; laid on orange crate night-

stands, displayed on cable spool coffee tables in bay-windowed flats along Stanyon Street. You could flip through it waiting for the drugs to take hold when the wild chemical rush turned the tiny print into vibrating hieroglyphics.

Manly P. Hall first published *An Encyclopedic Outline of Masonic, Hermetic, Qabbalistic and Rosicrucian Symbolical Philosophy*, popularly known as *The Secret Teachings of All Ages*, back in the fall of 1925. Two specially prepared editions were presented to the Crown Prince of Sweden and the Scottish Rites Bodies of Oakland, California, in 1928, and since then, the oversized digest of religious and mystical arcana has gone through at least twenty printings. A glance through the tome—which purports to interpret "The Secret Teachings Concealed within the Rituals, Allegories, and Mysteries of All Ages"—immediately explains its appeal. A kind of spiritual Sears Roebuck catalog, *The Secret Teachings* peddles an exhaustive array of myth, legend, and pseudoscientific humbug, giving vent to every nutty cult and esoteric cosmology to which Manly Hall—an acknowledged expert in the field—had ever been privy.

Crammed with ancient charts, anagrams, and sundry theosophic pictographs, the magnum opus sports essays on "The Life and Writings of Thoth Hermes Trimegistus," "Hermetic Pharmacology," "Freemasonic Symbolism," something called "The Chemical Marriage," and the indispensable "Fundamentals of Qabbalistic Cosmogony." One full chapter was devoted to the assertion that Shakespeare was actually Francis Bacon, another delved into the "Theory and Practice of Alchemy," a third into ceremonial magic. Lurid illustrations filled gaps in the reader's imagination: "Oannes the Fish Man," "Abraxas, the Gnostic Pantheos," and the "Heraldic Arms of Jesus Christ" were displayed in all their musty splendor.

"To bring about this coalescence of Beauty and Truth," wrote Hall in an introduction to the golden anniversary edition of his book, "has proved most costly, but I believe that the result will produce an effect upon the mind of the reader that will more than justify the expenditure." He wasn't kidding. *The Secret Teachings* had little to do, of course, with the somber verities of the World's Great Religions; discipline, ethics, morality, good works. . . . anyone could aspire to these mundane virtues. Hall's great accomplishment was to assemble, in one cracked-brain compilation, every spell-casting shortcut, spiritual sleight-of-hand, and esoteric shell game ever hawked as instant enlightenment. *The Secret Teachings of All Ages* was a handbook for ersatz religious revelation.

No wonder it was the Summer of Love's best-seller, a hippie gospel that espoused one of the great philosophical preconditions for enlightenment among the Flower Children. *The Secret Teachings of All Ages* had really only one lesson to impart. And even that could be summed up in a single phrase: Everything is everything.

If, during the balmy solstice of '67, you were under thirty, had hair below your earlobes, a disdain for the Man, your parents, and the Military-Industrial Complex; if you'd incinerated your draft card or bra and had a headful of ideas that were driving you insane; if, in short, you were part of youth's heroic usurping of art, culture, history, politics, and religion—that grand experiment raging out of control across the free world; if that was you, then there was only one place you yearned to set your dusty boots: the Center of the Universe, the magnetic Mecca, the anointed Jerusalem of the New Age: San Francisco.

And out there on the Baghdad By the Bay, along a hunk of genteel ghetto formerly populated by lower-middle-class Chinese and Russians and Irish, a great convocation had assembled to groove and grope. Flush to Golden Gate Park, spread in a hub around the fabled intersection of

Haight and Ashbury streets, was a knot of visionaries, charlatans and full-court consciousness cadets to baffle the fancy of a sideshow talent scout. For those who flourished in its teeming embrace, no less than for the tens of thousands who would flock there, Haight-Ashbury wasn't merely the youth-culture theme park so cynically characterized by media hounds; it was the first tantalizing glimpse into an *übermensch* wonderland of the future. More than just "What Was Happening," it was "How It Would Be," now and forever, *in excelsis*. The kids had taken over. The inmates were running the asylum. The earth had been inherited not by the meek but by the mercurial.

Like other ballyhooed spiritual eruptions in the later half of the twentieth century, the peace and love *jihad* of the sixties was a hyperkinetic variation on themes stated many times and long before. The world had shrunk to the size of a crowded waiting room; ideas caught on quickly and vanished even more quickly. The global electronic village was hardly the place for quietly unfolding life-style experiments. Not anymore. In the increasingly claustrophobic confines of modernity, everyone, it seemed, was looking for a way out or a quick thrill or some kind of a center that would hold. The Haight-Ashbury almost overnight became a trapdoor to the other side, a reality interface charged with possibilities.

Among the Haight's most revealing antecedents are the utopian communities of the American West which began to take root in the late nineteenth century. In the 1880s, for example, Thomas Lake Harris, poet, libertine, and spiritualist, founded a 1,700-acre spread north of San Francisco called Fountaingrove. There, among English, Japanese, and American acolytes, he propounded the secrets of "divine respiration," a form of breathing by which man was supposed to achieve direct communication with God. Harris also revealed, at long last, the history of the planet Oriana, the source of all earthly evil.

Theosophist communes flourished up and down the coast for half a century. Originally inspired by the mystic meanderings of Madame Blavatsky, confidant to the Great White Brotherhood of Tibet, the Theosophists constructed lavish communities with names like Krotona and Halcyon, where a fanciful mix of Greek mythology, Eastern religious thought, and medical quackery abounded. The marriage of plants, promoting the Indian guru Krishnamurti (a fourteen-year-old boy at the time) and the elevation of Mother Purple and her cocker spaniel, the Purple Inspiration, were among early Theosophist activities.

"Not a reading man but has a draft of a new community in his waistcoat pocket," wrote Ralph Waldo Emerson, himself no slouch in the utopian musing sweepstakes. "One man renounces the use of animal food and another of coin and another of domestic hired service and another of the State." Emerson, who once proclaimed "Whoso would be a man must be a nonconformist," and his disciple Henry David Thoreau, whose *Walden* would become another counterculture textbook, were grandaddies of the peculiarly American pastime of planting heavens on earth. Founder of the Transcendentalist movement, Emerson also championed Eastern mysticism over what he termed "historical Christianity."

"The early Hindu cults that flourished in California," writes Paul Kagan, "stressed the divinity of human nature rather than the sin and guilt that is the substance of East Coast American-European Protestant Christianity." This aversion to the careworn axioms of the Judeo-Christian consensus, over and against the stunning novelties of a multilateral Eastern revelation, would became the leitmotif for virtually every utopian communal venture from the

191

Emerson-inspired Brooks Farm all the way to the Haight
Ashbury itself.

What the Haight bore in common with the brave new
worlds before it—aside from the thrall of the Eastern world
and the warm, nurturing California sun—was the conviction that here human history would begin again. Seekers
of like mind and spirit, disenchanted with institutionalized
cant and mediocrity, would refashion their little corner of
the weary world in their own image, lighting a beacon to
show humanity the way. It is, of course, simply another
version of the American Dream. Paul Kagan: "We may
easily judge this faith as naïveté—faith that there is time,
that one has one's freedom, that man is naturally good
and that the function of the earth is to support that goodness—but something similar seems to be believed by most
Americans."

In the late sixties, what was believed by most Americans—those under thirty, at any rate—was that a threshold had been crossed and there was no turning back. By
a twist of fate, act of divine intervention, or genetic mandate, a point in history had been reached at precisely the
moment when a uniquely gifted generation had accelerated up the evolutionary ladder to seize the time. Change
was on the wing. What was significant about this particular promise of upheaval was not its social or political dimensions but its spiritual consequences. So complete a rejection of established order created a vacuum. And into
that vacuum, chaos was sucked. At the speed with which
events unfolded, at the risk of being left behind, there was
no alternative but to embrace the chaos.

Utopianism may have been the tradition from which the
hippie dream was constructed. But what rose on that foundation was something so fantastically articulated that it
bore no resemblance to any familiar spiritual architecture.
There was nothing premeditated nor any single illuminating

principle engendering the birth of the Haight-Ashbury. Whatever significance it had for the millions whose lives it changed occurred only in communion with the spirit of the time and place. It wasn't what you brought to it, it was what you got from it. In that respect, Flower Power took on the contours of a religious revival, a kind of heathen Azusa Street, where the blind and lame came and saw and were healed. There were no forefathers to draw up the charter or bring truth down the mountaintop. The mass harkening wasn't in response to messianic allures but to the promise of saving oneself; of self-discovery, self-actualization. And whatever that might mean became the colony's mandate for self-government. "Do your own thing," and as long as it didn't interfere with the thing doing of a fellow creature, your citizenship was assured.

Ken Kesey divided humanity into those who were "on the bus" or "off the bus." It was as close to a hippie doctrine as anyone would ever come, shorthand for one of the most influential metaphysical "awakenings" in modern times. Of course, a working definition of "spirituality" was something no one dared delineate, and therein lay the paradox that gave the community its sense of ever-verging enlightenment. For each man to discover God by nosing down the path of least resistance or quickest results or flashiest visionary fireworks was the antithesis of traditional religious discipline. The Almighty chose the terms of revelation; by accepting those terms, the individual achieved transcendence or was granted salvation. That's how it had always been. Those were the rules.

But the rules don't apply when things happen backward. Psychedelics and the brotherly communion of seekers caught up in the pulsing aura of impending nirvana conspired to turn the religious process on its head. Revelation, the mind-blowing Big Picture, came first, in huge, gulping doses of LSD-25 or mescaline. Countercultural cosmologies were extemporized on the spot as blown minds tried to piece themselves—and reality—back together. Existential doctrines were birthed from the foreheads of the new believers; ferocious truths were forged in molecular crucibles: the whole, certifiable Godhead experience had been laid bare, liberated from the prison of agonizing religious toil. The direst biblical warning had come to pass: Every man was doing what was right in his own eyes.

It was hard to believe unless you stood there, right smack in the middle of that horde of callow prophets, all drenched in the juices of their own spiritual afterbirth. But among that great company there was no mistaking the hum and throb of mutating karmas. The Haight-Ashbury signaled a startling transfiguration in Western spirituality: beyond cynicism, absurdity, technophobia, and paranoia was a brand new bag: a faith not of God or of man but of a huge burning wheel hurling both the sacred and profane through time and space.

Even a cursory examination of the religious tenets of the sixties counterculture reveals an unmistakable Eastern lure: the implacable, impersonal creative force, the potentiality of Godhead lurking in every human animal, the sanctity of life no matter how insignificant or unpleasant, the cycle of birth and death, the balance of good and evil. Yet for all their busy yinning and yanging, true Himalayan epiphanies eluded the New Age adepts. The simple fact was that like Christianity, real Buddhism, Hinduism, Taoism, whateverism was simply too much like a nine-to-five grind. Why spend twenty-five years in a cave learning to open your third eye when acid could *grow* one for you? Why strain toward immortality when you could sit back and let it come to you, on waves of patterned color? Why follow the narrow path to truth when you could pave your own superhighway?

"Bohemians have a tradition of what bohemia means," remarked Mike Prichard, an astute observer of hippie behavior, in *San Francisco Nights*. "It was centuries old, really, and it meant being sensitive, willing to suffer for what you believed in. We were more eclectic. We had no real roots. We attached ourselves to whatever was available, picked up on whatever caught our attention." And in the Haight-Ashbury, in the Summer of Love, nothing was more attention-getting than loud electric music.

Jerry "Captain Trips" Garcia, chunky, taciturn, and awesomely prolific lead guitarist of the Grateful Dead, had a strange way of contacting his muse. He'd be up on the flatbed truck, beneath the towering eucalyptus trees along Panhandle Park, playing fast and hard for the lucky love children who had tripped into one of the band's impromptu free concerts, and suddenly he'd just lean over, his eyes flicking back and forth, scanning the crowd. Then, with the whole, whirling musical machine rumbling behind him, he'd catch someone's gaze, lock stares for two electric seconds, and reel back, sending off a shower of babbling notes, like a bursting seed pod.

People would swear by it. They'd come early to dance concerts at the cavernous Fillmore auditorium or in the womb warmth of the Avalon Ballroom, and they'd gather right up in front, clustering close to this unlikely guitar hero with his Brillo hair and nascent double chin. And they'd wait, their faces mirroring the rapt attention Jerry gave to every jittery glissando that tumbled from his fingers. They'd wait and they'd watch, and if it was their special night, they'd catch his searchlight stare. The power would surge between them, and then, like a vampire lover, Jerry would play *them*, turn them into music and send them flying out across the room or up through the fragrant, rustling leaves, bound for glory. Then, almost before it started, it was over, and the axman would again stalk the stage, sweeping the crowd, his relentless fingers hunting the fretboard. . . .

The Grateful Dead embody not only the cultic potentials historically inherent in rock 'n' roll, but the entire submerged linkage between rock and religion. It's the personification of rock ritual, the mythic confluence of drugs, electricity, and music, a sum much greater than its parts. In the over twenty years of its existence, the group has become, in fact, less a musical assemblage than an elixir for the ferocious spiritual thirst of its followers. The Dead are, in short, the most complete amalgamation of music and mysticism in modern times and, perhaps, of all time.

The fusion of rock and spirituality the Grateful Dead wrought in San Francisco in the late sixties was, in itself, so complete and self-sustaining that it has remained virtually unchanged ever since. While they may tinker with peripherals, incorporating folk or funk into this or another number, their music and persona is a finished work. Their gospel is inviolate to the last jot and tittle.

Like acid, like all other subcultural fetishes, it's hard to apprehend the essence from outside the fold. The fact that the Dead's legendary live concerts bear uncanny resemblance to religious festivals is no help in cracking the secrets of the ceremony. Nor, for that matter, does the Dead's musical appeal make any sense from a pop context. "Even among musicians we're an acquired taste," admits Dead rhythm guitarist Bob Weir. Like any true religious movement, they have defined their own mandate on their own terms. "I am the way, the truth and the life," asserted Christ. "No man cometh unto the Father, but by me." "If you really want to see a leaderless collective," says Jerry Garcia, "with no real plan, which is utterly formless in the highest sense . . . then come see us, because we have it and it's working."

It started working almost from the very beginning. The Dead originally coalesced out of the miniature music orbits the San Francisco Bay Area has hosted for most of its garish history. Garcia, for example, began his career as an earnest folkie, plying the Stanford University club circuit with a banjo and goatee. "We all have musical backgrounds that are quite different from each other," he explains. "Each one of us brings together our various influences." The interests of percussionist Mickey Hart, Garcia continues, "include extremely primitive kinds of ethnic and ritual music." Bassist Phil Lesh harkens to "classical and avant garde, from the world of highly trained musicians." Bob Weir "is into rock and roll and rhythm and blues and that sort of modern American music. . . . So, we've been extensive dabblers and collectors. There is really an enormous amount of synthesis going on in the Grateful Dead."

In 1966 the fledgling quintet changed its name from the Warlocks to the Grateful Dead, choosing the evocative handle, according to legend, by flipping through the dictionary while they were on acid. "One of the things about the name," recalls Jerry Garcia to David Gans in *Playing in the Band*, "right from the beginning it had a lot of power. It was kind of creepy." It was also precisely suited to the tone of the times. As was the band's rapidly evolving music. Stylistic synthesis had combined with free-form improvisation to create some highly promising advances in the state of the pop music art. The hub of the new sound was San Francisco, serving as the locus for yet another colorful underground in the grand tradition of the Beats. Disaffected middle-class kids, politically precocious college students, old-school beatniks, bohos, and other assorted malcontents had scraped together the beginnings of a small, tight scene. They threw communal parties, and when lofts and railroad flats got too small to accommodate the overflow, they got together to promote dance con-

197

certs, featuring local rock talent lately sprung from elitist jazz and folk circles. Wide-open and freewheeling, these events quickly became the social focus of the flourishing subculture. Psychedelics, still legal and unregulated, fueled the fires. Overnight, a new kind of partying filled faded glory ballrooms. Poster artists, light show luminaries, dancers, costumed revelers, hustlers, and gawkers all converged to freak on each other, feed on the fun, and formulate a clever eye-and-ear–catching diversion.

Fun, initially, was all there was to it and more than enough. San Francisco in '64 and '65 was a haven for any soul hearty enough to cash in his chips on the bland American dream for an adventurous fling in this wicked outpost. The Barbary Coast was one slice of the Old West that more than a few new frontiersmen were intent on resurrecting. The dance concert phenomenon provided a modern corollary to the fabled pleasure houses of the Gold Coast, nineteenth-century emporiums like Abe Warner's Cobweb Palace, sporting a thousand nude paintings, cages of live monkeys, and cobwebs artfully draped everywhere.

Frisco's new pioneers were cooking up an endlessly entertaining pastime; all-night, interactive encounter sessions set to music, where everyone was explicitly encouraged to be either themselves or someone they'd always wished they could be. Participation was the key: dress from your fantasies, dance like a dervish, do something . . . anything to let 'em know you're out there.

In this supercharged atmosphere, rock 'n' roll was transformed from short, three-minute bursts of radio fodder to lengthy and convoluted workouts. The improvisation and stylistic blends that came to characterize the drug-induced San Francisco Sound weren't the result of sophisticated musical savants stepping boldly into the unknown. For the most part, ballroom regulars were inept neophytes, making up with sheer gall what they lacked in experience.

"I was somewhat older than the people who were starting to delve into his thing," remarks Ron Nagle, founder of one of the Bay Area's earliest underground aggregates, the Mystery Trend. "I was aware of songwriters and I knew there was something else beside all this psycho-babble in A-minor."

But Fillmore and Avalon faithfuls weren't interested in skill, at least not in the conventional sense. All they required was bands that could play loud and long. And the longer the better. Suddenly people wanted to dance; twirling around in tight circles all by themselves, fruging and shimmying with ever-changing partners or undulating across the floor in a Saint Vitus snake dance. Their stamina was daunting, and the early bands simply didn't have the chops to keep up with the demand. Folk and r & b chestnuts, along with rock standards and the occasional half-baked originals, became points of departure for jam sessions that were considered successful if they could stretch a single riff over twenty minutes, a half hour, or longer.

Improvisation would loom large in the development of much subsequent rock 'n' roll, eventually displacing all the hoary commercial maxims of Tin Pan Alley. It was license that would, in time, lead to horrific excesses as musicians indulged in noise orgies for art's sake and rock became a bloated parody of itself. But for the blitzed ballroom hordes, it was strictly musical manna, approximating the sustained roar of an acid rush. Here was rock not only designed for the Light Fantastic but for the fantastic lights and colors and the exploding aural galaxies of chemically induced euphoria. Everyone, artists and audience alike, was experiencing the same jolts and jitters to rusty old reality. "The stage," claimed Grace Slick of Jefferson Airplane, "is just the least crowded place to stand."

A handful of remarkably diverse groups quickly emerged, each with a handle on a different part of the elephant and often eloquently describing what they held on to. The Jefferson Airplane fashioned an enormous billowing sound full of light and air and anchored to the canny pop sensibilities of its prime mover, Marty Balin. Big Brother and the Holding Company, before they vanished into the shadow of Janis Joplin, their blues-madonna front woman, was among the quirkiest and most entertaining of Frisco's freak brigade. Big Brother featured the cacophonic genius of guitarist Jim Gurley and bassist Peter Albin, who was given to hopping around the stage like an over amped amphibian or lapsing suddenly into his alterego, the LSD Preacher. It was a noisy good time, a crowded, raucous chunk of the Western rim, reserved for a handful of flakes.

And then there were the Grateful Dead. The band's reputation as first among equals was assured by their prodigious ability to play longer, louder, faster, heavier, and more stoned than all the rest put together. Their repertoire of blues, r & b and folk standards—"Dancing in the Streets," "Viola Lee Blues," "Midnight Hour," "Good Morning Little Schoolgirl," "I Know You, Rider," "Morning Dew"—was no more or less original or inspired than tunes culled by other groups and sent roaring down the psychedelic highway. Nor, initially, did the sum of their individual talents offer an explanation of their extraordinary performing prowess. As promising a picker as was Jerry Garcia, his tendency to fussiness and noodling should have rendered him simply another overqualified technocrat. As bold and unorthodox a rhythm section as Phil Lesh and drummer Bill Kreutzmann combined to create, all the *Sturm und Drang* could too often seem simply indulgent. As colorful a character as vocalist/keyboardist Ron "Pigpen" McKernan appeared onstage, his marginal talents rendered him musically superfluous. The Dead, in other words, didn't earn its reputation on the strength of self-evident virtuosity.

But together . . . put them together and the analogies began to flow, hotly and heavily. "Rolling thunder," was what critic Ralph Gleason, an early supporter of San Francisco rock, would call their sound. "A picture window onto the true landscape of the worlds hidden just behind the real one," wrote one reviewer. "Mammoth epiphanies," stammered another. What was obvious immediately about this particular rock 'n' roll band was that it wasn't a rock 'n' roll band. Not really. Other groups, even in the heady haze of mid-sixties Frisco, would take the stage, do their songs, and judge the outcome by such ephemeral variables as audience response or personal satisfaction. Musicians would interact, play off of one another, even, on a really good night, summon up something extraordinary from their collective effort. It might be art or it might be show business, but one thing was for sure: it was on purpose.

The Grateful Dead weren't on purpose. They rehearsed and worked out arrangements and wrote songs and got paid a percentage of the gate. But none of that guaranteed anything, except the same five musicians together on a given night at a given gig. What would happen after that bore only the vaguest resemblance to cause and effect.

A Dead set most often would begin tentatively, as the musicians seemed to circle one another, feeling for openings, picking up cues from melodic fragments or quick rhythmic spurts. There was a laid back, almost mincing, feel to these exploratory feints; a patient accumulation of expectations, the slow concentration of coincidence. Whatever was happening to the group internally during these long warm-ups, the music they were making—loose-ended and distracted—matched precisely the scattered attention of the audience. People milled around, goggling each other or waiting for various pills and potions to take effect; the sound from the stage exerted a pull as inperceptible as the tides.

At a point, usually when it seemed that this vaguely pleasant muttering might continue all night, increments of tension would begin to develop in the music. The rest was as inevitable as an avalanche. Fugue state lift-off was signaled by a thickening of the atmosphere and sudden star filter glints off any reflecting surface. Bone-contusion thuds rattled rib cage and clavicle, and a sense of delicious dread, not unlike being in spark-showering proximity to a Bessemer furnace, pervaded. The Dead had opened the throttle on a cosmic combustion engine, hurling itself along at terrifying velocities, spewing notes like overheated lubricants. At its frenzied peak, the sound transubstantiated, becoming a particle accelerator, an electric chair, or something like an insatiable appetite.

It was the sheer heft of the music, its looming bulk, that eventually punched out the hole, creating a vortex that sucked the throng through to the eerie Other Side. When that happened, the sound would lose shape and texture, atomizing into the clotted air to settle as dust and fog on upturned faces. Everyone took on the dazed look of innocent bystanders moments after a bus wreck or a terrorist bombing. Onstage the group stumbled through the blinding ozone, looking for each other. Then, as slowly as they had begun, the Dead would reassemble the pieces, fitting them back into a song and laying it gracefully to rest.

A good part of Grateful Dead lore is dedicated to explaining what, exactly, happens at these concert encounters. "I don't think I was stoned," wrote fan Paul Grushkin in *BAM* magazine, ". . .maybe something like hash or peyote. . . . anyway, that click, whatever it is . . . going into hyperspace where suddenly everything is quite different . . . it's unnatural, not your normal course of events, and I couldn't decide through the next three or four hours whether it was me feeling that way, or if it was because of the band or the audience or the drugs. And I started to, if not hallucinate, really fantasize on some things associated with such a monumental experience in music making." Those associations, it turns out, are common among those who have had the "experience." "The Dead," remarked *Musician* magazine, "are a living, evolving phenomenon . . . capable of acting as channels for the special quality of energy that can transform an ordinary concert into a transcendent event." "Everyone who's ever altered his consciousness and gone to a Grateful Dead concert," explains Deadhead Tom Davis, "has had the feeling that he affects the band." "A Dead concert is a symbiosis on the grand scale:" asserts journalist Blair Jackson, "the Deadheads feeding positive energy to the stage and each other, while the band tries to fuse that energy with their own creativity to synthesize an entertainment that, at its best, transcends every notion of what a 'rock concert' is or 'should' be."

Among the most perceptive theorists are the Dead themselves. Reams of interviews, rap sessions, and off-the-cuff remarks comprise an exhaustively introspective meditation on the meaning of their music. "It has to do with creating a situation in which miracles can happen," ventures Garcia, "amazing coincidences that all of a sudden put you in a new musical space." And again: "It's a furious manipulation, man, and it's coming from my mind. It's what separates us from 'It.' I'm curious because I've had my mind blown. What is 'It'? I can't image being alive and not wondering about 'It.'" And again: "There's a feeling about 'It' which I fundamentally don't trust. I have the feeling it's somewhere along the road of losing your will." And once more: "We're in the same position as Deadheads are, fundamentally, about this phenomenon—the magic side of 'It'. . . . I'm not trustful about stuff like that. I'm the first one to worry about it. Maybe we're opening doors for some demons from the ninth dimension of something."

Could be. Or perhaps 'It,' as Bob Weir suggests, is "Gestalt linkage. We try to make ourselves of one mind or one mind out of many. What we're going for is the whole being more than the sum of its parts and, depending on the muse, it sometimes works."

"It's when the wolf comes out," says percussionist Mickey Hart. "When the wolf shines through. That's what I call it and that's what it feels like. When I look around, I see the music getting to larger proportions than was intended, or even expected. Now, we might induce altered states, which only happens when you get that many people seriously doing the same thing. We know what the Grateful Dead is. We know that it's not just a rock 'n' roll band."

Miracles. "It." Ninth-dimensional demons. Gesalt linkage or the wolf. Numbered among their own biggest fans, the group seems genuinely puzzled over the astounding effects of their music. What they don't seem able to do is regulate or direct the results in the slightest. A bad night for the Dead can be an utter disaster, an interminable masturbatory indulgence that glaringly points up the limitations of their specialized talents. Even more puzzling is the band's performance as recording artists. The Dead's copious album output—nearly twenty releases, including no fewer than five double-album live sets—has failed not only to tap into the band's super-reality gestalt daisy chain but is only occasionally able to muster the most rudimentary studio mix.* Their best effort remains their first, *The Grateful Dead*, recorded in under three days in 1967 and

* The band's studio ineptitude has long kept them from Top Forty success.

featuring some taut blues/rock fast takes—"The Golden Road to Unlimited Devotion," "Cold, Rain, and Snow," Cream Puff War"—ironically notable for both their brevity and pop accents. The album remains a classic of psychedelia's golden age, while two subsequent studio efforts, *Anthem of the Sun* and *Axomoxoa*, failed to corner the live sound and cage it on vinyl. The 1970 *Live Dead* was perhaps the group's most successful effort at explaining what they did to those who hadn't the opportunity or inclination to catch a show, but even here the sound was muddy, the vocals ragged, and the songs too dense to penetrate.

Two more LP's that year, *Workingman's Dead* and *American Beauty*, found the band veering sharply away from their dismal bring-it-back-alive strategy to showcase a collection of folk, country, and bluesy originals that were mildly endearing, occasionally whimsical, and generally well crafted. "Uncle John's Band," "Casey Jones," "Friend of the Devil," and "Truckin'" remain among the band's best songs, primarily because they *were* songs, not interstellar voyages, and a few of them even earned a modest berth on AM radio. But the Dead's early seventies output also incorporated for the first time the lyrics of hired poet Robert Hunter, whose way with a phrase was deadened by his penchant for bombastic gestures in vain approximation of the Dead's music. A kind of Walt Whitman on acid, Hunter's pompous doggerel immortalized the Psychedelic Everyman, for whom a bus ride, a glimpse of desert scenery, or the love of a good woman spawned mind-melting insights into life's refulgent cosmosity.

The Dead continued gamely churning out product (their last, a two-part live set spread out over four albums, was released in 1981), but the handwriting had long been on the ballroom wall. Whatever it was that made the group's concerts among rock's most indescribable experiences clearly wasn't translatable. Even a documentary film of

205

their annual New Year's Eve ritual at San Francisco's Winterland, shot in 1976, failed to conjure the mythical beast. The failure, in itself, is a cause for wonder. It could be a rock physic Uncertainty Principle in which whatever is measured, observed, or recorded is inalterably warped by the process. Or perhaps, more accurately, it relates to wives' tales that ghosts can't be photographed or that an image, once rendered, captures a piece of the subject's soul. "What we do is play for people, for warm human bodies. We don't play so good for machines." So says Garcia, leaving it at that. "We can prepare ourselves to be proper vehicles," adds Weir, "but we can't guarantee it'll happen on any given night." "We raise the sails," adds Hart, "but we can't make the wind come." Realizing that what they do is most potent in its purest form, the Dead have poured vast sums into gargantuan, stadium-devouring sound systems, featuring three-story banks of speakers hauled around the country in a fleet of semis; a portable rock 'n' roll Wailing Wall.

Of course, the most obvious explanation for the exclusive nature of the Grateful Dead's entertainment is the one they're most reluctant to acknowledge. The following exchange was recorded by David Gans for *Playing in the Band*. In one of the journalist's extensive rap sessions with the group, a sticky subject was broached. "When the Grateful Dead True Religion incorporates," jokes Weir, "I get to be in charge of making mitres and stuff like that. . . . Maybe the band'll get together every three hundred years or so and reincarnate and make an appearance."

"We used to say that every place we played was church," muses Lesh. "It was a pretty far-out church, but that was how we felt."

"This is a pretty tolerant religion, isn't it?" ventures Gans.

"Well," snorts the acerbic Garcia, "That word has a lot

of . . . *negative* to it. . . . I don't think a religion is what this is. We're not saying what it is: we're not creating dogma. There's no central thing which is absolutely true that everybody can know about it."

"But," insists Gans, "it does fulfill the role of religion for a lot of Deadheads. Many belong to this to the exclusion of . . ."

"That's okay, too," snaps Garcia, "because on a certain level it's a religion to me, too. But I don't like the word *religion*. It's a bad word."

"Bad word" or not, religion is precisely what the Dead and their followers have been engaged in from nearly the beginning. And ritual is precisely what infuses their concerts with revelatory surges. Putting Grateful Dead music on record is like a TV evangelist telling his invisible congregation to lay hands on the screen for a dose of the Holy Spirit. A few hapless souls may get a tingle, but for anyone who's actually danced in the aisles under the sanctifying power, among the company of the elect—well, there's simply no way to approximate *that*. In the same way that Christians comprise the Body of Christ, Deadheads are bricks in the temple of the Dead.

"A considerable part of the Mystery rituals," intones *The Secret Teachings*, "consisted of invocations and intonements, for which purpose special sound chambers were constructed. . . . The very wood and stone used in the creation of these sacred buildings eventually became so thoroughly permeated with the sound vibrations of religious ceremonies that when struck they would reproduce the same tones thus repeatedly impressed into their substances by the rituals." All of which would sound just about right to the repeatedly impressed substance of a Deadhead: reverberation as the meaning of life.

Garcia may have cringed at the mention of the Dead's religious credentials, and who can blame him? The specter of gurudom weighs heavily. "It's not something I'm making happen," he insists; "I'll tell you that. I can't take the blame for it, or the credit either." When asked to comment on the off-quoted remark that "The Grateful Dead is immortal, but the men who play in this band are not," the guitarist eagerly agreed. "That's exactly right. It takes the responsibility out of our hands, which is comfortable. It's scary if you feel like you're responsible for it." And finally, to *Crawdaddy* magazine in the spring of 1979: "I don't want to be a leader, because I don't want to be a mis-leader. I can't multiply fishes and loaves and turn water into wine."

Fair enough, but Garcia does seem able to turn music into manna, and the more he and his cohorts vehemently deny their divine appointment, the more insistently the faithful make the connection. "Deadheads flock to Grateful Dead concerts like cripples to Lourdes," writes Blair Jackson, "for a spiritual shot in the chakras, and few leave disappointed."

It is, in fact, nearly impossible *not* to draw the connection between religious ritual and the rock concert as perfected by the Dead. Sociologists and cultural anthropologists wear themselves out drawing parallels between primitive worship and rock spectacle, while those who have received the anointing of the electric church firsthand seem barely able to separate belief from the backbeat.

It has all been revealed to them in the throes of "The Other," "Saint Stephen," "Dark Star," "Caution," "Cryptical Envelopment," "The Faster We Go the Rounder We Get," or any of twenty years' worth of the Grateful Dead's thunderations. And once the central premise of the Dead as a path to spiritual enlightenment is accepted, the rest falls easily into place: the power of their presence, the tattered band of faithful pilgrims who follow them from concert to concert year after year, the persistent use of religious imagery to describe the band's music, the permeating aura of oneness, and an appeal that transcends taste and time.

Which leaves but one nagging question: if the Grateful Dead are a religion, what are the tenets, the doctrine, the rules, regulations, and way? The answer turns back on the basic belief system formulated in the halcyon days of the Haight-Ashbury.

A blending and bending of music styles came to define the San Francisco Sound and subsequently much of what would follow in rock music. A blending and bending of every spiritual path on the human road map was what would also define the counterculture's search for truth and subsequently an entire generation's religious impulses. What is remarkable, if not astonishing, about the sixties is the coincidental juxtaposition of an almost universal hunger for truth among the young with a spiritual harvest that laid out so exotic and abundant a table from which to taste, sample, and gorge. At the very moment that the psychedelic experience meshed with a discontent for the status quo and the rise of a vital and creative underground, the flood of alternatives to the Judeo-Christian consensus had breached the dike and poured unchecked across the Western world.

The response to this dazzling variety of options was in direct proportion to the philosophic energies that had been mounting for nearly fifty years. From the erosions of Hegel/Kierkegaard/Nietzsche to the theory of relativity to dadaism to the Axis powers, the first half of the twentieth century had delivered one devastating blow after another to the common view that had God in His heaven and man and woman in the service of divine will. "Throughout these years," writes historian Paul Johnson in *Modern Times*, "the power of the State to do evil expanded with awesome speed. Its power to do good grew slowly and ambiguously." The very ambiguity of good—of order and the rule of law and the sovereignty of God—threw the darkest doubt into the human heart, and in that darkness seeds sprouted that would eventually bear the fruits of relativism, cynicism, and a deeply rooted paranoia. Since nothing, least of all the existence of God, could be certified in the face of such contradictory chaos, truth itself was demythologized. Absolutes simply ceased to exist. It was every man for himself.

Initially, the response was a disillusionment that diminished the spiritual in favor of a hard-nosed respect for what man could, and must, accomplish on his own. But the search for the meaning dies hard, and the sixties counterculture, fueled by acid and an unshakable belief in its own manifest destiny, resurrected the quest. But with a single and profound difference. Organized and institutional faith had for so long been bankrupt, serving as handmaiden to all the oppressive social tyrannies of the Western world, that the new seekers entirely circumvented tradition. The spiritual had become irrevocably separated from the religious. Ritual, ceremony, ordained writ—the entire cultural context of belief was cut from its moorings and swamped in a flood of customized mysticism.

The hybrid weeds that sprouted in the Haight yielded wild and exotic blooms that would wither after the first promising blush. However genuine may have been the yearning for eternal verities among the young, the thrill of novel and endless variety at first distracted and ultimately destroyed the noblest of impulses. Significantly, the Haight, and its global outposts, would serve as incubation chambers for the most influential religious movements of the next decade: the Hare Krishnas, Jesus Freaks, Gurdjieff adepts, and various technoid EST permutations. But none of these would have nearly the impact that did the wholly original spiritual consensus that is the true legacy of the sixties.

A bustling traffic in symbolism characterized the kinesthesia of the sixties. What a thing meant was of far less importance than how it looked and sounded and felt— how it blended on the palate of the senses. Spirituality became a tactile experience, and what set the nerve endings tingling were exotic symbols, talismans, and charms gathered from the far corners of the earth.

It is unusual for even a primitive culture to so thoroughly sustain itself on symbols alone—religion is nearly always underpinned by pragmatic needs for good crops or victory in battle. The hippies' postlogical penchant for emblematic mysticism reflected only a narcissistic obsession with all the Aquarian wonderment they had invented. The Onyx, the *I Ching*, tarot cards, and God's eyes. *Steppenwolf*, *Siddhartha*, Middle Earth, and Merlin. The peace sign, yin/yang, astrology, and yoga. All the incredible, intricate coronets and orbs and chevrons that comprised the subculture's coat of arms compensated for the great hollowness at the core of its quest. Devoid of the substance of spirituality, the hippies became masters of the form, constructing their own periodic table of symbols, feverishly consulting this absurd jumble of runes and nostrums for flimsy clues to their own immortality.

Initially the portents looked promising. From the welter of American Indian lore, Arthurian daydreams, Oriental smoke rings, science fiction ciphers, and their own growing compendium of psychedelic syllogisms, the hippies seemed on the verge of achieving a grand synthesis, striking the final harmonizing metachord. The "furious manipulation" of the mind-bending dance/concert experience was the initiatory ritual of the New Age. San Francisco rock 'n' roll was alloyed from blues, jazz, folk, and all the other elements in that bubbling improvisational stew. The alchemical fusions of the new faith transmuted the base metal of pop music into prayers, profundities, and Pythagorean mystery.

"To an insider, Garcia is magic," wrote one music critic in a 1980 edition of *College Papers*. "The Dead's music is positive, electric, high-energy. The obscure lyrics of Bob Hunter . . . are on the order of prophesy and their very obscurity shows a kindly respect for the listener's spiritual growth. Dead Heads usually see themselves as searching souls on a journey that's a little hard to explain except that it's definitely with the Dead."

From the beginning, The Grateful Dead's intuitive grasp of their music's power led them to brilliantly exploit its religious potential. They became the preeminent symbol mongers of the era, personifying both the chronic lust for spiritual prowess and the cultic pedagogy of the flower children. This dazzling transmutation of words and music was enhanced by visual elements that began with the band's own front line. The swarthy, stocky Garcia, rail-thin and razor-angled Phil Lesh, and the sweet androgeny of Bob "Ace" Weir: it was a pantheon of demigods, a triad of mutually dependent attributes.

Added to the mix were album art, logos, bumper stickers, and T-shirts, all underscoring the band's provocative mystique. Among the best-known and most-enduring of the Dead's symbolic resonators was a festooned skeleton dancing in a field of roses. It was an astonishingly potent icon, first conceived by poster artist Alton Kelly for an early Avalon Ballroom poster. "The rose is *the* most prominent image, as far as I'm concerned," asserted Robert Hunter in *Playing in the Band*, "as to beauty, delicacy, short-livedness . . . thorniness. . . . There is no better allegory for— dare I say it?—*life* than roses." Allegorically speaking, however, skulls better suited the Dead, and over the course of their career, grinning death heads appeared in various images; in the lightning bolt logo of the mid-seventies, the carefully rendered cyclops skull of *Terrapin Station*, a skeletal Uncle Sam, a fiddle-playing mummy. . . . The group made incessant use of Grim Reaper visages, not only for the obvious connection to their name but for the even more persuasive connotations of the death and rebirthing cycles implicit in both psychedelics and Dead music.

One artist was especially attuned to the secret teaching of the Grateful Dead. Before he became a Born Again Christian, painter, cartoonist, and illustrator, Rick Griffin had created Murph the Smurf in the early sixties and had gone on to establish a reputation as one of the most original and distinctive poster artists of San Francisco's rock renaissance. His work for the Dead was the perfect visual counterpart to the band's mystical allure. The 1969 *Aoxomoxoa* was Griffin's first album cover for the group, a luminous acid-etched depiction of the everlasting grave-womb, meshing magic mushrooms, embryos, earth mother vaginae, the trees of Life and of the Knowledge of Good and Evil, scarabs, and, unfurled beneath a glowing winged globe, the group's moniker, rendered in the nearly indecipherable Gothic calligraphy that Griffin pioneered. At the center of this spooky mandala, a phallic skull, spurting cosmic sperm into the heart of a fertile sun. In its bony grasp—a pair of eggs.

Rich grist for the Dead's symbol mill, Griffin's work came to personify the free-associative iconography in which the band habitually wrapped itself. The artist drew heavily from Manly Hall's *Secret Teachings* along with a host of other holy and profane texts. His canvases teemed with flying eyeballs, bleeding, thorn-pierced hearts, Mayan warrior gods, exploding fetuses, eight balls, tumbling dice, sand clocks, gravestones, smoking censers—anything and everything that whispered hidden significance. "Line up the cross hairs of the brain," Griffin wrote in *Man from Utopia*, a grotesque, fascinating portfolio of drawings and paintings published in 1969, "pull the trigger of the mind, hit the bull's eye of the being."

For the Dead, nothing was more on target than the intricate arcana of Egyptology. The decorative motifs and occult phantasmagoria of the ancient civilization appeared with increasing frequency in Griffin's work for the Dead, but the visual component only made explicit the longstanding if unspoken connection between the Dead and ancient Egypt. The uncracked secrets of the Pyramids, the animism, the bustling host of deities, and above all the implacable, monolithic *solidity* of Egyptian theology exerted a mesmerizing pull on the band and its followers. Here was an intimidating mythology, rendered in vast necropolitan monuments, impassive monitors of time's slow unwinding. Egyptology delivered up a kind of immortality, half-submerged in shifting sands, mute and omniscient. It was a fitting metaphor for a band that, some said, would live forever, even as its members passed into oblivion.

In August of 1978 the Dead spent a half-million dollars to ship themselves, their equipment, and their extended family to Egypt to play a series of concerts at the base of the Great Pyramid. In practical terms, the Egyptian performances made absolutely no sense. The Middle East was hardly a bastion of Deadheads and the political situation made the journey distinctly dangerous. *Symbolically*, however, it was a master stroke. "The journey was something we took very seriously," remarked Hart to David Gans. "This was something we'd wanted to do for years. Without sounding too mystical, I'd say we felt *drawn* there."

It was, of course, impossible *not* to sound too mystical when dwelling on the concept of the Grateful Dead weaving their spell under the gaze of the Sphinx. "This would be a real test of the power of the music," Hart continued, "to play in a place where nobody had any expectations of us and we didn't have the safety net of conditioned responses. We weren't there on our terms, nor on the audience's terms. We were all there on the desert's terms— and the desert had never seen amplified Western music, not to mention the Grateful Dead." Asked by an Egyptian official if their music changed depending on where they played, Phil Lesh replied, "Precisely, and that's why we want to play at the Pyramids." That, according to the bassist, "changed it in their eyes from somebody jacking off to somebody meaning business."

The Dead's "business" at Giza was tantalizingly obscure. There were rumors that they intended to use the King's Chamber of the Great Pyramid as a kind of giant echo chamber. Their third and last concert at the site occurred during a total lunar eclipse. Deadheads were well within their rights to expect a megaperformance, perhaps even a guest appearance by Egyptian gods Osiris or the Ibis-headed Thoth. The Dead playing the Pyramids—what heavier trip could possibly be concocted? It was a triumph of gratuitous symbolism, imbued with portentous significance not because of what happened or what might have happened but simply because it *had* happened, one more gong-banging, oracular feat to thrill the illuminati.

Even before the Grateful Dead had attained their exalted status as Keepers of the Flame, the counterculture's promiscuous spirituality had debased the very symbols it had so lovingly fingered and fawned over. Even Manly Hall's eccentric deceptions could no longer do justice to the folly of the flower children. It was, instead, a comic book hero that would eventually become the most fitting metaphor for the era's transcendent pretensions. Appearing regularly in Marvel Comic's *Strange Tales* Dr. Strange, Master

215

of the Mystic Arts, was an underground favorite, the disciple of a Tibetan cave-dwelling avatar known only as the Ancient One. The good doctor, furled in his Cloak of Levitation, regularly battled with such supernatural fiends as Kaluu, Dormammu, and Umar in a vast dreamscape. Written and plotted by comic masters Roy Thomas, Steve Ditko, and Stan Lee, Dr. Strange delighted his legions of fans with utterances like, "The eternal Vishanti do ever protect me!" "By the Vipers of Valtorr!" or "May the Hoary Hosts of Haggoth defend me!" One of the most original characters in Marvel's teeming roster, Dr. Strange personified the four-color mysticism of the sixties, hurling magic bolts, magnifying this "mental energies," sallying forth in his ectoplasmic alter ego into a distinctly psychedelic fantasyland. Along with Silver Surfer, another Marvel hero keyed to hippie values, Dr. Strange aptly summed up the extravagant thrill seeking that had become the grail of youth culture.

Similarly, psychedelic music, once promoted as the path to enlightenment, had been steadily reduced to a glitzy fraud. Musicians became enthralled with their own importance, and their music simply collapsed under the weight of hot air. San Francisco's operative art form was no longer acid rock but the dance/concert light show, a hurling, maniacal barrage of images, an entertainment where meaning occurred only in the accidental associations of a drug-dazed mind. The vaunted quest for truth had become a befuddled funhouse ride full of feverish distortions, mirrored cul de sacs, and scary but ultimately empty apparitions. An enervated generation, politically spent and spiritually poisoned, fell back mumbling as its vision faded in the chemical haze. It had indeed been, as the Dead proclaimed, "a long, strange trip." And it was over.

Nearly. "The Grateful Dead have proved that you *can*

216

get there from here," insisted drummer Bill Kreutzmann. "It's just that there's no tickets available." But it wasn't only the tickets that were missing. The destination, the timetable, the stops along the way were decided as the train rolled on. Little wonder so many got lost. The Dead would continue to blaze the trail even as the seventies ground down to a bleak new decade—and they would be rewarded with the fanatical allegiance of their followers. Out of the inchoate frenzy of their time, the band had ultimately emerged as the rock 'n' roll equivalent of musty, hidebound denomination: liturgical, bound in tradition, performing ceremonies that had long since lost their spiritual significance.

It may have seemed like betrayal. The Grateful Dead had championed a whole generation's faith in the formlessness of faith, had perfected the "leaderless collective" and charted a trip through the signifying cosmos. Ultimately, they became the high priests of a de facto religion. The cult of the Dead proved, finally, that faith without substance could drive men to distraction and, from there, into the comforting embrace of familiar ritual.

Jim Morrison, 1966

Chapter Nine

A GARDEN OF
EARTHLY DELIGHTS

> You never know what is enough unless you know
> what is more than enough.
> —Wiliam Blake, *Proverbs of Hell*

> It's a mighty long way down rock 'n' roll,
> from the Liverpool docks to the Hollywood Bowl.
> And you climb up the mountains and you fall
> down the holes.
> —Mott the Hoople, "All the Way From Memphis"

Washed ashore on a desert island. Palm fronds, presumably, sway, sunsets are monotonously spectacular, the scent of rotting breadfruit wafts across the reef. All is utter stillness, an enveloping silence . . . almost.

In 1979, Greil Marcus, one of the designated deans of rock criticism, proposed an intriguing hypothesis to the cream of his profession: stranded on a desert island, what one rock 'n' roll album would you want with you? "It's an old question and a good one;" Marcus wrote in the introduction to *Stranded*, the volume that resulted from his challenging conjecture. "Absurd, but irresistible." He was right. The same premise had once launched a radio show called *Desert Island Discs*.

The notion of eking out one's days with nothing to keep you company but the shriek of gulls and one rock 'n' roll album may not seem to some a fit topic for polite conversation. Who, after all, would want to contemplate endless repetitions of "Please allow me to introduce myself" or "It was twenty years ago today" or "We carried you in our arms on Independence Day" or "The screen door slams, Mary's dress waves" or "Once upon a time you dressed so fine" or "We skipped the light fandango" or even, God help us, "You know, the day destroys the night, night divides the day"?

However, his fellow critics rose to the challenge. "Call me Gilligan," began Nick Toches's meandering essay in which, after rejecting *The Doors*, Irish troubadours the Chieftains, and an obscure Lynyrd Skynyrd album, he finally settled on the Rolling Stones' *Sticky Fingers*. Simon Firth chose *Beggar's Banquet*, while Langdon Winner opted for Captain Beefheart's cacophonous *Trout Mask Replica* for the perverse reason that it "offers none of the qualities of a 'good' record." Joe McEwen made the wise choice of *Little Willie John* while John Rockwell selected, for motives still obscure, a Linda Ronstadt album. Paul Nelson liked Jackson Browne's *The Pretender*; Tom Carson, The Ramones' *Rocket to Russia*. Two LPs from Van Morrison finished in the desert island derby, along with Neil Young's *Decade*, the Eagles' *Desperado*, and the New York Dolls' neurotic debut. The premise of *Stranded*, Marcus ventured, was "less to head off into exile with a single piece of rock and roll than to bring it home, along with a story good enough to make others want to listen."

Why not? Each of the twenty writers offered a well-tendered defense of their particular choice, employing the desert island metaphor to dust off in droll or declaratory fashion their favorite theory on the Art of Rock. But no one in Marcus's salon, save one, latched onto the central, unsettling dilemma at the core of the experiment. "I never thought rock 'n' roll was fun. I thought it was hard work, triumph and failure." So critic Dave Marsh was once quoted, while elsewhere he avowed, "To me, rock 'n' roll was always the function of a certain kind of idealism. That idealism is important because that's what I base my whole philosophy on." Faced with what, from the evidence, must have been the frightful prospect of selecting the one, ultimate, and final example of all the philosophic idealism, the tears, laughter, and travail of the whole rock world view, Marsh balked, then cheated. He elected to ignore the rules of the game and concocted his own album of Greatest Hits of Deepest Meaning. Marsh's LP consisted of carefully culled, exhaustively justified selections from Elvis Costello, Bob Dylan, the Who, Roy Orbison, Otis Redding, Jerry Lee Lewis, the Beatles, the Stones, and others.

Who could blame him? Marsh, in his gut, understood that what Marcus was asking no dedicated rock aficionado could countenance. A single album, plucked from the galaxy of the twentieth century's grandest art form, the very music that Patti Smith had once called "the highest and most universal form of expression since the lost tongue"? May it never be! Forcing such a choice was tantamount to confronting a true believer with death or renunciation. Between the lines of Marsh's tongue-in-cheek *Stranded* essay was the unspoken horror inspired by the very thought of that solitary island existence, cut off from the rich and nourishing fecundity of rock 'n' roll. It was the cruelest kind of abuse, or, in Marsh's case, self-abuse, as he implied that if deprived of the philosophical moorings provided by popular music, he could find no greater fulfillment than a life of constant masturbation.

For those whose grasp of reality isn't dependent on large and regular doses of pop music, the deadly earnestness of Marsh and other chroniclers of the faith might seem either charming or dangerous. And if all this exaltation of rock sounded like nothing so much as graduate students blowing steam, well, chalk it up to an enterprise that, by the time *Stranded* hit the racks, had been going strong for more than a decade. Welcome to the world of formal rock crit.

It all started innocently enough in 1966 when a gaggle of college rock fans started writing about their favorite subject. It seemed like a good idea at the time—promising East Coast writers like Richard Goldstein, Paul Williams, Sandy Perlman, and Richard Meltzer with something to say and the boundless enthusiasm to make it stick. It wasn't their fault, exactly, but by '67 rock was getting serious, and you didn't have to be a social linguist, historian, or Ph.D. candidate to know it. But it sure helped.

Take, for example, Daniel Gannon's review of the Supremes' "You Keep Me Hangin' On" in *Crawdaddy* magazine in January of that year. The scintillating chart buster, Gannon insisted, "draws more inspiration from Prokofiev than from earlier Motown." The spoken line at the end of the second verse, if you will, "borders on the vocal style used by Arnold Schoenberg in *Pierrot Lunaire*, in which the soprano speaks the text, following in exaggerated high and low pitches on a printed line of music."

Come again? Prokofiev? Schoenberg? What happened to Holland-Dozier-Holland, Berry Gordy, and "don't forget the Motor City?" Never mind that precious few Supremes' fans, or any one else for that matter, knew the difference between *Pierre Lunaire* and Pepe LePew, or that a working knowledge of exaggerated pitches enhanced an appreciation of Diana Ross's baby doll breathlessness not one whit. Suddenly, according to Dan Gannon and like-minded highbrow popculturists, rock was coming of age.

The release of *Sgt. Pepper's* in June found the critics frothing. *Newsweek* hailed the Beatles as Britain's new poet laureates. They were unabashedly compared to Tennyson, Dame Edith Sitwell, playwright John Osbourne, and Wordsworth. Their music was on an aesthetic par with the films of Chaplin, the books of Donald Barthelme, and the drama of Harold Pinter. They even drew comparison to T. S. Eliot: "A Day in the Life" was nothing less than "the Beatles' 'Wasteland.'" The race to profundity was on. Critical dissections of rock music began popping up in the unlikeliest places, including *Esquire*, where Robert Christgau inaugurated his "Secular Music Column." By the turn of the decade, every Middlesex hamlet had its resident pop pundit. Rock 'n' roll, it was revealed, could illuminate the entire pulsing spectrum of human experience.

The question of which came first—leaden rock progressivism or self-aggrandizing critics, is moot. The point was, it had suddenly become possible to evaluate popular music from all sorts of intriguing angles. As a business, for example, rock had turned the traditional music industry on its ear. In San Francisco alone by 1970 a Bank of America financial analyst was predicting that "hard rock" would shortly become the city's fourth largest industry. In 1965 RCA Records had stunned their competitors by offering a $25,000 contract to the Jefferson Airplane. Two short years later, no one blinked when Atlantic Records offered $200,000 to an unknown British ensemble named Led Zeppelin. Rock's commercial growth curve was exceeding all sorts of expectations for a very simple reason: prior to the advent of real rock artists, the coin of the music business realm had been the 45 RPM single, sold for around a buck. Albums, if and when they were made, were simply ancillary marketing tools, collections of radio hits rounded out with often embarrassing filler. Suddenly, it was no longer deemed necessary, or even desirable, to churn out Top Ten contenders. If a musician couldn't embellish two sides of a long player, he didn't deserve serious attention. The entire smarmy recording industry was, in fact, disdained by the self-ordained musical elite. What had crass enterprise to do with the triumph and struggle of real art?

As it turned out, plenty. Albums, peddled at steadily escalating prices, overnight became rock's chosen medium of expression. Instead of raking profits off the dollar-per-unit rate of singles, record companies were taking slices from a pie three, four, or even five times as large. Through the tinted shades of music moguls, musicians began growing webbed feet, bills, and feathers, dropping golden eggs with clockwork regularity. It's hardly surprising that the geese were coddled and stroked and pampered. Huge sums were spent while artists, proven or otherwise, dithered around in expensive studios searching for the lost chord. Even larger sums were spent *constructing* studios for the dithering to take place. Pitched battles were joined over artistic control, song length, promotional, advertising, and marketing budgets, but it was all mock heroics. Art and commerce were snuggled tightly on a money-stuffed mattress. Everyone even vaguely associated with the rock industry was prospering, and if they weren't, well, there was always the next album, the next tour, the next contract negotiation.

But the business of rock was only part of the story. Long before the close of the sixties, the music was having a cultural effect out of proportion with its humble origins, proving, with the possible exception of television, to be the most influential pop medium of modern times. The reli-

gious establishment, noticing the emptying pews, a dwin-
dling donor base, and a steady seepage of credibility
among the young, began taking another look at its long-
standing crusade against the pernicious influence of rock
music. Some denominations began opening fellowship
halls and basements to local garage bands for safe and
supervised youth nights. More radical wings held hap-
penings, became politically involved and actively sought
to realign themselves with the mutating values of the counterculture. Fundamentalists held firm, especially (and not
surprisingly) the Pentecostal and Methodist sects of the
Deep South. But elsewhere, interesting if uneasy alliances
were being struck. In Southern California, for example,
the Jesus People—Born Again hippies who had fused an
innate mistrust of authority with a genuine devotion to
essential Christian doctrines—had begun retooling traditional worship. Introducing mild but unmistakable pop
music elements into the sanctuary, they attracted large
numbers of disaffected flower children, creating the basis
for a new and hotly controversial expression of Christianity. In time this ground swell would support its own
cottage industry, but contemporary Christian music's
struggle to break down the barriers between the church
and culturally relevant pop music styles would prove both
frustrating and inconclusive. The breach was too wide.

More startling still was the failure of Christian doctrines
and values to find voice in the rock 'n' roll mainstream.
The sixties spawned no major rock group espousing hearth
and home, monogamy or monotheism. Considering the
sheer diversity of what *was* being propagated, the exclusion is revealing, and the exceptions only prove the rule.
If Jesus or the devil, sin or salvation, heaven or hell were
ever evoked in song, it could safely be chalked up to one
more aesthetic contrivance or literary allusion. The studied
indifference and ill-concealed contempt could be only

partly explained by the long-standing antipathy between rock and Western religion or, for that matter, the violent rejection of Christian pieties in the widespread counter-culture. Here was the flowering of some deeply rooted, uncompromising hostility.

It is pointless to trace rock's development for the seeds of this alienation. The gospel nurture of black music and thus of all rock 'n' roll had faded so far into the distant past it had become completely irrelevant to the portentous undertakings of the Sixties. What was considerably more relevant was rock's quite remarkable power in the lives of countless individuals. When Dave Marsh spoke of an idealism worthy of a whole philosophic construct, he was putting words in the mouths of millions of enthralled fellow travelers, precisely articulating their attachment to this special music.

What, it might well be asked, gives? Hadn't there been moments of ecstatic affirmation through music before Elvis ever slung a guitar? What of the classical world? What of the codified drama of opera or the rarefied pleasures of jazz? How about folk or country music? Each certainly had its gaggle of devotees, but put all that music together, add up its individual appeals, and you'd still be light years away from the Rock Effect.

In the face of such an overwhelming phenomenon, rational analysis fails; one enters the realm of the numinous and immanent. And that suited the purveyors of Sixties rock just fine. Through accretions and transferences, acts of rebellion and reformation; through processes dependent on and superior to history, philosophy, and wishful thinking, rock 'n' roll had reached for and achieved the status of incarnational faith.

Nineteen hundred years before all the excitement, Saint Paul was being propelled hither and yon through the wilds of Macedonia at the prompting of the Holy Spirit. During a layover in Athens, a kind of first-century spiritual swap meet, he spent an afternoon with some Epicureans, Stoics, and various other erudite pagans up on the windswept heights of Mars Hill. As the Book of Acts tells it, this mixed bag of philosophers, deep thinkers, and professional seekers used to "spend their time in nothing other than telling or hearing something new." Paul gave them an earful, pointing to the altar of the Unknown God and announcing that what they worshiped in ignorance, he proclaimed in no uncertain terms—the One True God, creator and sustainer of the universe. Some listened and followed; most were mildly amused. Life on Aeropagus hummed blithely on.

As an early church anecdote, the episode serves to underscore the central challenge faced by the fledgling Christian faith: a diffuse but entrenched religious enterprise that not only tolerated diversity but prided itself on the harmonious coexistence of any and all metaphysical credos. There were, of course, other considerations that kept the arrangement in balance. Later in Acts, Paul's message threatens the thriving idol-making business of some Epicurean silversmiths. Convinced that this one-deity hoax might cut into their profits, they drag the evangelist before the proper authorities, howling for blood. Religion, then as always, was big business. By rejecting the appealing notion that the cosmos crawled with gods and demigods— all of whom could be appeased and appealed to—the first Christians were flying in the face of the most comforting kind of conventional wisdom. There was one truth, they insisted, not a myriad; one way, and not the one that seemed right to man. This was as close to heresy as anyone could get in the ancient anything-goes carnival of concepts.

What goes around comes around. The great and engaging surge of spiritual energies that transformed rock music centuries later was not destined to benefit from the clarifying reductionism of any latter-day Saint Paul. Plunged deeply into the music's spectrum of doxologies, dogmas, and mesmerizing diversions, the rock 'n' roll philosophers had long since tossed off the asphyxiating restrictions of the Judeo-Christian ethic. Rock and Jesus had been weighed in the balance from the days of Elvis; Jesus had consistently come up light. It wasn't just the thundering denouncements of pulpiteers that had soured rock 'n' roll on Christianity. It was the very *exclusiveness* of the religion, the antithesis of rock's resplendent diversity. Truth be told, rock had long since ceased to be any one thing. Already stylistically splintered, the music's varied offshoots played host to a formidable array of genuine, quasi and artificial spiritual come-ons. The music had indeed become a religion, supplanting and deriding the old Western faith; but more than a religion, it was a great, overarching aesthetic, under which nothing was forbidden. Windy Aeropagus, hosting all manner of bemused and beguiling speculation, had found its modern counterpart in electric music: something for everybody and no rules to follow.

Is it any wonder then that Dave Marsh, the voice of rock's faithful, shuddered at the notion of Marcus's desert island banishment? Never mind that all the pomposity of the new rock priesthood was systematically choking off the music from its source of combustible spontaneity. Forget the dangerous presumption which elevated guitar players to sages and necromancers, imbuing their every utterance with prophetic heft. Finally, ignore the bizarre mélange of mysticism and menacing hedonism that was infecting the core of the new faith. Preserve, instead, the conviction of all that can be known, could be known, instinctively, through the music that "can set you free."

228

There may once have been a time when you could live out your days on that awful island with one Elvis or Little Richard memento. But this was the new age: rock was all things to all people, contained not on an island but strewn across a vast archipelago. This wasn't music. This was *epistemology*, determined to test the limits of human knowledge.

"Jim's trip was about life. If he had to kill himself to get there . . . that was alright." That's how Danny Sugerman sees the strange and pathetic saga of Jim Morrison the Lizard King, an alcoholic and leather-clad personification of rock 'n' roll's monumental self-absorption. In a way he hit it right on the mark. Sugerman was the favored gofer, aide-de-camp, and, eventually, myth guardian of the Doors, a band whose quick ascendancy and sudden stomach-turning plummet to oblivion marks a grimly instructional chapter in sixties music. At the age of thirteen, Sugerman had fallen under the influence of Jim Morrison. There was ample opportunity to observe all the contradiction, hypocrisy, and shrieking excess that attended the singer/poet's fleeting moment in the sun. If, when all was said and done, Danny could somehow pull life from meaningless death or revelation and art from wretched deception; if somehow he could believe that paradox . . . more power to him. "You can straddle the fence between life and death, between 'here' and 'now' for only so long," he wrote in the introduction to the best-selling Morrison biography *No One Here Gets Out Alive*. "Jim . . . went on alone, without us."

For a minute there it seemed as if he'd take us all along with him, down the twisted, creepy path of our own darkest impulses, a Bataan death march of self-discovery with Morrison at the head of the column, swaggering and leering and full of spiteful, secret knowledge. The Doors' aus-

229

picious and surprising arrival into the midst of the paisley wonderland of the late sixties was the occasion for all manner of wide-eyed pronunciamentos' from the critical establishment. "Anyone who disputes the concept of rock literature," warned Richard Goldstein in *New York Magazine*, "had better listen long and hard. . . . this is Joycean pop." "His songs are eerie," chimed a wide-eyed *Vogue* reviewer, "loaded with Freudian symbolism, poetic but not pretty, filled with suggestions of sex, death, transcendence." It was January 1967 and the Doors' eponymously titled debut album had burst out of the warm concrete expanse of Los Angeles like an act of God. What the world was shortly to discover, a handful of Hollywood club crawlers had been hip to for over a year. That's when the Doors had first galvanized the provincial Hollywood music scene with a threatening and theatrical stage show, emitting something completely hostile to San Francisco's soothing vibes.

In the small, insular world that revolved around all-night summer cruises down Sunset Strip for a stop at Fred C. Dobbs, Ash Grove, It's Boss, or, naturally the Whiskey-a-Go-Go, many of Lotus Land's pop cognoscenti knew all about Morrison. A fomer UCLA film student and son of a Navy admiral whom he would later claim was dead, Morrison had corralled three itinerant musicians to form his own rock band. At the time he had never sung a note for fame or money. Doors music, suggesting a brooding confluence of parking lots and casual depravity—the Los Angeles of such early originals as "Twentieth-Century Fox," "Crystal Ship," and "End of the Night"—seemed very much a local phenomenon; some kind of weird, slightly unsavory variant on the basin's prevailing ennui. It was a strangely distancing sound, dominated by the smoky interplay of Ray Manzarek's keyboards and Robby Krieger's slithery guitar; sort of adventurous cocktail music until you began to sink beneath the surface, where all sorts of sinister innuendoes lurked. The contrast to prevailing psychedelic antics was bracing; here were cool, calculated songs, neatly targeted.

And brazenly provocative. The Doors' singular contribution to rock was less evocative of Freudian undertows and sex-drenched nightscapes than of their own sense of drama; big, sweeping musical gestures that attracted attention by virtue of their sheer theatricality. Morrison would never be the thespian Mick Jagger was, but his play-acting in many ways was better suited to rock 'n' roll. Overwrought, chest-thumping, full of enraged bellows and whispered asides, Morrison never underestimated the enhancing power of the proscenium arch. "It was Jim's job to make sure he got the audience hot," explains Sugerman. "He once explained to me about the pregnant pauses the band incorporated into their shows by saying, 'You either have the audience or you don't. If you don't have them . . . well, I just stop the music and get them.'"

With the certification of "Light My Fire" as one of the half-dozen genuine anthems of the era, Morrison and his band was getting them but good. In the summer of '67, the Doors were the market's hottest commodity. In light of their overnight coronation, it seems poetically just that audiences and critics should just as quickly turn ugly. It was whispered that *Strange Days*, the group's eagerly awaited follow-up album, released in October of that year, sounded awfully like the first go-round, up to and including the extended rant "When the Music's Over," a pale approximation of the genuinely scarifying surrealism of "The End"—the first and still the best example of why the Doors had created such a stir. By '68 with *Waiting for the Sun*, the floodgates of ridicule were wide open. Morrison had become, in Nik Cohen's memorable phrase, "a marvelous boy in black leather made up by two queens

231

on the phone." His lyric poetry, another critic sneered, was "third rate Rod McKuen and Kahlil Gibran." The Lizard King, for *Time*, was "a psychedelic pushcart salesman hawking Oedipal nightmares like Good Humors."

So what was the problem? Other bands had fallen out of favor before, rudely awakening to empty halls and a snide press. Doors records were, in fact, continuing to sell respectably, and their skirmishes with the critics were only the opening rounds in an escalating battle of wills between writers and rock stars. Why was the blush so suddenly off the rose?

The answer was as plain as the smoldering embers in Morrison's eyes. *The guys actually believed the act.* He wasn't just pretending; all that mute nostril agony was from the heart. On permanent display was an actor in the grip of his own masquerade, playing it for all it was worth clear back to the cheap seats. It was, well, embarrassing. No wonder the patrons turned tittering away.

Or egged him on, taunting him with their unflagging lust for spectacle and outrage. On March 1, 1969, in Miami, Morrison reportedly pulled down his pants and wagged his genitalia at thrill-thirsty fans. It was an incident that wrenched his grip from whatever credibility he still clung to, and the exhausting obscenity trial—with comparisons to similar ordeals of Henry Miller and D. H. Lawrence a little too neatly drawn—further sapped his flagging energies. Not long afterward—overweight, muddled, and dissolute—Morrison retreated to Paris to die a lonely death of heart failure in his hotel bathtub.

It might be hard to imagine the lion-maned rock poet in any other context, but it's worth a try. If Jim Morrison had been a gas station attendant, a Naval lifer, a beach bum, or a pro fullback, could he have so recklessly summoned the demons that turned and swallowed him whole? Perhaps. "Morrison soaked up influences like a sponge," recalls Richard Blackburn, who traveled in the same circles at UCLA as Morrison. "He'd read books, passing over pages like a Geiger counter, finding the stuff that supported his world view and filing it for later." The fact that Morrison *had* a world view hints at precocious processes of self-invention. Sadly, he had the chance to play himself out against the hallucinatory backdrop of rock stardom. Rock 'n' roll *created* Morrison, filling in the blanks and giving meaning and significance to both his talents and his awesome delusions.

As a fledgling legend, Morrison set about early pumping himself up to cast a long shadow. It wasn't enough—it never was—simply to be famous because of some serendipitous ability to entertain people. And Morrison, more determined than most rock stars, was in the business of proving that his fame was founded on a supreme supernatural mandate. Sugerman reverently recounts one of destiny's earliest taps on Morrison's shoulder: "When Jim was five, six years old, he was driving down the highway with his parents and they came upon an overturned truck of Pueblo Indians, and they were dying, they were scattered on the highway bleeding and dying. . . . One of the souls of one of those dead Indians was just freaking out and jumped into his soul because he was the youngest and the most vulnerable. . . . What Jim did by describing that incident was he gave credence to his shaman theory . . . that he was a shaman. Not just by mental belief, but by spiritual transmission he had received the shamanistic spirit."

Lurid hokum, maybe, but to a newly minted star perched on the pedestal of fame, it sounded just about right. Shamanism was the face Morrison had taken from the ancient gallery, and he freely employed shamanistic lore to justify both his art and his brakeless life. His role as possessed priest/poet of the rock church wouldn't become fully fleshed until after his death, but it was obvious from the singer's own ruminations that he regarded himself as the anointed vehicle for some grand synthesis of religious and theatrical rites. Doors music, he mused, was a striving to "break through to some cleaner, freer realm. It's like a purification ritual in the alchemical sense." Shortly before his death, he told writer Digby Diehl, "Sometimes I look at the history of rock and roll like the origin of Greek drama, which started out on a threshing floor at the crucial seasons and was originally a band of worshippers dancing and singing. Then one day a possessed person jumped out of the crowd and started imitating a god. I think rock serves the same function."

What the singer would only flirt with in the press and in his music (the 1969 ludicrous *The Soft Parade* highlighted a tune called "Shaman's Blues") was spelled out in no uncertain terms by his disciples. Citing the influence on Morrison of author Carlos Castaneda's best-selling (and unauthenticated) series on the Yaqui Indian sorcerer Don Juan, Doors keyboardist Ray Manzarek remarked, "Don Juan takes place in Mexico. You can't take it out of Mexico and plug it into L.A. Don Juan was a shaman, you know, and what people needed was an electric shaman, a contemporary city shaman, and that's why they turned to Jim. He was an electric shaman and we were the electric shaman's band, pounding away behind him." Manzarek, who, after the Doors' demise, would release a dismal series of albums detailing his fascination with Egyptology and reincarnation, goes on to describe the band's performances as a "mystical journey to a darker psychic realm that people today would just be scared to enter. . . . In tribal times, the shaman was kind of an ecstatic visionary who would go into trances and act out the psychic life of the tribe while all the people were beating on drums and shaking spirit catchers. A shaman has to have a rhythm to go into a

234

shaman's dance, and we were doing the exact same thing."

All this shamanizing well served Morrison's inflated self-image, handily explaining, at the same time, his prodigious self-indulgence. Elected rock's own "erotic politician," Morrison was also the worst kind of drunk: loud, abusive, totally out of control. His life, writes Lester Bangs, "could be written off as one of the more pathetic episodes in the star system or that offensive myth that we all persist in believing which holds that artists are a race apart and thus entitled . . . to generally do whatever they want."

Jim Morrison didn't generally do whatever he wanted: he *explicitly* did whatever he wanted, to whomever he wanted to do it, regardless of the consequences. *No One Here Gets Out Alive* abounds with tawdry feats of bravado and a pathological disgust for the humblest social amenities. Incident followed incident: Morrison forcing a girlfriend to drink his blood; Morrison passed out time and again in a deathlike trance induced by booze and drugs; Morrison dangling precipitously from balconies; Morrison abusing his friends, his wife, his audience, himself.

Could Morrison, a man of ephemeral but promising talents, have been saved from the hideous consequences of his own fame? Might truer friends have served him better and loved him more? The questions evoke, in turn, the profound isolation, the whole distorted hyperreality of life on top of the rock pile. Morrison, perhaps more than most, was susceptible to believing his own hype. It's safe to assume that the mask of electric witch doctor—in touch with elemental magic, persecuted by cruel authoritarians—never fell away to reveal the sodden spiritual derelict.

But even *had* Morrison been inclined to listen to a still, small voice of conscience, it's doubtful he could have heard it over the sycophantic clamor of his entourage. In an attempt to justify—to him, to themselves, for the

235

record—Morrison's addictive personality, Doors mythologizers added to the incessantly repeated role of shaman another dubious honor, the very incarnation of Dionysus. "The Dionysian spirit, ecstasy, enters through the ears," explains Manzarek, "so you had to come to a Doors concert and listen." Michael McClure, in his maudlin afterword to Morrison's biography, writes: "Jim was a metamorphic hero who thrilled us with his energy and daring. He perceived with his senses and altered them with alcohol (sacred to Dionysus, the god of drama and intoxication), with acid, with the interior elixir of his ebullience and exuberance." Consistently left unmentioned was that the Greek demigod's attributes also included that of lawgiver and promoter of civilization, not precisely a role model for a man "attracted to revolt, disorder, chaos."

When alcohol, acid, and the "interior elixir" dispatched the hero, it served only to crank up the ghoulish hyperbole. His death, intoned Sugerman, assured him "a place in the pantheon of wounded, gifted artists who felt life too intensely to bear it." In a statement that leaps the bounds of the rational, Sugerman adds that the suffering his addictions brought him "were incidental, and indeed, insignificant compared to the visions and powers one would receive. In other words, Jim didn't get loaded to escape. Jim got high to become a high spiritual human being."

For Morrison, slipping the mortal coil was, apparently, an unintended by-product of spiritual transcendence. But more illuminating than the feats of devotion performed by his legatees—death is life, destruction is creation—is the sobering realization that Jim Morrison was nothing more or less than a product of his times. Sugerman, Manzarek, and company can hardly be blamed for sanctifying delusions that meshed so neatly with the staggering vanity of their generation. Manzarek: "We're always looking to worship outside ourselves. You've got to worship yourself. We are all gods, and Jim was able to tap that. . . . Everyone is capable of entering the same state that Jim Morrison entered into, where you're free and alive and capable of doing anything without bonds and without restrictions."

Unrestricted and unbound, the story of the Doors had the thudding directness of a morality play written for retarded children. Yet while such hair-raising rock 'n' roll fables weren't exactly the exception, they weren't precisely the rule, either. Sometimes simple silliness offset the grimmest cases of cause and effect.

The Moody Blues, for example, proved conclusively that you'd never go broke underestimating the spiritual sophistication of rock audiences. Erstwhile r & b hacks, the British quintet hit the big time conjuring up a loopy melange of Prince Valiant chivalry, low-grade occult blather, and symphonic wheezing that scored big with the starry-eyed set. Album titles like *Days of Future Passed*, *On the Threshold of a Dream*, and *Seventh Sojourn* pretty much summed it up, as did their drippy tour de force "Nights In White Satin," which charted no less than three separate times over a twelve-year span. Quintessentially goofy, the Moodies' matchbook-cover mysticism would nevertheless set the tone for dozens of other groups, anxious for their own slice of the round table or the wheel of reincarnation. Druid and Celtic lore, the whole blowzy Arthurian soap opera, and every other chestnut from yesteryore would become stock props in rock's metaphysical road show.

Of considerably more interest, and substance, were the gloomy candle-and-cobweb meditations of Procol Harum. The British band's intriguing pretensions were underscored even by their name, Latin for "beyond these things." Progenitors of "classical rock," with a penchant for cantata frills and Bachish lilts, the group could also flex a hard, electric blues muscle. But it was the subject matter of their original material—penned primarily by lyricist Keith Reid and keyboardist Gary Brooker and spread out over ten albums and eleven years—that set Procol Harum apart. For once rock music's high literary aspirations were in competent hands: the Reid/Brooker partnership at its best achieved the pop music equivalent of a good nineteenth-century novel: mordant fatalism, mixed with a healthy dose of Old Testament fear and loathing, an obsession with sin, self-abasement, and moral decay that would warm the cockles of a flagellant's heart. Even when they overdid it, wallowing in melodrama or dipping into the trough of bastardized Eastern dogmas, Procol Harum remained a cut above the best efforts of many rock pundits.

It was a *raison d'être* not immediately evident in the band's early efforts. The 1967 "A Whiter Shade of Pale," their first and most successful (and still best-known) hit, could be interpreted as an exquisitely painful tale of regret, but its appeal as a slice of psychedelia lay in a doomy surrealism couching the obscure message.

It was a different story with *A Salty Dog*, the group's 1969 stroke of genius and one of the few real accomplishments in the benighted realm of Rock Concept. A ghostly guided tour through the feverish hold of a sailing ship, *A Salty Dog* was peopled with a cast of haunted, deluded, and deranged characters, each with a cautionary tale to tell. The band's deft handling of the most venerable seafaring metaphors was enhanced by a wonderfully entertaining storytelling skill. "The Milk of Human Kindness," "Juicy John Pink," "The Devil Came From Kansas," "Too Much Between Us"; the songs are, at once, character cameos, one-act psychodramas and beautifully rendered judgments on the human condition. Interspersed were evocative nautical interludes; the title cut with its echos of Melville and the wind-whipped mock operatics of "Wreck of the Hesperus" set the rolling seas under this fated musical clipper.

A Salty Dog closes on two luminous compositions that speak as clearly of Procol Harum's melancholic genius— and their unique place in modern music—as anything they ever did. "You better listen, anybody," says the character in "Crucifixion Lane," "Cause I'm gonna make it clear. That my life is unimportant. What I've done, I did through fear." Bitter self-reproach dissolves in a moment of existential terror, as the blues riff builds to an anguished crescendo. "Can't you hear me, mother, calling you? I'm cold, I'm deaf, I'm blind." This stroll through the valley of the shadow of death is contrasted with an ineffable sense of loss in the majestic "Pilgrim's Progress," where still another shipboard stranger laments life's futile journey:

> In starting out, I thought to go exploring,
> and set my foot upon the nearest road.
> In vain I sought to find the promising turning,
> but only saw how far I was from home.
> In seaching I forsook the paths of learning,
> and so did stead to find some pirate's gold.
> In finding I did hurt those nearest to me;
> still no hidden truths did I unfold.

"I sat me down," concludes this sadder-but-wiser penitent, "to write a simple story. Which maybe in the end became a song. The words have all been writ by one before. We're taking turns in trying to pass them on."

Procol Harum would themselves, in time, pass on, and while they would never regain the lofty heights of art and metaphysics attained on *A Salty Dog*, their recording career remained one of the most consistently intriguing in modern music.

So, too, was the fetishistic vinyl output of the Velvet

Underground, whose music offered a subversive alternative to the increasing sanctimony of late Sixties rock, elevating them, with a handful of torturous LPs, to the status of blood-sweating heretics. If the Doors peered arrogantly through a glass at the sprouting hippie-dippy utopia, the Velvet Underground took the glass, shattered it, and slit their wrists. Featuring a female drummer and a front line of classically trained musicians, the band would have an incalculable effect on much of the music of the impending Seventies. But more than recherché decadence, gender-bending, and drug culture glam, the Velvets accomplished a truly remarkable feat of musical imagination during their five-year fling. David Bowie, Roxy Music, Patti Smith, the Sex Pistols, the Cars . . . any of the artists that would come to huddle in the shadow of this unlikely New York aggregate (and it's been said that every Velvet Underground fan eventually went out and started a band) could approximate the sleaziness and raunch, the gutter snarls and homoerotic mantras that mottled the music of the Velvets like bruises. But what could only be alluded to by others was the jolting authenticity of their songs, the pitch of flayed emotions, and the drone of narcotized lust.

The band's near lack of commercial success—even during their tenure as Andy Warhol's house band—is hardly surprising considering the perverse pleasure they took in slaughtering the sacred cows of the counterculture. Malicious spoilsports, the Velvet's version of free love and sexual liberation was sadomasochism and fellatio-crazed drag queens. The Day-Glo pleasures of acid popping and reefer toking were tranformed into diseased celebrations of unbridled mainlining. "Heroin" and "White Light/ White Heat," the most enduring of the band's grotesque needle fantasies, seemed, late in the decade, to have materialized from some other world completely—an alternate universe hung with portraits of Dorian Gray. Psychedelic pied pipers handing out candied doses on the streets of San Francisco had become the heartless smack peddler in "I'm Waiting for My Man," doling poison in Harlem alleys. Peace, love, and understanding were tidily laid to rest in the band's 1969 "I'm Set Free." "I'm set free," chief songwriter and guitarist Lou Reed crooned, "to find another illusion."

Reed was, according to critic Kurt Loder, disinclined to "judge his troubled urban characters." But that wasn't the half of it. Suspending sentence on all this moral gangrene was one thing; infusing the penchants and predilections of his creations with positively religious passions was quite another. A junkie's love for his habit; the yawning maw of sexual obsession and the lethal potential of love: Reed appeared intimately acquainted with it all. The contrast couldn't have been more startling. The Velvet's transcendence-through-pain musical motif brought Aquarian daydreams crashing down on flower-decked heads. Life wasn't an unfolding lotus of love beams; it was a nasty, dangerous bit of business where oblivion was the only sure escape. This Velveteen manifesto had the unmistakable ring of truth, and at its best, the band was devoid of the cynicism and despair that would've stripped its music of its power. This was raw-nerve stuff that caught both terrible and beautiful echoes of the human condition.

Significantly, the Velvet Underground captured these anguished moments best not simply by singing them but by playing them. As explicit as the lyrics to Reed's songs may have been, it was the band's ensemble work that most succinctly expressed the furtive revelations of their fallen world. Individually, the Velvets certainly *knew* how to play their instruments—they had served time in all sorts of standard-issue pop bands, and could prove their skills anytime it suited them (as, for instance, in the folk-rock interludes on the 1970 *The Velvet Underground*). That they chose most often to flail, trash, and clang like musical therapy patients in the multiple offenders' block, was to have a lasting effect on rock 'n' roll in the late seventies. Defiantly primitive, relentlessly crude, the group eschewed the fussy mannerisms and baroque studio techniques of the time, depending on volume, distortion, and their own churning innards to get the message across. Here was a small but special turning point: one needn't be a bluesologist, have a degree in sound engineering, or a denful of finger-picking trophies to play rock 'n' roll. Conviction and audacity would suffice. Just strap on the Stratocaster, crank the dials, and peel rubber on the noisy road to self-expression.

It worked. The Velvet Underground could wring more from a crunching four-chord progression than from a whole sound stage of phased and filtered harpsichords. It was an early warning of the rabid backlash waiting in the wings.

In much the same way, the guitar playing of Jimi Hendrix spoke a powerful new language. One of the first and still most enduring guitar heroes, Hendrix was a self-invented rock icon. He playfully manipulated the sideshow appeal of a psychedelic Negro, deflating much of pop music's pompous self-absorption and perfecting a gloriously fluent electric glossolalia, full of fun and thunder and certified transrational pith. In 1966, when the twenty-four-year old music veteran (he'd played with everyone from Little Richard to Sam Cooke to the Isley Brothers) came roaring in on a tsunami of white noise, the world hardly needed another riff-and-lick virtuoso. The group Cream, fronted by Eric Clapton, was strutting its indulgences and mangling the blues, while San Francisco was sprouting gee-whiz stringmen at an alarming rate. What the world *did* need was what Hendrix brought to the art of amplified guitar—a gut feel for the tremendous power of electronics to unlock new realms of expression and the imagination to fit the key to the lock.

Hendrix could never wield a lyric with anything like the audacity and breathless abandon with which he threw notes and chords and blistering wah-wah effects against each other. For the most part pedestrian excursions into extraterrestrial life, voodoo machismo, recreational politics, and sundry mystic musings, Hendrix songs—with rare but startling exceptions—seemed to swing between bad Dylanisms and street jive, never quite reaching either perch. The fact that "Foxy Lady," "Purple Haze," and "Are You Experienced?" are classics of the era says nothing about their content, and everything about their delivery.

Hendrix was as completely mired in the cosmic quagmire of the sixties as any other self-respecting rock star. In 1970, for example, he hosted the Rainbow Bridge Vibratory Color-Sound Experiment on Maui in Hawaii. Playing to an audience assembled according to their astrological signs, Hendrix sported a magic Hopi medicine man's shirt and used the Crater of the Sun on the Olowalu Volcano as his resonator. "The purpose of humanity for being on this planet," announced the Rainbow Bridge MC Chuck Wein, "is to build a bridge between the heart and the high mental and spiritual centers of the planetary being. . . . So instead of just being like a reflective groovy audience that we have at every love-in and concert forever and ever up to now, if we just turn on harmony so Jimi can stick it to that and lead us across the bridge . . . everybody all over the world is going to pick up on that." Wein exited with the serene Hindu chant "OM." Whether any of this coaching registered with the reflective groovy audience—by all accounts as completely blitzed on drugs as the cast and crew on stage—remains a matter of speculation. What can be determined by this and similar slices from Hendrix's career is that on the enlightenment scale, Jimi rated with the Moody Blues, a postacid Eric Burdon, and any of a dozen second-billed Frisco bands.

Which is all, finally, beside the point. "I'm standing next to a mountain," Hendrix sang on "Voodoo Chile." "I chop it down with the edge of my hand." It was a good line, as good as "'Scuse me while I kiss the sky" or "Is it to-morrow, or just the end of time," or any of a handful of snippets from his collected works. But what infused these snatches with quaking significance was what Jimi Hendrix was doing to his guitar at the same time. The music—that huge, liquid cacophony—actually was the bridge for su-pernatural energies that struck folks like bolts from the blue. Hendrix could evoke the surface of Neptune, the submerged skyline of Atlantis, or the déjà vu of recycled lives; could elicit magnificent mindscapes and magical ter-rains. In short, he could approximate that very moment when the shuddering Other swims into view. He could do it all, and better than anyone, with only the clarion blast of his ax. If it all only signified the fill-in-the-blanks spirituality of the masses, well, what did that have to do with the brash pleasures at his fingertips?

His music invites, of course, inevitable parallels; trance mediums and other unwitting bearers of otherwordly gifts. Could be. It's certainly true that Hendrix's music often seemed the work of a possessed man, in the grip of a powerful, perhaps even demonic, master. It's also true that his de rigueur diet of drugs and various occult jolts may well have opened him up to the legions. The guitarist might even have welcomed his hoary houseguests. What remains unsettled is the unmistakable stamp of person-ality, the wit and bravissimo at the root of his best work. Jimi Hendrix may have taken his spiritual pursuits seri-ously, but it's clear that playing electric guitar was a source of great joy for him, and it's that joy—a childish delight in flashy noises and dexterous trickery—that's the real source of his genius. It's probably inevitable that his music would underscore the inarticulate urgings of the generation. Hendrix was, after all, a poet for whom words were a second language. But it's the euphoria, the lingering spirit of play that remains his legacy. It had once been fun to let your hair grow and your inhibitions down, to shock the elders and "wave your freak flag high." By the late sixties, Hendrix was the last reminder of those innocent beginnings. His routine rock-star death by drug overdose and the posthumous 1971 release of *Cry of Love*, full of eerie omens of the impending end, only italicized the irretrievable loss of the sixties' best impulses.

No more absurdly obvious example of what had become of those impulses can be found than in the spectacular rise of Led Zeppelin. Whatever else would follow the twelve-year reign of the first real supergroup—no matter how calculated, vacuous, or trendy—there is no moment in modern music that can attain to the sheer triumph of form over content achieved by this British quartet. As with all of rock's biggest successes, there was an inevitability to the emergence of Led Zeppelin, a causality dictated by the accelerating spiral of fame, idolatry, and incandescent egos. The bad-boy blusterings of the Rolling Stones, the hermetically sealed studio sorcery of the Beatles, the religious trappings of the Dead; it all came together in Led Zeppelin. With a vengeance.

The magisterial guitar-playing of Jimmy Page was the pump that kept the lumbering edifice of his band afloat. Page, an English studio veteran who'd provided some distinctive moments on dozens of hit records by everyone from Donovan to the Yardbirds (as one of the more auspicious alumni of that seminal outfit), is among the most facile and technically polished instrumentalists ever produced by rock 'n' roll. Rail thin, dour, and obsessively aloof, Page was everything Hendrix was not. Even though he pioneered feedback freestyle, guitar-string bowing, and every kind of phased and filtered effect available in the growing arsenal of electronic gimmickry, Page remained studiously removed from the passion of playing. English blues brutalizers like Ten Years After may have corrupted the emotional purity of American black music with ham-fisted excesses, but Page's crime against the blues was more insidious. Isolating elements of menace and mourn-ing and thumping sexual frenzy, Page upped the voltage, sent bent notes and delta chording screaming down a maze of enhancements, and spewed out a grotesquely over-wrought parody of the real thing. Augmented by the rhythm section of Bonham and Jones, who early on con-fused stamina with finesse, along with the lugubrious howls and Regency primpings of vocalist Robert Plant, Page was laying the foundation for heavy metal, the most ritualized of all rock offshoots.

Led Zeppelin's credentials as white blues boys were im-portant in the late sixties, when authenticity, however ten-uous, could make or break reputations with the critical establishment. Page had, in fact, hung in the same purist circles as Jagger/Richards, Clapton, and John Mayall. The band's 1969 debut album highlighted turgid renderings of Willie Dixon sides and some hot-breathed originals in the prevailing British blues mode of the period—lots of show-ing off around a fundamental riff. "Whole Lotta Love," released the following year, was a turning point for both the group and rock's self-respect. The breakthrough hit that would remain the band's signature tune until the in-carnation of "Stairway to Heaven" three years later, "Whole Lotta Love" managed to embody both Led Zep-pelin's mastery of bombast and their soulless exploitation of the blues idiom. With a bludgeoning riff that equated sexual intercourse with a drilling rig, the song's famous middle eight was an extended echo chamber orgy of fret scratches and mewling, designed to either simulate or stimulate a teeth-rattling orgasm.

The band was catapulted to the top even as the critics turned up their noses. A pattern was set: enormously popular groups, selling out coliseums and churning out platinum sellers, spurned at the very threshold of immortality by rock writers who lived with their mothers and saw the world through Coke-bottle bifocals. Led Zeppelin would complain bitterly about the regular drubbing they received in the press, sullenly withdrawing into their moated country estates to drum up new sounds to win the fickle critics. No matter that millions flocked like lemmings to have their ears split by the group's industrial strength decibles, respectability lay in the hands of those who wrote rock history, the very ones who were relegating Led Zeppelin to a footnote.

The search for respectability along with the barren finesse of their music would come to define the career of Led Zep and scores of others who came after. Reducing the blues to the stuff of adolescent male fantasies became, as the seventies wore on, a diminishing ingredient in Page and Co.'s recipe for success. It was replaced, not surprisingly, by mystical conceits that brought them unheard-of adulation. Led Zeppelin's brand of spirituality best represented both their frustrated quest for status and the resounding void at the heart of the music.

Touring incessantly during their first two years, the quartet gained a well-earned reputation for reckless debauchery. Hotel-room demolitions, harrowing drug and alcohol consumption, and the sadistic humiliation of groupies became as important to the band's image as their marathon concert appearances, often lasting three hours or more. Drummer John Bonham especially became infamous as a man with a tenuous hold on sanity, a kind of rock Rasputin, given to astonishing feats of liver abuse and sudden psychotic violence. It was all, of course, simply a sur-real burlesque of the Rolling Stones' patented snotnose routine.

In sharp contrast to all this malignant tomfoolery were Led Zep's mystic reveries. By '71, their dabblings in British fairy lore, Viking demagoguery, and, of course, the occult, coalesced on an album that didn't even have a name. Marked only by four Druidic runes, supposedly selected by Page to embody the essence of each band member, the LP contained "When the Levy Breaks," the last word in blues overkill, the title-tells-all epic "The Battle of Ever-more," and an eight-minute homage to all things ethereal, "Stairway to Heaven."

As songs go, "Stairway to Heaven" had a haunting melody and an unusually restrained performance going for it. By this time, Page had perfected a sure-fire formula that began with folksy acoustic strumming, resolved by incremental rock intrusions and finally sweeping into the billowing beyond by a final assault of furious technique. "Stairway to Heaven" stands as the best example of these innovations, but nothing can quite explain the stupefying significance the tune took on for millions of the faithful. The all-time most requested rock song ever, "Stairway" is a perfect welter of dreamy mythological imagery seeming to reveal truth of priceless personal import. If you've heard it once, you've heard it a thousand times, and so have a thousand dewy-eyed pubescents and downer–dazed rock freaks. "It makes me wonder," sighs Plant as he picks his way through the ticket of deep meaning. He wasn't the only one. "It's about sophisticated people," says one long-time fan of the anthem, "the power groupies, and how they try to buy the truth that can't be bought. It could be the Catholic church or any power structure. The signs of the truth are everywhere, but the signs are hard to follow. The spirits are there, pointing the way, but they're hard to hear. One day, if we all become one, God will lead us. When we get the message, the spirits will rejoice. If you hear the spirits, don't be afraid, you can go down any path, but there's still time to change. The piper is wooing us all. Our path can't be bought, only sought by the guiding of the spirits or the Spirit. When we're all one, the truth will be revealed and we won't be swayed. I could show you the Eastern side or the Christian side. It depends."

"'Stairway' crystallized the essence of the band," Page enthused. "It had everything there and showed the band at its best. . . . It was a milestone for us. Every musician wants to do something of lasting quality, something that will hold up for a long time." Led Zeppelin had succeeded with "Stairway to Heaven." Unquestionably stirring, the song was also the era's quintessential slice of all-things-to-everybody symbolism. Even Plant, who wrote it, seems unwilling to take final responsibility for its meaning, or even its authorship. "Pagey had written the chords and played them for me. I was holding the paper and pencil, and for some reason, I was in a very bad mood. Then all of a sudden my hand was writing out words. . . . I just sat there and looked at the words and then I almost leaped out of my seat."

Rock lore is chockful of supposed episodes of automatic writing. Chalk it up to helpful muses or just writers unwilling to admit their latest hit was penned in a bar on the back of a cocktail napkin. In Plant and Page's case, there's good reason to believe an ethereal hand may have been moving. Whereas Mick Jagger may have picked up a tome or two by the nefarious Aleister Crowley, Page went the whole hog, or, in this case, the whole beast. "By 1970," writes Stephen Davis in his Zeppelin biography, *Hammer of the Gods*, "Jimmy Page had already been preoccupied with the life and work of Aleister Crowley for several years. He had a growing collection of Crowley books, manuscripts, and memorabilia, and that year he collected one of the most Crowleyian artifacts of all—Boleskine House on the shore of Loch Ness in Scotland." Formerly the country residence of the self-proclaimed "Wickedest Man on Earth," Boleskine had all the cozy charm of a crypt. Built, according to Davis, on the site of a church that had burned down around its parishioners, Crowley had used the estate for all kinds of sleazy satanic rites, including some notorious "sex magick" orgies and attempts to summon up the Egyptian demigods Thoth and Horus. A groundskeeper, local legend had it, went berserk and slaughtered his family there, and the place is so crammed with dark spirits that no sunlight, it's said, penetrates the windows. Back in London, Page purchased another weird abode, Tower House, replete with a Catholic confessional and thematic room decor. In the basement, the ubiquitous Kenneth Anger was ensconced, working on his long-delayed masterpiece *Lucifer Rising*, which Page, following Jagger, had agreed to score. Page was also involved in financing an occult bookstore in Kensington, where he spent hours poring over priceless black magic manuscripts.

If anyone, in short, had the ability to call forth dark powers, it would seem to be Led Zeppelin and, indeed, an occult luster attached itself to the band. There were persistent whispers, writes Davis, "of something more sinister than a rock group's after-hours vices. . . . Led Zeppelin had sold their souls to the devil in exchange for their instant success, their addictive charisma, their unbelievable wealth." Davis goes on to point out that during the Fundamentalist furor over backward masking in the early eighties, it was Led Zeppelin's "Stairway to Heaven" that was most often cited. When played in reverse, the words

"Here's to my sweet Satan" are said to emerge from the slur.

Taking all the haunted real estate, hidden messages, and public relations strokes into account, Led Zeppelin end up the most likely finalists in rock's Minions of Beelzebub Competition, even though the only documented case of spirit meddling attached to the band was when a crazed fan broke into Tower House claiming that the ghost of Jimi Hendrix had ordered her to marry Jimmy Page. And, as with the Stones, it's fair to conclude that the devil had gotten the better deal. In 1975 Plant and his family were nearly snuffed in a serious car accident on Rhodes. Two years later his son, Karac, succumbed to a virulent respiratory virus. John Bonham was to follow in 1980, checking out in the time-honored rock star manner of choking on his own vomit. Led Zeppelin dissolved in drift and confusion. The terms of their contract had, apparently, expired.

So what did the devil get in the bargain? Aside from, presumably, four souls ripe for roasting, there was the legacy of ten years' worth of music that further devalued rock 'n' roll's already inflated currency. At Led Zeppelin's feet can be laid artistic crimes that hundreds of copycat bands would happily emulate. It wasn't just the nature of their strange and senseless music, which would reach a repugnant apex in heavy metal. It was the *scale*. Already well on its way to becoming a depersonalized industry, rock music, in the grip of Led Zeppelin and their ilk, lost all human dimension. Certainly other groups had played to screaming hordes in vast arenas, but who could even hear the Beatles' tinny twenty minutes at Shea Stadium? Simply being in the same general proximity of the Fab Four was entertainment enough.

You couldn't help but hear the anguished roar of Led

Zeppelin as it crashed against the shoals of a capacity crowd night after night in one faceless metropolis after another. It was music created to fill enormous, darkened voids, to overpower and dominate by the sheer tonnage weight of amps and equipment and money. And behind it all, the sloppy grin of banality.

David Bowie

Chapter Ten

TWILIGHT OF
THE GODS

I can see for miles and miles.

—Pete Townshend

I never thought I'd need so many people.

—David Bowie

—Before becoming a Born Again Christian, Roger Mc-
Guinn—founder of premier folk rock group the Byrds—
had been an ardent follower of Subud, a tony Indonesian
cult centered on ecstatic rituals.

—Following their visit to the maharishi, The Beach Boys
retrieved the torch of transcendental meditation dropped
by the Beatles, promoting mantra chanting at every
opportunity.

—Cat Stevens, a singer/songwriter who enjoyed substantial success in the early seventies with albums like *Tea for the Tillerman* and *Catch Bull at Four* dropped abruptly from sight after contracting a raging mystical bent, marrying a girl he met in a London mosque, and subsequently converting to Islam.

—Influential British folk artists Richard and Linda Thompson, who'd worked with the cream of the British folk set, announced their conversion to Sufism by appearing on the cover of the 1973 *Pour Down like Silver* in the headgear of the Middle Eastern sect.

—Carlos Santana, San Francisco's pioneering latin/rock fusionist, flirted briefly with Christianity before falling headlong into the embrace of Indian guru Sri Chinmoy.

Expressed in the music of a growing number of bands for whom mysticism was its own reward, the evolution of rock's own religious credo was accented by the emergence of popular artists who had found themselves, God, or some combination of the two by enlisting in a variety of exotic cults. Scientologists and ESToids abounded among the white musical echelons, while blacks wandered to more esoteric expressions of Christianity such as Jehovah's Witnesses and assorted Adventist offshoots. Few explicitly proselytized through their music, but those that did created a new category in pop music's already hefty cosmic catalog.

In the early seventies, for example, an entire branch of music became the exclusive turf of a bizarre cult that worshipped a wizened African monarch as the direct descendant of King David. While reggae had been slowly incubating beneath the Caribbean sun since the close of World War II, its trance rhythms and distinctive deep echoing "dub" arrangements didn't reach white audiences until established artists like Eric Clapton, Paul Simon, and Stevie Wonder copped the licks and scored hits. Celebrated briefly as the new rock 'n' roll, the sudden popularity of reggae among trend setters introduced an assortment of Jamaican artists into the mainstream, led by the Wailers and their militant front man, Bob Marley. A fervent prophet of Rastafarianism, Marley's pungent music was laced with the teaching of Marcus Garvey, who had founded the faith around a wild-eyed revelation that elevated Ethiopian emperor Haile Selassie to messiah status, proclaimed marijuana a direct path to the Godhead, and practiced a euphonious secret language that formed the text for reggae's strident, back-to-Africa message. At the height of his popularity in America and England, Marley was setting to music whole speeches by Selassie, "King of Kings, Lord of Lords, the Conquering Lion of the Tribe of Judah" and letting the white oppressors have it right between the ears.

Long before Marley succumbed to cancer in 1981, reggae's moment in the sun had passed. While he was still enormously popular in the islands, Africa, and South America, it's doubtful that any music tied so intimately to an arcane and aggressive third-world cult could have supplanted rock 'n' roll's spiritual joy ride.

Considerably more to the point was the curious case of The Who. If rock and religion made strange bedfellows, there were no weirder companions beneath the comforter than Pete Townshend and a what-me-worry Indian avatar by the name of Meher Baba.

In simple terms of influence—records sold, concert grosses, inches of print—The Who ranked with any of the great sixties rock bands. But it was hardly an overnight vault to the top. For a while The Who's very Englishness kept them from the transatlantic appeal enjoyed by the kingpins of the British scene. The Who's early sixties success in their homeland was founded primarily on their status as rowdy champions of the fashion-conscious Mod movement. Modified Modism would eventually yield the Beatles and Merseybeat, but as expressed by The Who, the Mod way of life was a humming little rebellion with the very strictest codes of dress and decorum. The Who's earliest output—dubbed "maximum r & b"—was a cheeky amalgam of primitive performance art and crudely rendered soul and Motown standards. The underdeveloped musical abilities of the quartet, especially lead guitarist and songwriter Pete Townshend, forced them to compensate by honing their onstage image with brilliant pop art costumes and calculated acts of violence, especially Townshend's famous guitar demolitions, conceived, according to legend, to avoid playing encores.

It was all in the spirit of the time and place—a wide-open scene, sucking energy and inspiration from the unlikeliest sources. It was also definitively British and a long way from the American shores. Even as the Stones and Beatles scampered across the cultural bridge their music created, Stateside success for The Who remained tantalizingly out of reach. It was 1967 before the band began making inroads across the ocean, with an appearance at the watershed Monterey Pop Festival and the release of *A Quick One*, retitled *Happy Jack* in the U.S. The LP contained a ten-minute miniopera that scooped the Beatles' *Sgt. Pepper* as rock's first stab at a concept album. A year later, the band landed its first American hit with "I Can See for Miles," but by then their best work was already behind them.

The spark that lit The Who during the first heady years of their rise was struck from the same source as Hendrix and the earliest San Francisco bands. The unself-conscious pursuit of fun, a flippant derring-do, and an instinct for glorious overstatement, plus Townshend's captivating teenage song stories, underscored the adenoidal transitions that make genuine rock 'n' roll a passing fancy. The

Who, in the best sense of the term, was a "pop band," brazenly faddish and devilishly clever. And the best of their music, a firecracker string of singles that included "I Can't Explain," "Anyway, Anyhow, Anywhere," "The Kids Are All right," and the landmark "My Generation," hit on the feverish conviction that anything worth saying was worth saying at the top of one's lungs while the hormones were pounding. There was a wonderful *temporariness* to The Who, the fractious essence of flaming youth, threatening always to blow apart in a burst of furious immaturity. It was the very disposability of The Who's initial singles that make them rock 'n' roll classics; off-the-cuff and immediate, these songs captured an elemental and epic impatience.

But The Who's innocence could hardly survive the times. It was, after all, 1968, and psychedelia was stalking the land. Acid and grass evoked in Pete Townshend one of the most towering preoccupations with mystical questions in rock history, unveiling at the same time a complex personality almost as fascinating to its owner as to the group's followers. Given to voluminous self-analysis, free with the secrets of his creativity and profligate in his spiritualizing, Townshend was hardly your standard rock icon. He may well be one of the most verbose musicians ever to agree to an interview, viewing the press as a kind of sounding board on which to test his vast-ranging theories on any number of subjects. His rap session with *Rolling Stone* founder Jan Wenner in 1968 was a classic Townshend mystery tour, with the guitarist expounding endlessly on the philosophy of rock music ("it's got to undulate"), getting stoned ("To get stoned in England is an entirely different trip"), and fame ("I always used to work with the thought . . . that The Who were gonna last precisely two minutes"). At one point in the interview, Townshend is apparently so aglow he asks Wenner if he's

259

been slipped LSD in his orange juice. About the only thing the guitarist *didn't* get around to discussing was his large nose, a subject that would consume him in subsequent interviews. "When I was in school" he told one writer, "the geezers who were snappy dressers and got chicks . . . would always like to talk about my nose." To another: "When I was a kid I had this enormous hooter and I was always being baited about it. So I used to think, '. . . I'll push my huge hooter out at them from every newspaper in England.'"

The picture that would emerge from these reams of introspection was of an insecure artist in search of some complete and uncritical acceptance. Townshend's torrent of words was often too painfully honest, too earnest and unguarded; he was a man who wanted desperately to be known and loved. It was a facet of his character that would play a major role in his music.

During his confessional with Wenner, conducted in the middle of the band's U.S. tour in support of *Happy Jack*, Townshend went into great detail concerning The Who's projected new album. In light of the significance that album would take on in contemporary music, the details are worth hearing.

"We've been talking about doing an opera," Townshend begins, intriguingly. *Rock opera*: there was an idea whose time had finally arrived. "The package I hope is going to be called 'Deaf, Dumb and Blind Boy.' It's a story about a kid that's born deaf, dumb and blind and what happens to him throughout life. The deaf, dumb and blind boy is played by The Who, the musical entity. . . . But what it's really all about is the fact that because the boy is 'D, D & B,' he's seeing things basically as vibrations which we translate as music. That's really what we want to do: create this feeling that when you listen to the music you can actually become aware of the boy, and aware of what he's all about. . . . Yes, it's a pretty far out thing, actually."

Actually, it all sounded like one more preposterous presumption by a rock star convinced that his music could breach the barriers of the senses. But there was more, lots more. The boy, Townshend continues, "sees things musically and in dreams, and nothing has got any weight at all." His father, frustrated by this smiling vegetable, beats him up, and a lecherous uncle fondles him. The weight of these experiences gradually change the hapless hero of Townshend's opera. "Slowly but surely the kid starts to get it together, out of this simplicity, this incredible simplicity in his mind. He starts to realize that he can see, and he can hear and he can speak. . . . The music has got to explain what happens, that the boy elevates and finds something which is incredible. To us, it's nothing to be able to see and hear and speak, but to him, it's absolutely incredible and overwhelming. . . . The second important event is when he sees himself in a mirror, suddenly seeing himself for the first time: he takes an immediate step back, bases his whole life around his own image . . . not knowing, of course, that what he saw was him but still regarding it as something that belonged to him, and of course it did all the time anyway. . . . It's a very complex thing," he sighs, "and I don't know if I'm getting it across."

"You are," breathed Wenner.

You probably had to be there. Townshend's high-fa-lutin' fable would, in time, of course, become *Tommy*, The Who's love-it-or-hate-it rock opera. What, exactly, *was Tommy* about? The consensus opinion ran something like this: an autistic child, the toddler Tommy, is plunged into his sight, sound, and speechless existence by the trauma of seeing the murder of his mother's lover by his vengeful dad (although Townshend also claimed it was the lover

261

who killed the father). His first glimmers of self-conscious-ness come when his dad yells out his name; later the youngster wows the locals with his pinball-playing prow-ess. Tommy (Townshend picked the name because, ac-cording to Dave Marsh, it was common, British, and had "OM" for a middle syllable) is subjected to various trials at the hands of the drooling pervert Uncle Ernie, the sa-distic Cousin Kevin, and the Acid Queen, a psychedelic gypsy who tries to snap him out of it with a stiff hit of LSD. Finally, he's taken to a specialist who announces that the boy's malaise is pyschosomatic and, to prove it, places him in front of a mirror. Fascinated by his own image, Tommy has another revelatory awakening, rudely inter-rupted by his mother, who smashes the mirror, releasing him at last from his affliction.

At this point, *Tommy's* tale takes a startling turn as he becomes a religious figure, attracting masses of converts who are sent to some sort of camp where they're instructed to play pinball corked, plugged, and blindfolded, in a rit-ual approximation of their messiah's path to enlighten-ment. In the last hurried minutes of the opera, Tommy becomes a fascist bully and is roundly rejected by his dis-gruntled followers. That, at least, is what seems to occur over the opera's hour-plus length. Townshend would fuel the confusion by giving countless interviews explaining his work and then explaining his explanations. "Nobody knew what it was all about or how the hell it was going to end," claimed Who bassist John Entwistle, reflecting generally the ambivalence the rest of the group felt toward Townshend's diffuse psychodrama.

While it's perhaps unfair to judge the ultimate content of *Tommy* by Townshend's early sketch, the guitarists' form-ative ruminations do confirm two unmistakable conclu-sions. First: between the time of his *Rolling Stone* interview and the release of the double-album magnum opus a year

262

later, the various texts and subtexts of *Tommy* didn't exactly gel into a cohesive whole. "The dialogue in Tommy is suggestive rather than discursive," writes John Swenson, laboring to put the best face on the bewildering sprawl comprising the pop opera's libretto. Dave Marsh, in his Brobdingnagian biography of the band, *Before I Get Old*, fills page after page contrasting and comparing the varied, often contradictory interpretations presented by both critics and by Townshend himself. Marsh ends up with the best of both worlds, finally deciding that while the story fails as drama, "being too corny to succeed as that rigorous and cold formalism that is all that modernism wishes to recognize as art," it is also "glorious and may move any listener to accept it joyously to the core of his or her being."

Formalistic failure or a core-moving experience, *Tommy* marked a point of no return in rock's ardent inward seeking. In its final form as both an album and a concert performance, *Tommy* enormously enhanced popular music's credibility as a medium for deep musings. *Time*, for one, took it all very much to heart. "*Tommy* strikes a responsive chord not as a living musical drama but as a hopeful sign that pop forms like rock have the vocabulary and the expressive scope to deal with important subjects on a broad symphonic and operatic range. Every troubled society or social group needs its own encouraging myths and fables. . . . for the rock world, *Tommy* is at least a start."

There's more than a little truth to this claim. *Tommy* was, at the very least, a good idea, a clever play on prevailing notions of self-discovery and, at least potentially, a revealing contemporary parable. The problem arose in execution. Musically, *Tommy* was either too long by half or, as some would assert, too short by a third. It was, by all accounts, a hulking collection of tunes, strung together by recurring melodic themes, swinging wildly from the ethereal ("I'm a Sensation," "Amazing Journey," "Sparks") to the embarrassing ("Sally Simpson," "I'm Free," "We're Not Gonna Take It"). One of the many functions in Townshend's grandiose scheme for *Tommy* was to serve as a vehicle for hit singles, but "Pinball Wizard," a nicely turned bit of vintage Who dynamics, was the only real song to emerge from the mix. On the whole, *Tommy* often sounded thin and distant, as if all the various uncertainties surrounding the project, amplified by Townshend's ceaseless speculating, had drained off the band's legendary energies. No matter. *Tommy* arrived at precisely the right moment in both the band's career and rock's spiritual ascent. The opera established The Who as major international stars of impeccable mystical standing. Whatever else they did or didn't do from here on out, it would be attended by the most rapt and reverent attention. The Who had scaled Olympus.

The second conclusion to be drawn from *Tommy* and from Townshend's in-print maunderings on his creation was that beneath the hodge-podge of half-baked symbolism lay some significant spiritual stirrings. Whatever else it may have been, *Tommy* was far removed from the glitzy iconography of acid rock. Townshend *was* saying something, or at any rate trying. A point of view lay hidden in the story of *Tommy*, some kind of instruction or moral or guide to better living. But no one was sure what it was.

It would be a while before Townshend felt comfortable enough about his spiritual convictions to reveal their source, even though the liner notes for *Tommy* offered an early clue by listing "avatar" right along with "producer" and "chief engineer." *Tommy*, it turned out, was indeed inspired by a very specific religious experience.

A year before the opera's advent, at the tail end of an exhausting tour, Townshend was introduced by a friend, Mike McInnerney, to the writings of Indian guru Meher Baba. "I was bitter, cynical and angry most of the time," the guitarist recalled. "But most of all I was really very stupid." At the time, Townshend had taken up the theorizing of George Adamski—who propounded the existence of extraterrestrial spirit beings. The guitarist was also downing regular dollops of acid. As was his habit, he regularly and tirelessly chronicled his latest insights to friends and journalists. McInnerney apparently recognized spiritual 'birth pangs' when he saw them and invited Townshend to check out the benign philosophy of Baba. It was a turning point in the musician's life.

The son of Persian parents, Merwan Sheiar Irani, aka Meher Baba, had the first inkling of his destiny as the Avatar of the Age as a college student in his native India. Sitting at the feet of Perfect Master Hazrat Babajan, he was launched into cosmic consciousness when the guru kissed him on the forehead, an act of such perfect validation that the dazzled acolyte spent the next several months without food or sleep in favor of zeroing in on his Godheadness. Upasni Marharaj, one of the five perfect masters under which Merwan subsequently studied, sometime later threw a stone at his disciple, hitting him in exactly the same spot as Babajan's kiss. From little acorns . . . something about the smacking of lips and pebble convinced the young Baba that he was not just another guru but, in fact, the Original Enlightened Soul who visits this planet every ten centuries or so to straighten out humanity's collective karma. Dubbed by his followers Meher Baba ("compassionate father"), the reincarnation of Christ, Buddha, Moses, Mohammed, and sundry assorted deities, he roamed the subcontinent eating vegetables, scorning money, and gaining prestige. In 1925 he took a vow of silence, which remained unbroken until his death forty-four years later.

"Baba only asked people for their love," Townshend would later explain. "Not their possessions or even their lives. Just their love." And love was something Townshend was ready to surrender willingly. Whatever else may be said about his utter devotion to Baba—its effect on his music and the vitality of his band—it is apparent that for Townshend, deep needs were being filled. "In retrospect I needed something in my life, but at the same time I was not aware of the need." In Baba, the long struggle to be accepted was finally resolved. All that striving to be noticed and approved, to look good in other people's eyes, could be laid to rest. The bliss of Baba marked the end of Townshend's nasty struggle with his own identity. "For the first time in your life," he would say, "you actually acknowledge the fact that you've got problems instead of futilely trying to solve them."

Problems—and there was an awesome assortment of them stemming from both Townshend's obsessive personality and the pressure cooker of stardom—were never solved so much as dissolved by the ministering spirit of Meher Baba. A focus for all the unrequited emotion the artist had ever felt, Baba also held out the most alluring of all paths to salvation: to do nothing. "If someone says to you 'How do I find God?'" Townshend extrapolates, "and you say 'Just keep on doing what you're doing,' that would really make them angry. They want to know what book to read, where to meditate and that sort of thing. Baba didn't talk about meditation. . . . But he did say it was important for people to hear his name, because at this time he's the highest possible manifestation in human form of Consciousness. He's the highest, most advanced soul in the Universe."

"Don't worry. Be happy." It was a contraction of the Sadguru's maxim "Do your best, then leave the rest to me and don't worry. Be Happy." Neatly summing up the whole of Meher Baba's philosophy, the motto appeared beneath his famous portrait, his wide grin spread under

a Groucho Marx mustache. "Rama Krishna, Buddha, Zar-
athustra, Jesus and Meher Baba are all divine figures on
earth," Townshend rhapsodized. "They all said the same
thing: yet still we trundle on." Christians, Buddhists, even
Zarathustrians might take issue with this glib slogan, but
for Townshend it was from divine authority. "Previous to
being involved with Baba I tended to weigh things up very
carefully whereas now I'm much more impulsive," he explained. "I just sort of chase my Karma around with the
feeling that Baba's got his thumb on my head, so everything's all right."

The wisdom Meher Baba dispensed dovetailed neatly
not only to the knotty psyche of Pete Townshend but the
values of his generation. The guru's teaching, writes Who
biographer Dave Marsh, are "quite consistent with other
great spiritual teachings, although well adapted to modern
language and custom." No argument there. Baba was a
repository for a kind of homogenized Eastern spirituality
that flicked every switch on the sixties seeker's circuit. Not
only was man capable of ascending the stairway to heaven,
not only did the path lay within, but, finally, there was
no discipline, no dogma, no authority, no unpleasant exercises necessary for the climb. Don't worry. Be happy.
Do what thou wilt. What goes around comes around.
Nothing to get hung about. Marsh: "Baba refused to establish anything resembling a church. . . . The simple values Baba taught—compassion, love, intense introspection—are discipline enough."

The impact of such values on a youth culture already
fascinated with its own image cannot be overstated. While
it could be argued that "intense introspection" was the
last thing self-absorbed artist types like Townshend
needed, there's no denying that following one's own destiny—especially down the paths of rock stardom—was a
delightful avenue of least resistance. Baba's brand of tran-

scendence spread the glittery veneer of eternity over the base realities of life in the material world. "It's something inside," said Townshend, "where all you want is for the things that seem so simple and fundamental to your life to mean something more than they appear to mean."

The appearance of meaning was what lent *Tommy* a significance far outweighing its real worth, as either art or truth. "*Tommy* has got a mystical thread running through it," insisted Townshend, "and it's about the spiritual evolution of man rather than about the sub-teenage frustrations I used to write about before." Actually, *Tommy* was a frustrating subteen version of spiritual evolution based on Townshend's understanding, however accurate or inaccurate, of the teachings of Meher Baba. It could be argued that the rock opera trundled out the very concepts that best supported the subculture's consummate vanities only because Townshend understood imperfectly or not at all the depths of Baba's teachings: The illusory veil of the senses, Godhead through self-realization, the inevitable corruption of established religion, the truth that waits at the end of being to thine own self true. But then, how insightful did a love-starved neophyte like Townshend actually have to be to grasp a philosophy that summed up all human endeavour with "Don't worry. Be happy."?

Baba's teaching did have an immediate and important effect on Townshend's life beyond simply affirming impending transcendence. For one thing, the guru frowned on the use of drugs as "harmful mentally, spiritually, and physically." Townshend, adept at abusing substances, struggled briefly and overcame his habitual use of grass. Yet even though he'd had a life-threatening trip on the super pyschedelic STP not long before, he refused to warn others of the dire effects of drugs. He understood only too well that to do so would have violated the sacrosanct doctrine of Do Your Own Thing. "[It] was very unfashionable," he confessed, "because dope, acid in particular, was still a happening thing."

Tommy would go on to become a stage production, a nightmarish film by Ken Russell, and a fixture in rock history. It also effectively destroyed The Who as a band. Having released the demon of rock profundity, with parables, classicism, and deep inspiration sprouting like hydra heads, it was impossible to send it back to the darkness. *Live at Leeds*, a ferocious album released in 1970, can be viewed as a belated attempt to capture rock's lost innocence in the form of an exorcism of the infernal deaf, dumb, and blind boy. But Townshend, by now consumed by the grandeur of transcendental rock—he once referred to selections from *Tommy* as "the quiet explosion of divinity"—could not resist the length and weightiness of the rock opera. *Who's Next* was an album of flotsam from a scuttled multimedia extravaganza of interstellar proportions called *Lifehouse*, which planned to feature banks of lasers and holograms, a hero named Bobby, and a plot that revolved around a six-month long rock concert. It was his attempt to launch *Lifehouse* that finally sent Townshend spiraling into nervous collapse. By 1973 he'd recovered sufficiently to conceive and record *Quadrophenia*, an astonishing muddle of clotted metaphors and overheated ambitions that made *Tommy* look positively minimalist in comparison.

The Who stumbled through the remainder of the seventies refusing to give up the ghost and subjecting fans to the agony of the band's every wheezing death rattle. Even after drummer Keith Moon succumbed in yet another Death By Misadventure, the remaining members stubbornly hung on. Townshend, alternately trading on and agonizing over his status as the elder statesman of rock 'n' roll, cut a series of increasingly obtuse albums; each waded further into unseemly self-analysis and pointless political and social conjecture. His fervor for Baba has apparently never waned, but like everything else once associated with The Who, it's a devotion that's fallen on hard times. The sixties, at length, have passed away, leaving those who survived wondering what, after all, the excitement had been about.

The industrialization of rock 'n' roll had ensured, by the mid-seventies, the solidifying of broad movements in popular music into which dozens of groups were slotted. No longer could a single band or any one scene exclusively embody a particular credo or aesthetic. There was too much money out there, too many canny careerists vying for attention, and too diffuse an audience scanning the record bins and ticket brokers. An increasingly large pie was being cut into increasingly smaller slices; each new wrinkle in the pop music formula was a potentially profitable new market, with not only its own demographic but its own orbit of stars, each putting a slightly different spin on his specialty.

The question was no longer which you liked better: the Beatles or the Stones, or even the Grateful Dead or the Jefferson Airplane. Well before 1976 and the long-overdue arrival of the punks, the question had become whether you preferred country rock or fusion, singer-songwriters or heavy metalists, glitter rock or art rock or disco. This proliferation of hyphenations ushered in what is generally considered to be the nadir of rock 'n' roll's legitimacy as either an art form or a good time. The "vast-wasteland" view of the seventies is, by and large, accurate. It was a dire stretch for anyone interested in the fundamental thrills of pop music. It was also, for all its high-flying hybrids, a period of remarkably little real creativity.

Remarkable, because the seventies were the palmiest salad days the music business had ever experienced. Peo-

270

ple bought albums by Fleetwood Mac, Elton John, the Eagles, Rod Stewart, and the Bee Gees in record numbers. Record labels, radio stations, and retailers were functioning like a well-oiled machine, pressing and promoting and pumping each Big New Sound in a widening cycle of profits. There was an inevitability to rock's spiral of success, with its vast talent pool and well-trained consumers. Moguls could throw it against the wall all day, simply scraping off and packaging whatever stuck. There was room, it might well be imagined, for endless refinements on every variety of musical mysticism—a rock band for every cult, a new race of philosopher superstars.

But as rock 'n' roll became more institutionalized, its willingness to take risks withered. The sixties had been a harrowing, heady time, jittery with big leaps of faith and even bigger tumbles into disillusionment. In a very real sense there was nothing left to say. Rock music, even as it ballooned into a heavyweight entertainment contender, contented itself with the most conventional wisdom. This museum of old masters had its occasional jarring bit of prescience or nose thumbing or honest workmanship. Steely Dan, a misanthropic duo with an obsessively crisp sound, had a rapier wit and a knack for poking unfair fun at their generation. The Swedish quartet Abba, one of the most successful Top Forty acts in history but generally disdained for their middle-of-the-road music, fashioned a string of exquisitely filligreed pop classics and the first real pan-European music. Roxy Music glammed it up to occasional good effect, and the odd country rock group got lucky. Fleetwood Mac transcended the superstar shtick long enough to produce two pieces of first-rate radio fodder; the '76 "Go Your Own Way" and the '77 "Don't Stop," both from the fifteen-million-seller *Rumours*. For the most part, though, it was merely nostalgia and gleanings.

Art rock, a category whose title told all, was a primarily

271

British invention in direct line of descent with the studio probings of *Sgt. Pepper*, the arid virtuosity of the guitar heroes, and the warmed-over sword-and-sorcery mysticism that had been a staple of English dandies since Sir Walter Scott. Yes was probably the best known and best-selling of the art rock attractions. A band that went through no less then seven personnel permutations in its twelve-year history, Yes blended neoclassical posturings with unchecked virtuosity and middlebrow mythologizing and went on to earn the awestruck adulation of a mass audience. But, by far, the most intriguing group of art rockers of the period was a weird aggregate of first-chair players with an out-of-control passion for melodrama named Genesis.

Like their counterparts, Genesis was given to showing off their instrumental prowess at the drop of a beat, often playing their suite-length song stories in deliberately bizarre time signatures and filtering everything through so much circuitry that it took on a kind of ozone stench. Featuring singer Peter Gabriel (who wore his hair in a reversed mohawk—long on the sides, shaved down the middle) and singer/percussionist Phil Collins, Genesis created some of the strangest, most viscerally unsettling music of all time. To say that Genesis's work was distinctive was to widely miss the mark: it all sounded like it was issuing from one vast organism, chuffing and thumping and tootling along all by itself.

It may have taken a while to get used to what Genesis was up to musically, but nothing could quite prepare the unwary listener for the subject matter of their material. Over the course of four early-to-mid seventies albums— *Nursery Cryme*, *Foxtrot*, *Selling England by the Pound*, and the nightmarish *The Lamb Lies Down on Broadway*—the band inflated a ghastly universe full of monsters and ghosts and netherworldish wraiths of every description.

It was a Boschian musical landscape where the sacred and the obscene jostled for a foothold and nothing was as it seemed. Genesis created a genuine spiritual intensity, all right; the intensity of a bad acid trip or a medieval passion play. "Supper's Ready", occupying nearly the entire second side of *Foxtrot*, is as good an example as any of the band's creepy genius. The song cycle alternates between moments of mystery—as in the "Lover's Leap" and "As Sure as Eggs Is Eggs"—and dire Wagnerian thunderclaps, all meant to approximate the climactic last chapters of the Book of Revelation. As a musical composition, "Supper's Ready" has a dizzying centrifugal pull; as some sort of spiritual art, it borders on the lunatic.

The same might be said for the famous Genesis live shows, in which Gabriel would transform himself with elaborate masks and costumes into the characters peopling the band's convulsive fantasies. If there was anything more nerve-wracking than hearing Genesis perform, it was watching them perform, an event not unlike stepping defenseless onto someone's epileptic seizure. It all came to a head on *The Lamb Lies Down on Broadway*, Gabriel's last gasp with the group and a double album of inpenetrable density in which Rael, the hero, battles hordes of deadly metaphors. "Keep your fingers out of my eye," begin the copious liner notes of this astonishingly unpleasant album. "While I write I like to glance at the butterflies in glass that are all around the walls. The people in my memory are pinned to events I can't recall too well, but I'm putting one down to watch him break up, decompose and feed another sort of life." It was a positively sunny sentiment compared to what lurked on the vinyl.

Art rock, even in the hands of Genesis, added not one whit to the revelations accumulated by the psychedelians. It was all a rehash, a gussied-up version of the same old secret teachings. Which is both more and less than what can be said for heavy metal. The pathology of hard rock is easy enough to trace—the wanton blues mangling of the early sixties wed to the excesses of electric guitar technocrats, attended by the whole range of rock's nasty threats to the status quo. The Yardbirds, a blues-and-feedback band years ahead of their time, the Kinks—mannered art students who scored an early hit with a raw riff called "You Really Got Me"—and The Who are cited as progenitors of the metal sound, followed by Hendrix, Cream, and Led Zeppelin. Contributions were made by a short-lived San Francisco trio named Blue Cheer (second only to Vanilla Fudge as the original sludge rock band), Mountain, with their two-hundred-and-fifty-pound lead guitarist Leslie West, Grand Funk Railroad, a prototype for the Quaalude party band, and Deep Purple, a kind of hyped-up Moody Blues generally considered the low ebb of late-sixties British progressivism. A dozen other groups also had a hand in forging Heavy Metal: Ten Years After, Humble Pie, Bad Company, Free, Foghat; the list goes on.

But that isn't much help in explaining how the mostly interchangeable music of these groups—a mix of blues, bombast and deep bottom*—became an article of faith for an enormous cult of rock worshipers. Heavy metal, as it finally became codified in the middle seventies, owed less to the fundamentally hippie outlook of these early bands than to the meticulously refined imagery of glitter rock. Glitter, in turn, was simply the same old tongue that rock had always stuck out at the squares. Rock stars with girls' names (Alice Cooper) and rock stars in girls' dresses (New York Dolls) may have been one of the more transparent shock tactics employed by the status bashers, but the rogue and ratted hair of the androgynous corps would set

* Bass and drums.

off a chain reaction that would finally fuse hard rock and creative costuming into heavy metal.

The logic was irresistible. By the mid-seventies rock 'n' roll had become so debased a means of expression that only the most overblown gestures could attract attention. The sideshow appeal of glitter, matched with the numbing assault of hard rock, was a combination that couldn't fail. The subsequent fixation on fetishes, misogyny, and santanism was inevitable. Heavy metal was a masterpiece of reductionism, the parboiling away of style and personality and finally even the sexuality that had formerly defined rock music. The remains were only the gristle of violent spectacle. It was also the final triumph of a pandering, mass art void of content. Indeed, heavy metal was so big a gesture for so small an expression that the menace of its demonic imagery was essentially neutralized. Like chains and whips and leather bondage suits; like makeup and dog collars and writhing tattoos; the whole hellhound routine of the metallists was one more stage effect, contrived to assure the white adolescent male audience that here was something big and loud that would set their parents' teeth on edge.

It could be argued that prolonged exposure to the satanic trappings of heavy metal has the same noxious effect as if the bands actually practiced the black arts beneath a pall of dry ice smoke. This is essentially the tack of watchdog groups like the Parents Music Resource Center, whose Senate subcommittee hearings in 1985 raised the roof in rock circles and presented the droll spectacle of self-appointed spokesmen like Frank Zappa implicitly condoning lyrics that celebrate pursuits like sodomy, ritual murder, and pederasty, to name a few. But PMRS may well have missed the point. When Kiss bassist Gene Simmons spit blood and breathed fire, when Iron Maiden droned on about *The Number of the Beast*, when AC/DC sprouted horns on the cover of their best-selling 1979 LP *Highway to Hell*, they were only trying their best to entertain. Heavy metal, in short, is simply the punishment that fits the crime. Rock 'n' roll certainly isn't the only force at work in dismantling the religious consensus of Western civilization. That it should reflect so accurately the spiritual bankruptcy of so much of the culture is, in some perverse way, to its credit.

One of the curious ironies of heavy metal is its occasional if unintended reflection of the Judeo-Christian ethic, exemplified in the midperiod music of one of the genre's pioneers, Black Sabbath. The Sabs displayed a real flair for B-grade moralizing in their music, almost as if all this flirting with the supernatural had given them pause. On the 1971 *Masters of Reality*, for example, is the remarkable "After Forever," which asks the heavy metal question, "Have you ever thought about your soul—can it be saved?" The answer, surprisingly, is yes. As singer Ozzy Osbourne, who would later personify the very worst excesses of metal music, sings, "I have seen the truth. Yes, I've seen the light and I've changed my ways."

What was happening here, on at least a semiconscious level, was the rejection of the muddled sixties spirituality in favor of something more dramatically resonant, i.e., the old-fashioned battle of good and evil. This trend came to fruition in the 1973 *Sabbath, Bloody Sabbath*, perhaps the best, certainly most musical, heavy metal offering. A kind of Classic Comics version of *Pilgrim's Progress*, *Sabbath, Bloody Sabbath* took on the weighty themes of salvation and damnation and almost managed to pull it off, as much by virtue of some restrained riffing and adroit songwriting as by supernatural inspiration. After a decade of prattling on about karma and the wheel of creation, an album like *Sabbath, Bloody Sabbath* had a refreshing directness about it. Songs like the title cut, "Killing Yourself to Live," and "Spiral Architect" presented clear-cut choices between sin and some ill-defined salvation. The front and back covers of the LP, depicting a man on his deathbed alternately tormented by demons and ministered to by angels, would not have been out of place on a Fundamentalist tract.

Heavy Metal, nothing if not direct, has proven to be among the most durable of all rock hybrids, spawning an army of snarling cretins who refuse to go away. Grounded in the universal rites of puberty, its perennial appeal, despite occasional exceptions like Black Sabbath, is nurtured by a pervasive nilhilism. Heavy metal, wrote critic Lester Bangs, is "a fast train to nowhere, which may be one reason it seems to feel so good and make so much sense to its fans."

Pop music in the seventies would stumble down many more blind allies in search of its lost innocence. The singer/songwriter genus reached new heights of self-indulgence, occasionally producing an artist quirky enough to beat the smothering odds. Van Morrison, in particular, survived the decade to create some of his most affecting music in the early eighties. The 1980 *Common One*, for example, is one of the most intriguing anomalies in the whole religious rock hit parade. The incantatory title cut combined vintage r & b imagery with allusions to modern English literary figures and a potent dose of Irish mysticism, evoking the singer's ostensible Christian conversion. The emotional depths reached on the album were echoed two years later on *Beautiful Vision*, only to be drowned in the avant-garde jazz settings of the '83 *Inarticulate Speech of the Heart*, an album that singled out Church of Scientology founder L. Ron Hubbard for special thanks.

The disco phenomenon raised the hackles of rock's guardians with its attempt to sidestep the bloated carcass of progressivism and return to the good-time footing of an earlier era when pop music was an endless series of

277

dance crazes. Reaching its apex in '78 with the soundtrack to *Saturday Night Fever*, disco never entirely transcended its sweaty gay club roots. This brave attempt to breathe vitality and mindless fun back into music was choked off by the meddling influence of European synthesizer shysters such as Kraftwerk and the ubiquitious Giorgio Morodor, foisting off mechanized locksteps to the popper contingent. By 1980 the danceaholics had retreated back to the safety of their own subculture.

The entire decade's music might have mercifully petered out under the weight of its own inertia had it not been for the arrival of one last rock superstar in the tradition of the time. It was the crowning achievement of David Bowie's career that his mercurial persona, his ability to disappear behind his ever-shifting roles, his habitual detachment and flawless connivances were the personification of the wasteland across which he strode. "No other performer of this decade," wrote one critic, "has so cannily perceived and exploited the recurring susceptibility of the media to calculated outrage and extremes and manipulative self-dramatization." "It cannot be said that David Bowie rose to prominence strictly through his own merits or designs," ventured another. "The times were primed for him." "Bowie celebrated artifice," wrote a third, "elevated it." "I encapsulate things very quickly," said Bowie himself. "As soon as a process or system works, it's out of date. I move on to another area. Another piece of time." In an era of willfully truncated attention spans, Bowie was the last word in flirtatious enigmas. The man with no face, the chameleon in the kaleidoscope, Bowie was a brand-new kind of artist; one who simply ceased to exist after the curtain fell.

It's altogether fitting that "Changes" from the 1971 album *Hunky Dory* should have been the breakthrough song for Bowie, sending him hurling toward megastar status. Changes were what Bowie's music was all about—extravagant, surprising, and precisely calculated changes. Cultural observer Gene Sculatti offers a simple hypothesis to explain change, or the appearance of change, in modern music. His Binary Theory asserts that an artist or a group first attracts public attention with a particular style of music—hard, for instance, or progressive rock. They may have a hit or a string of hits before the consumer's interests starts to flag, at which point they announce the Change. If they started as a boogie blues band, they will usually make it known that they are introducing some "new elements" into their sound, bringing on Mellotrons, drum machines or the London Symphony Orchestra. If they're progressivists, then it's back-to-roots time, dropping all the frills for a fundamental approach. The Change will last for an album or two before a reversion back to the original stylistic stance. Entire careers of uncounted bands can be charted by this rhythmic swing between two poles, according to Sculatti.

Bowie escaped the Binary Theory by never doing the same thing twice. For that reason, a cohesive review of his music is virtually impossible. Each album and every tour entailed a completely new identity; each effort, the work of a brand-new artist with a vaguely familiar profile. Hailing from the grungy London suburb of Brixton and raised in the lower-middle-class confines of Bromley, David Jones was reared in the same fastidious, fashion-obsessed world of the Mods that had bred The Who. He apprenticed in a string of undistinguished pop outfits, including Davie Jones with the King Bees, the Mannish Boys, and Davy Jones and the Lower Third, before changing his name to Bowie in 1966 and going solo. A year later he flirted briefly with formal Buddhism, spending some weeks in a Scottish monastery and coming within a hair's breadth, according to legend, of taking vows. That, and a subsequent stint in a mime troupe, were both to loom large in Bowie's development as the seventies' preeminent artiste. The following year he scored a major British hit with "Space Oddity," a lushly mounted tune about an astronaut who decides not to return from orbit.

The song was typical of much of Bowie's early-seventies output. Reflexively clever, intriguingly derivative, his was a nifty repackaging of borrowed and stolen ideas. "Space Oddity," and much of the eponymously titled LP that followed, studiously echoed sixties dictates, celebrating peace and love with the mannered, effeminate flourishes of the hip London underground. *The Man Who Sold the World*, released in '70, was the first of many pace changes but nothing so radical as to upset the verging star's steady upward climb. This album introduced a theme that Bowie would employ incessantly over the course of his career: the disfunctioning future. "Assassins, madmen, occultists, deranged computers, dormant elder gods, children possessed of secrets beyond their parents' imaginings" was how one critic described the populace of *The Man Who Sold the World*, an album defined by a nasty undercurrent of contempt by the artist for the characters he had created. Dystopian nightmares had been a science fiction staple since Jonathan Swift, and what Bowie brought to the genre was, if not originality, a flair for detail and a sense of inevitability. "The world was doomed," he remarked, parroting the trendy pessimism of the time. "We're not capable of making it any better."

Another element Bowie tossed into the mix was the time-honored ploy of sexual ambivalence. Although one can never be sure with so agile a quick-change artist, Bowie's sexual orientation seems to be a matter of record. "Yes, of course," he responded to writer Mick Watts's blunt query. "I'm gay and I've always been." "He's as camp as a row of tents," Watts would write in 1972, "with his limp hand and trolling vocabulary. . . . And if he's not an out-rage, he is, at least, an amusement. The expression of his sexual ambivalence establishes a fascinating game: is he or isn't he?" In answer to the question of why he wore a patterned silk dress, color coordinated to match his shoulder-length blond hair, on the cover of *The Man Who Sold the World*, Bowie coyly replied. "Oh, dear, you must understand. It's not a woman's . . . it's a man's dress."

The cross-dressing cover art continued on *Hunky Dory* with a portrait of the artist as a young Greta Garbo and a collection of distinctly lisping songs that included, "Oh! You Pretty Things," "Andy Warhol," and "Queen Bitch." Along with "Changes," the selections on *Hunky Dory* positioned Bowie as a fey, ultrasensitive poet/singer, bewitched by fame and the famous (check "Song for Bob Dylan"), revising the future to fit the ideal of a glamorous new consciousness. All of this, in turn, concealed the fact that he was still trafficking in the rote assumptions of the time:"Changes" was simply a cute way of saying "The Kids Are All Right." The whole modernist baggage Bowie employed," writes critic Tom Carson, "was a dead tradition in literature, but it was new to rock."

So was *Ziggy Stardust*, Bowie's next charade and arguably the high point of his career. Certainly *The Rise and Fall of Ziggy Stardust and the Spiders from Mars*, released in the summer of '72, was the album that established Bowie's big-league status. It was also the precursor for all the self-referential rock works that were to follow in a flood. A nimble, smart, and perfectly timed concept album, *Ziggy* featured Bowie in the title roll as a superstar in yet another failed-future scenario, with the world this time only five years from some unspecified doom. Against the all-or-nothing backdrop, Ziggy, with "screwed up eyes and screwed down hairdo" rises to fame, suffers the slings and arrows of life at the top, and in the end either kills himself or doesn't, depending on how one reads the closing track, "Rock 'n' Roll Suicide." The potency of *Ziggy Stardust* lay not so much in the music, although there was plenty of high-end energy on display, as well as some of the sharpest writing of Bowie's career. What really set it apart was the *self-consciousness* the artist brought to this conventional fable. For the first time rock was talking about itself, if not exactly critically, at least cleverly. Here was a brave new world indeed: one where art lingered lovingly over its own image and the artist's most fitting subject was his own sweet self. "How else can you discover precisely what rock and roll stardom is like," wrote English critic Charles Shaar Murray "without actually going out and becoming a superstar?"

Good question. A multitude of rock stars would follow in Bowie's steps, singing forlornly of life on the road, the epic struggles to create hit music, the sacrificial surrender to fame, the whole star-crossed messiah bit. To the hilt. Modern music, with *Ziggy Stardust*, had descended one more notch into its own fatal allures. "Ziggy Stardust was the zenith of glitter rock," wrote one critic in *Trouser Press*. "It epitomized the trend, transformed the theatricality into spectacle and unleashed the ideal of decadence; a doomed world in which public image is all, where impotent messiahs are transformed into stars, where the only logical way of life was to live for fame and thrills until the end."

What followed, for David Bowie, were changes too fast and furious for any but the most dedicated to follow, much less comprehend. *Aladdin Sane* (1973) was the last clearly distinguishing image, if only by virtue of the bizarre and sickly effect it achieved. Again, the cover art commanded attention as a portent to what lay inside. Here, Bowie was almost completely obliterated beneath makeup and airbrush contours. The gatefold featured a full-frontal hermaphrodite coated in silver from the chest down, a lightning bolt cunningly etched down its face. Ice-cold, raw, and vindictive, the music of *Aladdin Sane* proved Bowie's willingness to put a venomous sting behind his dappling images. "The Jean Genie," "Watch That Man," "Cracked Actor," "Lady Grinning Soul"; here was a not-so-soft-cored mean streak that underscored Bowie's debt to the Velvet Underground.

After *Aladdin Sane* it was open season. If rock music in the sixties had flung symbols with no regard but for their aesthetic resonance, Bowie took the process one step further, incarnating a new set of symbols, equally meaningless and equally entertaining. Throughout the remainder of the decade, Bowie stepped into the spotlight as a gay pirate, a dog, a boxer, a gigolo, an anorexic sumo wrestler, a woman, and in an encylopedic array of intergalactic get-ups. He posed as a forties film star and a kind of Zen go-go dancer in a spandex leotard with a rising sun painted on his forehead. He stepped right into his film role as *The Man Who Fell to Earth*; a misunderstood alien in an existential tizzy. He cast himself in the starring role of his own alter ego: The Return of the Thin White Duke. At one point, during the quarter-million-dollar *Diamond Dogs* tour, he switched persona in midstream, dumping the elaborate stage sets and appearing in Fred Astaire Oxford trousers and no makeup.

There was music to match: the revisionist disco of *Young Americans*; the avant-garde elevator music of *Low*; the party-time ennui of *Let's Dance*.

"This kind of shadow-boxing probably comes a great deal easier to Bowie because of his periods of Zen Buddhism," wrote Roy Carr and Charles Shaar Murray in their biography of the star. "Most Westerners regard the concept of the individual personality as inviolable. . . . The personality is believed to be something passive, even in decisive, assertive, extrovert people: something that is acted *upon* by circumstance.

"Bowie, with this training and background," continue Murray and Carr, "is aware that much of what we feel to be part of the essential fabric of the personality is far more likely to be surface detritus, compacted mannerisms. When Bowie changes 'personality,' he conducts modifications in that area where style is considered to be a function of personality." Which sounds a little like the tail wagging the dog. Buddhism may or may not have given Bowie the rationale for his lascivious affair with his own multifaceted ego, but he hardly needed the excuse. Bowie was the supreme strategist of contemporary music, and if, eventually, the consumer's ephemeral hold on the real person simply slipped away in that rush of roles, it's only because Bowie hadn't cooked up a fitting end to his own career.

In Bowie's case, all's well that ends well, and he seems to have survived to prosper. When all the excitement had subsided, and with his best years clearly behind him, the real David Bowie finally emerged. And he seemed, surprisingly, a nice enough guy; bemused, a little shy, aware that the cost of survival is a diminished legend. That he chose survival was perhaps the canniest of all his calculations.

Which leaves only his legacy, one of the most influential in popular music. It was a matter of simple probabilities. Over the course of his career, Bowie had tried on so many different masks, struck so many poses, and warbled so wide an assortment of songs that much of the music of the eighties would echo, deliberately or not, one or another distinctly Bowiesque attribute. By being everything he ever imagined he could be, Bowie actually *did* anticipate the future. And it was him.

Johnny Rotten

Chapter Eleven

WITTENBERG ROCK

No Elvis, Beatles or the Rolling Stones
—The Clash

We spat on everything, including ourselves
—George Grosz on Dada

Unlike most of the big moves in rock music, if it hadn't
happened, there's no guarantee that someone would have
invented the punk explosion of the late seventies. There
was nothing inevitable about it, regardless of all the
dog-eared social and cultural causes and effects trotted
out to explain this brilliant flash of heat and light. Sure,
1977, the year of Britain's Silver Jubilee, was a particularly
jarring juxtaposition of officious hypocrisy and savage

street-level realities. As the Green and Pleasant Isle basked in the glow of its royal family, racial tension and a cancerous economy had gripped the post-industrial slums. But Britain had survived hard times before, kept her head high and her youth from turning into ravening wolves. And in the U.S., in the concrete chasms of Manhattan or out West along the smog-smudged earthquake line, middle-class kids seemed to be suffering more from a bout with botulism than a case of acne, banging heads and sniffing glue and playing all kinds of moronic tricks on their future. So what else was new?

The years 1976 to 1978 may not have been the best time in which to pin your hopes on the Western Alliance, what with embargos and stagflation and other evidences of mounting debilitation. But the Great Depression hadn't been a picnic either, and you didn't see flaming youth back then clearing a demilitarized zone of contempt between themselves and the rest of the civilization. In short, the punk apocalypse, when all was said and done, picked up where most other movements spurred by social malaise left off. Political causes sought redress of grievances; aetheticians challenged the stasis of taste; individuals adjusted or went mad. Punk perfected alienation as a party platform, rejection as an art form, and loathsomeness as a uniform.

In the process, the punks achieved one of those rare moments of originality that dot the pop cultural timeline: an originality that owes less to prevailing social and economic conditions than to an urgent creative surge. With plenty of reason to turn to crime, sink into despair, or follow in the footsteps of their elders—including their hippie siblings—the punks instead assembled the elements of a thriving, self-sustaining subculture and a flashy, threatening, and therefore successful, one at that.

The challenge to authority represented by youth rebellions is, according to Dick Hebridge in his revealing book *Subculture: The Meaning of Style*, "expressed obliquely, in style. The objections are laid, the contradictions are displayed . . . at the profoundly superficial level of appearances, at the level of signs." Punk was quintessentially a signifying phenomenon. But unlike the American juvenile delinquent or the English Teddy boy, punks were signaling something more than their deliberate differences with the social norm. The outrage that fueled the fury had an unmistakably *moral* character, a protest against sins so ingrained in human enterprise that the only way to exorcise them was to take them on—call them by your name and give them your face. Asked why she wore a swastika emblazoned on her forehead, a punkette explained, "Punks just like to be hated." It wasn't, in critic Greil Marcus's words, "a protest against the way things were, not that at all, but a protest against life."

Punkishness had a Hand of God directness that would prove itself in its galvanizing effect on popular culture. The fact that punks never seemed to grasp the full scope of their avenging mission was all the better. Working from instinct, a nothing-to-lose solidarity, and their own inspired sense of shock-value style, they emulated a corruption that was beyond corruption, attaining to the purity of pinheads and mongoloids. It was a brilliant stroke of intuition, the perfect medium for the cleansing work at hand. The punks took on the sins of their elders and went to the grave despising the shame. As the great reformation of rock 'n' roll, punk had one cut-and-dry purpose: to purge.

It hadn't started out that way, and it sure didn't end up that way. The dyed roots of punk could be traced clear back to the mid-sixties, when a handful of American garage bands kicked up some dust in the face of the British Invasion. But more to the point was the deadpan wall of sound erected by a quartet from Forest Hills, Long Island named the Ramones. Joey, Johnny, Dee Dee, and Tommy Ramone (no relation) first surfaced in a seedy East Side club called CBGB's, where they stumbled onto a long-lost principle of pop music. The rediscovery of what would later be dubbed by critic Richard Meltzer "offensive stoopidity" was a glorious disinvention of twenty years of rock progressivism. Forging valiantly backward to the hormonal jolt of loud, fast music, the Ramones cranked out two-and-three-minute anthems to mindlessness that, in '74 and '75—the era of Bowie and Zep—sounded like the work of lobotomized cretins. In fact, on songs like "Teenage Lobotomy," "Cretin Hop," "Suzy was a Headbanger," "Gimmie, Gimmie Shock Treatment," and their signature tune, the enigmatic "Gabba, Gabba, Hey," the Ramones, unbeknownst to everyone, had breached the edifice of artifice. Countless punk bands to follow would cite the quartet as a prime influence and, more importantly, an encouraging omen: blue-collar kids with no discernible artistic subtleties daring to wrench back the music from the fops and careerists and guitar priests. If they could do it, anyone could—a sentiment that was later sloganized in the British punk fanzine *Sniffin' Glue*, whose creator, Michael Dempsey, drew guitar-chord diagrams and announced, "Here's a chord. Here's two more. Now go out and start a band."

It was *Sniffin' Glue*, in fact, that ran a review of the Ramones' first album in its premier issue—a two-page, hand-typed broadside, back in summer '76. The adrenal rush of enthusiasm was a sign of things to come: "Their music is fast, simple and instantly likable," wrote the reviewer amid a blizzard of typos. "They haven't got much melody, but they've got enough drive to make up for it. . . . Everything's full on, wait till your mum and dad are out (or wife if you're unlucky) and turn it all UP!" After running down the cuts, which included "Blitzkrieg Bop," "Beat on the Brat," and "I Don't Wanna Go Down the Basement," the writer concludes, "By this time you're coughing up blood and spitting all over your Led Zeppelin albums."

The Ramones were generating the sincerest form of flattery in some pretty unlikely places. Southern California, for example, so long a bastion of enforced mellowness, erupted with a slew of home-brewed bands that were quick to pick up on the primal kicks. Dickies, Weirdos, Germs, Zeros, Mumps, Dils, Bags, and Screamers; all of a sudden Hollywood was crawling with forky-haired miscreants, followed closely by San Francisco, where a North Beach dive called Mabuhay Gardens became the focus for a new kind of fun.

And fun was what it was all about. Real fun . . . not paying fifteen bucks to sit in a blimp hangar and watch rich men in satin britches through binoculars, but getting up and doing it yourself, risking—in fact *inviting* derision—not knowing how to play and not wanting to know how, just making loud noise and sweat and . . . fun. The early punk practice of hurling spit and abuse at whoever dared to take the stage was one more brilliant signifying stratagem; it neatly reversed the insufferable adulation of rock stars by a conspicuous show of contempt. There was an unerring instinct at work here, a demented genius for deflating.

Take the pogo, for instance, or slam dancing. Jumping in place or butting heads with your partner may not have constituted a new dance craze, but it sure fired up some long-inert circuits. Loud rock music had originally been intended to get you hot and bothered and bring out all that, well, "offensive stoopidity." Punks had simply reinvented the rock 'n' roll wheel, taken the music out of the concert halls and back to the basement, where they thought it belonged. Throughout its short life, punk would always be attended by an electric aura of violence, real or rumored. After a decade of safe-and-sane rock, it's only surprising that the danger of the new music was so contained, so stylized. The squares were getting off easy.

The English punk's answer to the Ramones was the Damned, whose single, "New Rose," released in October '76, was the first recorded evidence of a scene that had already been thriving for more than a year. With a lead singer in Dracula drag, a drummer named Rat Scabies, and the fearsome Captain Sensible, who performed, on occasion, wearing nothing at all, the Damned's inspired incongruity reflected the movement's preoccupation with having a good time on its own terms. Self-parody was an essential survival technique, and the Damned excelled at making a joke, albeit a sick one, at the notion of rock swagger, setting early standards for repulsiveness and spontaneous displays of dementia. They were the best example of the spirit of blasphemous adolescent elation that sparked the early punk scene.

What was to follow had more serious consequences. Deadly serious. Dick Hebridge: "Punk claimed to speak for the neglected constituency of white lumpen youth . . . 'rendering' working classness metaphorically in chains and hollow cheeks, 'dirty' clothing (stained jackets, tarty see-through blouses) and rough and ready diction. . . . [It] described itself in bondage through an assortment of darkly comic signifiers—straps and chains, strait jackets and rigid postures. Despite its proletarian accents, punk's rhetoric was steeped in irony."

The initial object of that irony was fashion, the punk's own image. The garbage-heap chic developed by the subculture was to have a lasting impact on mainstream fashion sensibilities, but even more significant was the statement it made about fashionableness itself. By vehemently rejecting standards of respectability, beauty, and taste, all of which helped to conceal the inhumanities of the at-large culture, the punks invented a stylistic mirror reflecting the ugly truth. At the same time, they cast themselves in the role of despised and discarded, proud to be repulsive and unacceptable in every way. "Conventional ideas of prettiness were jettisoned. . . . Faces became abstract portraits," writes Hebridge, "sharply observed and meticulously executed studies in alienation. . . . The perverse and abnormal were valued intrinsically," reflecting, in turn, "the tendency toward wilful desecration and the voluntary assumption of outcast status." The ranks of the punk movement were comprised primarily of those who'd already failed to meet the prevailing standards of beauty or even acceptability: short, pudgy girls; dorky, pimpled boys—the victims of fashion's tyranny. In this new kingdom of the revolting, the geeks reigned. The beautiful people were suddenly second-class citizens.

Punk fashion accoutrements vividly underscored this inspired notion. Mutilation—the humble household safety pin stuck through the ear, cheek, or lip—quickly became the chief ornament of the new aesthetic, embellishing the ideal of anti-attraction. Zippers, S & M bondage equipment, cheap hair-dye jobs in the most outlandish colors, prom clothes with graffiti, defiled school uniforms, tampon necklaces, dog collars, chains, street-walker regalia . . . the punks had pulled off a coup of major proportions, dredging up their identity from the debris of the modern world. Elements of the punk look have since become so integrated into *haute couture* that it is easy to forget just how brilliantly unsettling the whole battered, frayed, and pieced-together image was at first blush. It remains one of the genuinely innovative fashion statements of our time.

The punk's effect on rock 'n' roll was just as brazen, if not as ultimately influential. Punk rock was essentially reactive and—as a slap in the face of progressive rock—it

293

really packed a wallop. Scorning texture, coloration, and dramatic tension, the punks opted for sheer nervous energy, reducing rock to a single equation. Played all at once and at a blinding tempo, formal punk had the simplicity and impact of a choice obscenity. Unintelligible lyrics were screamed into cheap microphones, every instrument was played as fast and as furiously as possible, and no song lasted more than a couple of minutes. There couldn't have been a more obvious negation, point by point, of rock's artistic mandate, and the rock establishment reacted with predictable pique. "It's a fad," insisted one rock talent scout, while another concluded, "The fact that it isn't disciplined prevents me from liking it." Eric Burdon, one of the true relics of the sixties, opined, "Their music is not important." Sniffed Phil Collins of Genesis, "A friend videotaped the group (the Sex Pistols) . . . and following all the publicity we played it over out of curiosity and all we found was a lack of talent." The fact that the punks weren't welcomed as a new branch on rock's spreading family tree is an indication of just how aggressively they were confronting the prevailing state of the art, and how, by flaunting their own rank aesthetic, they were exposing the pretensions of their elders.

Gleefully undermining rock's faith in diversity and dexterity, the punks exploded, at the same time, the myth of immortality. "Rock 'n' roll is over, don't you understand?" asked the Sex Pistols' Johnny Rotten, long after his band had itself imploded. "It's gone on for twenty-five years and it's got to be *cancelled*. The Pistols finished rock and roll; they were the last rock and roll band. It's finished now, *done with*. And that was all quite some time ago, when you think of it."

When you think of it, rock 'n' roll *could* very easily have finished with the Sex Pistols. The band's blink-of-an-eye saga had the symmetry of a self-fulfilling prophesy and the fanatic singlemindedness of a suicide mission deep behind enemy lines. It wasn't that the Sex Pistols had delivered the thunderous last word on what rock 'n' roll was or might have been. Rock, for Rotten (who with his tiny, ice-blue eyes and curdled sneer was the spiteful soul of punk), had always been a scam of insidious dimensions. Denouncing it, even for the pinnacle of fame, would have been too easy, just more cheap talk. The Sex Pistols instead staged a great, farcical fable, cast themselves in the leading roles as sainted fools, and concluded the performance with a real, resonating climax: an act of self-destruction so spectacular it should have signaled the honorable way out for the whole rock 'n' roll enterprise. The fact that business prevailed as usual wasn't their fault. The Sex Pistols had done their duty.

Formed in 1975, the quartet had the deceptive appearance of an actual band, with certified humble origins. Composed of London street kids, the Sex Pistols were assembled under the auspices of Malcolm McLaren, a latter-day Andrew Loog Oldham who operated a King's Road protopunk boutique called Sex. McLaren, who would later take full credit for inventing the Sex Pistols, and, by extension, the entire punk consciousness, was a canny manipulator who had gone to America to manage the pivotal glam rock band, the New York Dolls, in the last months before its demise. Returning home he began casting about for a group of his own, eventually stumbling on a trio fronted by a part-time Sex employee, Glen Matlock.

There was nothing to suggest the slightest hint of promise in these callow weekend rockers (drummer Paul Cook kept his job at a brewery even after the band began attracting national attention), because, in fact, they had no promise. Neither, for that matter, did McLaren's schemes, until the arrival of Johnny Rotten. John Lydon earned his moniker as a Kings Road hell raiser, spending his days on the street harassing the trendies. "I used to go up and down the Kings Road gobbing at the posers," he told journalist Caroline Coon. "I couldn't stand them. . . . they were weeds." It was around this time that, according to Coon, "after feeling particularly hostile to Chelsea's wealth and well-groomed finery Johnny bought (or acquired) a brand new suit, shirt and tie. He took it home and slashed it to pieces. He pinned it and stapled it together again. And then he wore it." Whether or not Rotten can be credited with displaying the first punk ensemble, there was no doubt that it was his charismatic nasty streak that induced McLaren to invite him into the fledgling band as a singer. "I couldn't sing," remarked Rotten. "I never ever bothered to sing in my whole life. I had absolutely no interest in singing." But sing he did, standing in front of the jukebox at Sex and mouthing the words to Alice Cooper's "I'm Eighteen." Whether or not it was apparent then, it was quickly to become clear that Johnny Rotten was one of the greatest gut-level vocalists ever. Rolling his *rs*, spitting his *ss*, enunciating each snarl, Rotten sprayed his words with venom before letting them loose. His voice escaped from the precise center of his scorn, there where all the bile was churning, aching to be lanced. With no introspection, no shadow of doubt or shade of compassion, the genius of Rotten's performance was in its *outwardness*, the musical equivalent of the accusatory finger or handwriting on the wall. "God, it's such a weird feeling," Rotten marvels, recalling the first time he rehearsed with the band. "For the first time in your life you get up in front of these people you don't know, who you've been very cynical about. I'd never done anything myself and I thought, 'Oh my God! I can't back up what I'm saying.' So I just grabbed the mike and *screamed*."

Whatever claims the Svengalian McLaren may have made on the band's extraordinary success, it was the loud-

mouthed Rotten—his anarchic rage and mangled innocence—that focused and fired the Sex Pistols. McLaren did
indeed have a flair for guerrilla flack tactics, relentlessly
promoting the band's unsavory image, but Rotten's appeal
transcended even such heavy-handed hypes. The manager's manipulations were no match for his artist's intuitions. Rotten understood exactly what his mission was
and, in fact, used McLaren to accomplish his ends. Despite
his insistence that he had "manufactured" the Sex Pistols,
McLaren could only capitalize on the shock waves generated by Johnny Rotten's words and image. "You know
what Malcolm's like," Rotten once told a reporter. "Ace
controller. Nobody controls me, dear." It was more than
teenage bravado. From the beginning it was Rotten's
show.

And for a while there it was the greatest show on earth.
Throughout 1976 the band steadily built steam, playing at
seedy London dives like the 100 Club, the Marquee, the
Nashville, and the Roundhouse and being systematically
banned from each venue after fistfights, furniture hurling,
and general audience provocation. Matlock, citing friction
with Rotten, left to be replaced by one of Rotten's Kings
Road cronies, Sid Vicious. "I don't understand why people
think it's so difficult to learn to play guitar," Vicious told
the English music press shortly after joining the band. "I
found it incredibly easy. You just pick a chord, go twang
and you've got music." Rotten and Vicious quickly became
the focus of the group—Vicious for his self-mutilation habits, which included rolling around onstage over broken
glass; Rotten for his blunt assessments of the intrinsic
worthlessness of everything, particularly rock music and
rock stars. It's a system, he claimed, "that doesn't work.
It gets you absolutely nowhere. It's not a solution for
us. . . . I listened to rock 'n' roll, but I had no respect for
it. It was redundant and had nothing to do with anything

that was relevant. Do people actually *listen* to that music? No! It's just background music while they buy their jeans—flared jeans. Is that any state for rock to be in? I just feel sorry for the people who try to apply their brains to it." It was the kind of incendiary overstatement that lapped over into all sorts of heavy topics, and as a punk spokesman, Rotten's consistent negation of any and all values presented to him served to define the punk anti-ethos, in the ideal if not in practice.

It was a stance beyond nihilism because it was so active, so aggressive, and so informed by the creative energies of punk. What Rotten so wickedly expressed was his generation's unwillingness to be suckered into a search for the meaning of life. By stripping away the phantasmagoria, the punks pushed through to ground zero, a reality where truth, if it existed, would be self-evident and meaning would stand out starkly against the backdrop of the absurd. "There's no love at all," Rotten told Caroline Coon. "I don't believe in love. And I never will. I mean, when you actually listen to a love song and try to relate it as something that happens in real life, it just doesn't work. . . . It's doesn't apply to humans." Marriage and family? "What about them? If you want a family you can go down to an orphanage." Sex? "By the time you're twenty you think—yawn—just another squelch session." Violence? "Pain doesn't hurt."

Later in '76 the group was interviewed on British television by a lugubrious talk show host named Bill Grundy who—depending on interpretation—either induced or invited the group to swear outrageously over the air. The episode created a sensation, with Fleet Street gleefully fanning the flames.

THE PUNK ROCK HORROR SHOW! BILL GRUNDY IN FOUR
LETTER POP OUTRAGE! TV FURY AT ROCK CULT FAITH!

The Sex Pistol's first single, threatening "Anarchy in the U.K." had just been released, and the combination of hysterical news coverage and a scathing chunk of hardcore punk lodged in the Top Twenty combined to turn the Sex Pistols into the first real British pop phenomenon since the Beatles.

It was a standing immeasurably enhanced when, as a result of the Grundy fiasco and other outrages, all but five shows on their first British tour were canceled. Shortly afterward, their record label, the prestigious EMI, dropped them. McLaren announced that EMI's £40,000 advance to the band was the price of the broken contract. A & M Records then stepped in, signed the Sex Pistols for £150,000 and fired them a week later. McLaren and the band pocketed half the advance in the bargain. Virgin Records was next up, offering £50,000. The band had released one single and had already "earned" over £150,000.

In May of '77 they released a second single in time for the Queen's Silver Jubilee. "God Save the Queen"—with the possible exception of the band's last recorded song, the harrowing "Holidays in the Sun"—was the Sex Pistols' finest moment. Despite its crashing condemnation of the "fascist regime" of the House of Windsor, the song is not a political diatribe at all. Instead, it is a brilliantly mounted punk manifesto, a cogent and lyrically stunning fire-and-brimstone sermonette.

> God save history. God save your mad parade.
> Lord God have mercy, all crimes are paid.
> Where there's no future there cannot be sin.
> We're the flowers in your dustbin.
> We're the poison in the human machine.
> We're the future. Your future.

Rotten's delivery is a moment of terrifying clarity. Punk

suddenly leaps from its narrow context, unmoored from its youth-culture lineage to become a medium for an explicit indictment of betrayal and a promise of revenge. "No future, no future, no future," is the great cycling chant on which the song fades. Here, in a little over three minutes, the Sex Pistols had finally consummated the promise of rock's prophetic power. Years and years of reaching for profundity had come to this. All the dead ends and blind alleys and desolate highways down which the seekers had forayed finally converged. Rock 'n' roll, at the very moment of its death, had finally transcended. "God Save the Queen," the punk's gift to dreaming England, was immediately banned from the airwaves, but went on to become one of the best-selling singles of the summer anyway. It was designated as a blank spot at the number-two position on radio charts. Later that year the band released their first and only album. The title and cover art—a ransom note paste job—of *Nevermind the Bollocks, Here's the Sex Pistols*, was yet another excoriation of rock presumption, while the music inside duplicated with stunning consistency the strength and sentiment of "God Save the Queen." In December of '77 the band embarked for America, where they played a handful of dates culminating with a performance in San Francisco's cavernous Winterland. There amid a couple of hundred local punks and the teeming ghosts of a thousand Grateful Dead concerts, the Sex Pistols played their last show. "Ever had the feeling you've been cheated?" were Johnny Rotten's parting words.

And that was it. The Sex Pistols had said everything they were going to say, had put up with the abuses of fame for long enough. They delivered the punch line. At the very beginning of their careers as rock stars—gazing into a future of recording and touring and earning and wondering when it would all slip away—they just stopped. They let it go. It was the perfectly timed perfect

300

ending, the final nose-thumbing slag off to the rock establishment. Was all this supposed to be a big deal? Was this what every kid dreamed of becoming? You've got to be kidding.

Of course, this was real life; nothing has the perfect symmetry of complete closure. Rotten reverted back to Lydon and plied his trade. Vicious ended up dead at the end of a heroin needle, and the rest of the band flogged a dead horse. McLaren, by nature, landed on his feet, masterminding one of the truly great swindles in modern pop: Adam Ant. What was left unfulfilled was the Pistol's legacy. What the punks had been about and what Rotten had put into words may have been impossible to ever completely live up to, but the fate of punk was marked by a singular failure of nerve for such a riled-up bunch.

"I haven't seen a hippie in two weeks," Johnny Rotten told Caroline Coon in November of '76. "That's something! They were so complacent. They let it all—the drug culture—flop around them. They were all dosed out of their heads the whole time. 'Yeah man, peace and love. Don't let anything affect you . . .' We say bollocks! If it offends you, stop it." Like most everything Rotten said, the implication of his words went far beyond the acrid snottiness of a disgruntled kid. Taken to their logical ends, the implications had the ring of reformatory zeal. If the punks' lock-stock-and-barrel rejection of the Aquarian age was serious, perhaps what they were calling for was a militant return to values that hadn't dared rear their heads for years. "No hippies" meant no more drugs, no more moral relativism, no more dallying in the mystical garden. It meant that what went around didn't necessarily come around, that doing your own thing wasn't necessarily the key to existence, that peace and love weren't necessarily prevailing. It meant, finally, that the dream really *was* over.

Initially, there were signs that this might be the case.

301

Although deeply into their brew, the early punks scorned psychedelics and the mellowing effects of marijuana. Hard drugs came into prominent use only later. On the Sex Pistol's album there appeared, of all things, an anti-abortion song, "Bodies." Punching through the rhetoric of the issue, Rotten drove to the heart of the matter, expressing in no uncertain terms the horror of "another discharge." Behind this appalling tune, a lurking indictment: the price of unchecked lust was murder.

In the end, the implications remained just that. The punks, like the rest of the at-large culture, proved unable to pull themselves from the mire of the sixties; the forces set in motion continued to grind out their conclusions. Had the punks attained to the purified status they preached, the results might have been even more spectacular than they ultimately proved to be. But much of their righteous rage was neatly sublimated by the oldest diversion in the book: politics. "We're more antisocial than political," ventured Glen Matlock with inadvertent insight, but as the seventies petered out, the line between the two became increasingly blurred. The Clash, another seminal English punk band, capitalized early on the movement's political potential. Their eponymously titled first album disguised their intent by masking it as anarchy. "White Riot," "I'm So Bored With the U.S.A.," "London's Burning," Career Opportunities," *sounded* like blistering punk attacks on the whole wide world, but in light of the Clash's later, highly touted work, the strident leftist agenda stood out in bold relief. Along the way to spelling out their Marxist solution to the punk's existential disgust, the Clash also abandoned the formal crudity that had given punk its protective exclusiveness. It was inevitable, of course: three chords and one emotional timbre don't comprise a musical style, but the Clash, for all their hard-core posturing, would play the progressive game to the hilt.

The double album *London Calling* and the *triple* album *Sandinista!*, while both containing some genuinely exciting music, reveled in the same profligate diversity that had sunk the last generation of rock stars. R & b, rockabilly, Zydeco, reggae, heavy metal, the Clash seemed intent on proving that the punk ethic could be applied to them all. As a result they defused much of the compacted power of punk. As Marcus points out: "[T]he Clash have always pulled back from the cutting edge on which the true punk movement was played out. . . . The Clash's very effort always to do the right thing, to make the correct choices, to define the problem properly, has kept them from ever being as dangerous as punk promised it would be—or as the Sex Pistols were." "What we do now is what we can do," reasoned Clash front man, Joe Strummer. "It wouldn't be fair to do ranting music, because we've mastered time-change." It was a long way from Rotten's boast: "We want to be amateurs."

Another group that misconstrued the punk mandate was Joy Division. Eschewing the exuberant status-bashing that had initially sparked the punks, this grim Manchester, England, assemblage wallowed in apocalyptic despair, droning on endlessly about the pointlessness of it all and generating music that one critic described as "brown bleeding into grey." Named after the prostitution wings in Nazi death camps, Joy Division were progenitors of deathly serious "Gloom Rock," the antithesis of the inventive and affirming energies of real punk. It was, of course, one more take on the rock musician as philosophical pontificator, only this time the message was "Why bother?" It was a question Joy Division founder Ian Curtis himself seemed unable to answer. In 1980, at age twenty-three, he hanged himself in his bedroom while his parents watched television downstairs. The suicide, predictably, was viewed a validation of Joy Division's callow pessimism, another heroic sacrifice at the altar of rock art. The Clash and Joy Division, for all their surly finger pointing, were new versions of the old guard, the first to venture out after the punk fire storm, check for damage, and begin the work of rebuilding the rock edifice.

The line, it turned out, formed to the rear. The Clash may have begun the rush to regain rock's artistic integrity, but they certainly weren't alone. Even as real punk sank back into the shadows, became 'hardcore' and the domain of hyperkinetic weirdos, the breach it had caused in rock 'n' roll's spiral to self-fulfillment was being alternately addressed, ignored, and papered over. Less than two years after the Sex Pistols' swan song, Pink Floyd surfaced with *The Wall*, a lumbering concept album that came complete with a multimillion-dollar stage show, reams of weighty critical interpretation, and, eventually, its own major motion picture. Anyone who doubted Big Concept Rock's determination to prevail had only to scale *The Wall* to discover otherwise. By the dawn of the eighties, the only traces left of the pugnacious subculture of the punks were the skinny ties around the necks of a huge new flock of posers.

It's unfair, of course, to sum up punk's influence as simply another round of musical chairs in which some old superstars were shuffled off to make way for some generally interchangeable new ones. Punk was a genuine and spontaneous protest against Pharisaic deceptions with a healthy disregard for the consequences. It also redefined the terms of rock's mandate as the ultimate expression of the popular will. Johnny Rotten was wrong, of course; rock 'n' roll wasn't over. It was too much a part of too many lives to ever simply go belly up, no matter how much anyone thought it deserved to. But by the same token, it was evident that the music could never again speak so presumptuously of final truths, at least in the lifetimes of anyone who'd witnessed its downfall. Rock's religious fixation had grown so mordant, so deep and dark and depressing, that quite aside from whatever fans derived from all this hectic questing, it was simply a drag to be around. Punk had proved that, and ironically, the result was a quick return to the ephemeral, trendy, and disposable. Rock once again became pop.

The first order of business was to declaw the nettlesome detractors. Punk was quickly retranslated to "New Wave" by record industry tacticians. The term was a catchall category for a potpourri of new arrivals who'd taken advantage of the recent house cleaning to stake their claim. Following the late unpleasantness, most dabbled in the derivative, seeking to simultaneously create the impression, if not the reality, of advance and change. The Cars' turbocharged glam rock, Elvis Costello's acerbic rendition of the singer/songwriter, and X's angst-ridden D.T.'s were all examples of artists creating, with varying degrees of success, edgy auras around repackaged goods. Drum machine majors, costume acts like Cyndi Lauper, reanimated discophiles, and any number of British ska/bluebeat bands cornered the good-time market, giving a new lease on life to the dance-your-buns off ethic. Synthesizers washed the music of the new decade with a shimmery, futuristic sheen, inducing the impression that a new tomorrow—hipper, cleaner, more self-aware—had dawned for rock 'n' roll.

It hasn't. The ballyhooed New British Invasion spearheaded by bands like Culture Club and Duran Duran, billed as the Fab Five indeed recalls the English incursion of the early sixties but with one significant difference. This time around there are no ground-breaking Beatles and Stones leading the pack, but only endless eighties versions of second-string trend jumpers. Culture Club is Herman's Hermits in drag; Duran Duran is the Dave Clark Five and in

the role of Freddy and the Dreamers. . . . take your pick.
A new pop category has come into its own: the Haircut
Band. Faceless, marginally talented groups by the dozens
can be distinguished only by the cut of their coiffures.
Naturally taken to the extreme, fledgling bands excelled
at razor cuts, ratting, henna rinses, and dreadlocks. Some
real pace-setters cook up do's that approximate the flight
decks of aircraft carriers or C-5As in midflight.

Meanwhile, music video has accelerated considerably
New Wave's tendencies toward cosmetic innovation. Deprived of its spiritual legitimacy, eighties rock has contrived a stylistic vocabulary in collusion with visual tech-
nicians who have no more regard for the simple pleasures
of pop music than do the rock stars themselves. The vacuity of progressive rock in the sixties and the vacuity of
New Wave in the eighties share a common fascination for
the power of symbols. If rock 'n' roll was ill-equipped to
bear the burden of cosmic truth piled on it by the progressivists, it is flattened to utter one dimensionality by
the accumulated weight of empty images heaved on by
the video-meisters. To watch one hour of MTV is to watch
it all: cheesy dreamscapes full of shattering mirrors, back-
alley liaisons and diaphanous blondes; endless enigmatic
rendezvous at desert gas stations; alternate universes
clogged with '57 Chevys, leather jackets, and flying guitars. It's a barrage of flashy pictures undermining the most
basic function of music—to spark the imagination. Video
is an unmistakable sign of the creative exhaustion that over-
took rock music after punk. Like a terminal patient
hooked to a battery of life support systems, rock needs
the ultimate enhancement, visualization, to survive. This
shotgun wedding of mediums is, of course, heralded as a
new art form, and in fact, it is: the art of inertia.

Video is also another indication that by the eighties, rock
music, despite its extravagant claims, has lost the will to

live. Not that it will ever exactly die; rock 'n' roll, like death and taxes, is here to stay. All it lacks is a *reason* to continue. Rock spokesmen in the new decade make much of a return to basics, to good feelings and fun.

The man who has engendered more of these qualities than anyone else is Bruce Springsteen, an artist whose most noteworthy accomplishment has been in overcoming the leaden self-consciousness capsizing popular music. Springsteen, an affable heartlander, has become an eighties superstar by virtue of his aw-shucks sincerity, a mythically proportioned stage show, and impeccable blue-collar credentials. Springsteen's inarguable genuineness is the foundation of his enormous appeal; there is, it would seem, not a calculating bone in his well-toned body. His music, on the other hand, is a veritable encyclopedia of iconic teenhood, a florid fantasy of main-street neon, Harleys by the reservoir, and sacred memories of innocence. Add to this a Guthrie-esque political stance, and a figure emerges to redeem rock's tarnished idealism, an exalted primitive dispensing the secret of perpetual youth.

The colossal ambitions critics and fans have for their favorite son have long since swamped the artist's own apparently modest ambitions. Whether Springsteen's sleep is disturbed by his millionaire, rock-idol status is a matter of conjecture. What's obvious is the heroic mantle with which his followers have long since crowned him. "Over the years, Springsteen's mandate has changed," observes critic James Wolcott in *Vanity Fair*. "In the beginning his mission was to restore faith in rock during a time of narcissism, power cords and dazed androids. . . . And as Springsteen became a fixture in the lives of his fans, they began to fashion a larger role for him. . . . So to the shining eyes of the faithful, Springsteen's task is to redeem the promise that Elvis fumbled." The idolatry that has attended the rise of Bruce Springsteen has tended to obscure

307

the fact that, as writer Richard Meltzer has it, the music of the Boss is not so much rock 'n' roll as it is *about* rock 'n' roll—a reflexive evocation of fleeting thrills that came naturally to Elvis and his ilk without the benefit of the sweeping mythological perspective. Critic Chet Flippo may evoke the "rock theology" of Bruce Springsteen, but such earnest affirmations lack the validation of spontaneity. Twenty-five years ago no one had to *explain* that rock 'n' roll was a wild joy: people were either too busy living it or too busy trying to stamp it out. Rock has traveled so far from those humble beginnings that not even Springsteen's best intentions can call it back.

Of course, there are exceptions: bands that, if not exactly important in the sixties sense of the word, are at least influential and at most entertaining. Talking Heads, an erudite gaggle of former art students, managed to fuse their own postpunk minimalism with selected eclecticisms to create a dry, self-referential music focused on the quick wit of their leader, David Byrne. The group attracted early attention with a commodity as rare in rock circles as humility: optimism. The albums *77*, *More Songs about Buildings and Food*, and *Fear of Music*, the first three and most representative of Talking Heads albums, presented buoyant Byrne originals that assured people not to worry about the government, extolled the joys of growing up, examined the decision-making process, and extrapolated a version of heaven that was like a big party where "everyone leaves at exactly the same time." Here, even the ironies were friendly and nonthreatening. In his more darkly textured tunes—"Psycho Killer" or "Life During Wartime"—a kind of gentleness prevails as well; a sense of humor and humanity. A mild-mannered iconoclast, Byrne seems less interested in explaining life than describing it. His compilation of small insights creates meaning through a heightened sense of the mundane. Talking Heads, fashioning a context in which normalcy is the strangest state of all, have helped a little to depressurize popular music a little.

Optimism also distinguishes U2, a young Irish band with a penchant for vast soundscapes full of echoes and sweeping wings. While their wall-of-sound approach is nothing new, the use to which they put it is surprising, and surprisingly successful. An avowed Christian, lead vocalist and songwriter Bono Vox seeks to inspire and edify with music that touches obliquely on doctrine and more directly on common aspirations for harmony and safe haven. U2's Christian sensibility might make more of an impact if more was made of it, but Bono and company, for reasons left unclear, have chosen to downplay their beliefs, rejecting suggestions that their music is either an evangelical tool or a two-edged sword. The impression left is of a band that has either not gone far enough in expressing what's on their mind or gone too far, by posing questions for which they're unwilling to provide answers. Still, the tremendous popularity of U2 suggests the intriguing possibility of a cessation in the longstanding feud between rock and Christianity.

Christian rock, meanwhile, continues to chart the largely ineffectual course it has followed since its inception with the Jesus People. Assiduously duplicating whatever prevailing mainstream rock mode is in vogue, contemporary Christian rock remains a musical subclass, adrift in its own contradictions. The paradox revolves around a series of unanswered and seemingly unanswerable questions. Is it wrong to preach the Kingdom in the language of the World? Is music a ministry, an entertainment, or both or neither? Is the Great Commission, in rock 'n' roll terms, to preach the gospel to the unsaved or to revive rhythm in the sanctuary?

There seem to be no easy answers to such dilemmas,

or at least none that are generally accepted. The result is a diversity of approaches, rationales, and philosophies from the top contenders in Christian rock. Singer Amy Grant, the most successful and accessible of the lot, seems completely comfortable with a strategy of breaking into the mainstream, there to prove to a skeptical world that the Christian message is relevant, well produced, and hummable. With songs deliberately written to be construed as either expressions of devotion or romantic love, Grant has been accused by fundamentalist fire-breathers of thinking that Jesus is her boyfriend, an uncalled-for canard that nevertheless points up the continuing schism in the church over the issue of popular music.

While old-timers thunder, a proliferation of new Christian artists struggle to throw off the weight of tradition and express their faith in the context of their time. The results range from the promising to the ludicrous. The absurdity of Christian aerobic dance music—Believercise—may or may not be offset by music that is trying intently to break through to a fragmented generation. What matters most to those who are spearheading the attempt is the conviction of their calling. "We don't want to be *of* the world. But we've got to be there as a light shining in the darkness of rock and roll arenas." So says Robert Sweet, front man for a raging dichotomy called Stryper, perhaps the world's first Born Again heavy metal band. The band, whose name, according to Sweet, stands for Salvation Through Redemption Yielding Peace, Encouragement, and Righteousness, is renowned in its native Los Angeles for throwing out pocket editions of the New Testament during its concerts. The group has been the target of special ire from the ranks of fundamentalists, yet Sweet seems assured of his mission. "If you don't associate with the world," he asserts, "you're not going to know what

310

the love of Jesus Christ is. That's what evangelism is all about."

"There's no 'look' to Christianity," claims Joe Taylor, founder of another eye-popping anomoly, the Christian punk band Undercover. "Yes, my hair is in a mohawk and my earrings dangle, but my Bible says that man looks upon man and God looks upon the heart. It's the people who are driving the normal cars and wearing the normal clothes who are conforming to the world. It isn't any less Christian to be involved in the punk subculture than it is to be involved in the middle-class subculture with its BMW's and everything else." With an unbridled hostility to church hypocrisy, matched by a breakneck brand of head-banging music, Undercover embodies a reformatory zeal revealing increasing impatience with the snail's pace of change within Western Christianity. "Once these kids become Christian," he asserts, "they're not going to throw away their Levis and boots to get wing-tips and polyesters. . . . People say we're arrogant. We're not arrogant; we're opinionated. Sure, we talk about abortion, but abortion and nuclear war and all the other issues are not what it's all about. For us, if people walk away from our concerts thinking about Jesus, then we've done what we're supposed to." It's an attitude in sharp contrast with wing-tipped and polyestered ranks of the church, which continues to decry the very notion of worldly music in the service of God. Referring to rock as "the cadence of decadence," they point to lurid newspaper accounts of teenagers committing suicide and mass murderers running amok at the behest of heavy metal taskmasters. With the lines so sharply drawn, Christian rock's evangelical potential seems, at best, a forlorn hope as long as the church refuses to support it wholeheartedly and the mainstream music industry continues to ignore it.

Meanwhile, the spiritual center of rock music in the

311

eighties lies far beyond the periphery of Christian pop. But the spiritual center of rock music in the eighties lies far beyond the periphery of Christian pop or the faint pulse-beats of optimism. The dominant strains of idolatry have bred new, powerful, and enigmatic media creations, men and women in the Bowie mold, swallowed up in their towering public personas, electronically enhanced for maximum adoration. Sting, a cold, bloodless archetype for a new kind of superstar, or Prince, in whom rock's narcissistic tradition has found a new face, are two examples of artists who have stepped outside the limits of pop music, laying claim to deeper, more demanding loyalties. The new role of rock stars can best be seen in the music's latest bid for legitimacy: rock in the service of mankind.

The run of rock 'n' roll fund-raising extravaganzas—superstar sessions like "We Are the World" and mega-concerts like Live Aid have been the signal events of the first half of the decade, proving conclusively rock musicians' willingness and ability to effect change—in common parlance, "make a difference." Rock 'n' roll has emerged at last from its long gnostic reverie to take up a social gospel. Even taking into account the ego-gratifying aspects of such endeavors, we can only applaud the results. Children are fed. Hope is rekindled. Rock has finally discovered a constructive use for its tremendous power.

For his work in helping feed starving Ethiopians, Bob Geldoff, former lead singer of the quasipunk outfit Boomtown Rats, has been nominated for the Nobel Prize. Jokes about Bruce Springsteen running for elected office are funny primarily because they seem so plausible. Miami Steve Van Zandt and a dozen like-minded artists have taken a stand against apartheid on the fund-raising song "Sun City." Elton John, Stevie Wonder, and others band together to battle AIDS. Part private citizen, part public domain, the famous lend the full weight of their influence to the cause that most deeply touches their hearts and minds, touching deeply, in turn, the hearts and minds of millions.

It all takes place in an unsettling mist of déjà vu. The question is not of rights, as in the right of a man to speak his mind, preach his faith, or rally to a cause. It's not a question of results—the good that is done, the inspiration offered. The question rather is of power and its corrupting capacities. It's a question of leaders and followers and what transpires between them. After twenty-five years, rock 'n' roll stars may still play the messiah's role. Not, this time, in the spirit, but in the flesh.

Bob Dylan, 1964

Chapter Twelve

GHOSTS OF 'LECTRICITY

Work out your own salvation with fear and
trembling

—Philippians 2:12

In the fury of the moment,
I can see the Master's hand.
In every leaf that trembles,
In every grain of sand.

—Bob Dylan

In the winter of 1979, Bob Dylan briefly attended classes
in the fundamentals of Christianity held in a small back
room above the realtor's office in Reseda, California. The
"discipleship school," under the auspices of the Vineyard
Christian Fellowship, began at 8:30 in the morning and
continued until noon, four days a week. During class
breaks Dylan would often walk into the parking lot in back
of the prefab building, dressed against the brisk morning

315

air in a leather jacket and stocking cap, smoke Marlboro cigarettes, and talk with his girlfriend, a singer who had toured with the legendary artist.

The year 1979 was the end of a long bad patch for Dylan. In 1977, his twelve-year marriage had crumbled. His film, the four-hour-plus *Renaldo and Clara*, a catastrophic indulgence, had been ridiculed by the critics and ignored by the public. It was followed by the album *Street Legal*, considered the nadir of Dylan's sixteen-year recording career, a work that, in retrospect, presents an agonizingly accurate portrayal of enervated genius. As if to ward off the pain and confusion of personal and public failure, Dylan launched a world tour, hauling along a full complement of backup singers and hired musicians, wearing eye liner, and incurring the wrath of fans old and new. "The Las Vegas Tour" was the kindest description some critics could muster.

Late in 1978, at the invitation of his girlfriend—a Born Again Christian concerned that she was living with an unsaved man who was not her husband—two assistant pastors from the Vineyard visited Dylan in his onion-domed Malibu Xanadu to talk about salvation. The Vineyard, a nondenominational congregation, combined a sunny southern California faith held over from the Jesus People era with a nonconfrontational charismatic program centering on the gifts of the Holy Spirit. The church had established a reputation for attracting young Christians alienated by the confining legalisms of the mainstream, offering instead an embracing acceptance assured by grace. Shortly after the meeting, Dylan converted to Christianity.

Attending the Vineyard's Sunday morning services, held in a borrowed Methodist church, was out of the question considering Dylan's towering celebrity. The discipleship school, a kind of crash course for new Christians, seemed a safe alternative. Among the subjects taught: The Psalms of Ascent, The Pauline Epistles, and The Sermon on the Mount. The students, numbering no more than twenty, included housewives, a fledgling film producer, an unemployed construction worker, a few lay ministers, and a man considered by millions to be the Poet of Our Time. Dylan fit tolerably well in the group considering the shadow he cast; he spoke little, listened attentively, and practiced the guarded glances of the famous.

One morning, a student stood to report a dream he had had the night before. In the dream, the members of the class were gathered in an upper room, a beautiful cedar-paneled loft lit golden by sun pouring through a skylight. One corner of the room, the student said, had been left unfinished, exposing insulation padding, ducts, and a tangle of dangerously frayed electric wiring. The hazardous wiring, it seemed, had to be pulled down before the room could be made safe for habitation. It was a difficult, dangerous job, and the dreamer was frightened until an unidentified man assured him that only boldness was required. Encouraged, the dreamer thrust his hands into the wiring and pulled. It fell away, and through the hole in the roof, fresh clean water began to flow.

From his seat in the corner of the room, Dylan's eyes were bright. He was nodding and smiling as a moment of unmistakable recognition passed between the student and the star. God, speaking to many men at different times and in different manners, had given to one a dream and to another its interpretation.

Bob Dylan knows about dreams and the power of speaking them out. "While riding on a train goin' west," he once sang in a voice bent with longing, "I fell asleep for to take my rest. I dreamed a dream that made me sad. . . ." Dylan knows the tenderness of dreams, he knows the haunted

317

sorrows and whispered promises and the still small voice of joy brought up from quiet pools. And he speaks them:

> . . . To dance beneath the diamond sky
>   with one hand waving free,
> Silhouetted by the sea,
>   circled by the circus sands,
> With all memory and fate
>   driven deep beneath the waves,
> Let me forget about today until tomorrow.
>
> Hey! Mr. Tambourine Man, play a song for me,
> I'm not sleepy and there is no place I'm going to.

Bob Dylan knows how to call from the deep and catch the answering echoes. He knows that justice and mercy embrace, that loving kindness endures. He knows that truth and righteousness are good gifts from the Father of Lights, and he knows the uncomprehending darkness of man. He's always known these things and he probably always will. But what makes him different—a poet, a genius, the apple of God's eye—is not the knowing but the telling.

It's the telling we remember even more than the man, a curious creature of lights and shadows indistinct in the glare of his legend. The legend, in turn, has grown brassy and harsh, ill-suited for middle age, revealing now less a mystery than a man who has outworn his mystique. Dylan has fared no better or worse than anyone else faced with the truth of what will live on and what will be interred with their bones. The Dylan of the summer of 1965, the cruel, cool mod-draped marksman, is immortal. The Dylan of today, all chin whiskers and crow's feet and hard-fought wisdom, is just passing through. He doesn't wear the autumnal mantle well. Temperamental, often tyrannical,

318

Dylan, particularly just prior to his conversion, was so far from the source of his art that he could slip into grotesque parodies of himself like a sick man slips into delirium. His affair with success has left him the cuckold many times.

Still, there are his words. The telling, which can never be diminished. "If you take away whatever there is to the song—the beat, the melody—I could still recite it," he once said, "It ain't the melodies that're important, man, it's the words. I don't give a damn about melodies." And what a lot of words there were; reams of words, booksful, a gushing flood of words that all taken together added up to a called-forth creation, Dylan's own. "A special gift," is what Janet Maslin called it, "a talent for making things real just by saying they were so."

And the reality that Dylan called forth was brighter, more terrible, and fulfilling than any that had been held before his generation. Popular music has reshaped culture in ways that are still being gauged, but the measure of Dylan's music is manifest already. It has the weight of tradition; not merely in the pull of nostalgia but in its summoning power. "Blowin' in the Wind" evokes what it meant to *believe* in the great struggle for racial equality as much as what it was like to have fought for it. "Don't Think Twice" doesn't simply recall love lost, it kindles the exquisite ache all over again. "Like a Rolling Stone" moves beyond the memory of betrayed illusions to lay hold of the terror of discovery. And in some similar way, "Visions of Johanna" or "To Ramona" or "It's All Over Now, Baby Blue" reveal their truths now as they did then; ceremonially. "It is in the physical world that the intangible meets us," writes theologian Thomas Howard. "A kiss seals a courtship. The sexual act seals a marriage. A ring betokens the marriage. . . . Only symbols, of course. But who will think lightly of his wedding ring and say it is nothing? Who will take a kiss lightly? . . . [I]n that small physical

319

act the great mystery is somehow bespoken." And in the physical acts of writing and singing, Dylan achieved something of that symbolic resonance. His songs don't remind us so much of what is—and may always be—true; they are themselves tokens of that truth.

It's no wonder Bob Dylan occupies a preeminent place in the development of rock's religious consciousness. The innovations he brought to both folk and rock 'n' roll would, by themselves, have set him apart. Long-form songwriting, social and political awareness, the display of a fully fleshed persona in music that reflected ecstasy and bathos, loathing and low humor, arrogance, compassion, and every shade between, together comprised as completely original a stroke as contemporary music had ever heard. His aphoristic talent and staggering poetic gift combined with underrated commercial craftsmanship to overwhelm the prosaic standards and practices of the time. Dylan's work became, in the astonishingly short span of three years, a kind of subtext incarnate in all kinds of popular music, from the Beatles and Stones to a thousand dusty-booted troubadours. In the truest sense of the word, Dylan liberated pop; not simply from its three-minute span or its June/moon/spoon conventions, but from *everything*. Suddenly the strangest metaphoric lexicons were made not only acceptable but mandatory. Any songsmith worth his salt proved it in twelve-minute word salads seasoned with three chords and a rusty harmonica. Dylan's impact on pop art was like nothing so much as e.e. cummings (a man whose capitalphobia Dylan emulated,) dropping in on an eighteenth-century salon of romantic English poets, all meter-bound and linear. People simply went wild with outrage, delight or confusion. Through it all, Dylan remained true to his nimble sensibilities.

His catlike grace for staying a leap beyond his own innovations was evident from the very beginning. Middle-class and middle western, Robert Zimmerman decided on his alter ego early in life. While still in junior high school he announced to a friend that he had "found his stage name," selected, of course, after the poet Dylan Thomas. It's a story Dylan denies, placing the event two years later, when he first began playing guitar at a coffeehouse in Dinkytown, the bohemian district of Minneapolis, where he briefly attended the University of Minnesota. The details are less important than what they suggest: a self-aware, self–styled folk singer concocting an image from the fragments of a dozen legends.

By the time Dylan arrived in New York City, in January of '61, the composite was already substantively in place. Cherubic, curly-haired, and shy, Dylan brilliantly concealed a steely ambition justified by a remarkable talent. In the sharply competitive Greenwich Village folk scene, he was careful to cultivate his middle-American twang and an image of innocence abroad. Yet there never seems a moment when he was not in absolute command of his gifts and goals. In December of '61, he recorded an evening of off-the-cuff music captured on tape by folk musician Tony Glover. At one point he stops to enthuse about some photos that had been taken of him. "Hey, man," he says to Glover, "you ought to see some pictures of me. I'm not kidding." He lets out an appreciative whistle. "I look like Marlon Brando, James Dean, or something. I'm standing up against this wall in a blue turtleneck sweater. All kinds of pictures! You oughta see me."

Seeing was, largely, believing. Dylan, opening with original material at Gerdes Folk City for John Lee Hooker, came across, in Jonathan Cott's words, "part Huck Finn, part Charlie Chaplin, part Woody Guthrie." To that list might be added Will Rogers, Parfisal, Hank Williams, and John the Baptist. It was a tremendously appealing image, a new American archetype, elements of which would be refined and exalted years later by Bruce Springsteen, John Cougar Mellancamp, and a dozen other heartland heroes of rock.

But rock was the farthest thing from the well-tuned aesthetics of the folk world, which was shortly to crown Dylan as the heir apparent to artistic authenticity and political correctness. By the time he had released his first album, *Bob Dylan*, in the spring of '62, Dylan, working off the small palette of the ingrown American grass roots scene, had wrought the same sort of transformation he was later to accomplish in rock 'n' roll. Essentially the domain of archivists, activists, and crew-cut sellouts, folk music was in the midst of its flirtation with the big time with hale-fellow trios and the network TV variety show, "Hootenanny." Purists predictably scoffed at the crassness of it all, glorying in the days of their McCarthyite martyrdom. Dylan neatly sidestepped the schism by redefining the rules of the game.

His model was Woody Guthrie, the Dust Bowl Conscience of America, the mythical wandering minstrel. Dylan, too, became a thing of rags and tatters, making up wild yarns about his boyhood that included meeting Guthrie in California, working in a carnival, and riding the rails. For Jonathan Cott, Dylan, "in his all-fusing character and his mythical recreation of his past . . . had made up for himself his own Great Depression and Dust Bowl to wander through."

The enduring appeal of the Guthrie myth, and its special appropriateness to the nascent counterculture, wasn't Dylan's only bit of shrewd image engineering. In fact, he correctly intuited and embodied several converging ideas at once. The engaging commercial ploy of playing off his own apparent lack of singing talent, for example, was a calculated risk that paid off spectacularly. By flaunting his coarse, rasping voice, Dylan overturned conventional show business norms and cleared the decks for music that could be judged by a whole new set of criteria. It's significant to recall that when he first gained national exposure, the controversy Dylan generated was not over his message but whether or not he could carry a tune.

As unique an entertainer as Dylan was, it was the tremors of social unheaval that provided the impetus for his appeal among the young, for whom issues of equality, peace, and butter over guns were to shortly become paramount. "This machine kills fascists," read a sign painted on Guthrie's guitar, a sentiment restated in the whole body of Dylan's caustic political broadsides. Dylan's social gospel is best exemplified in the 1964 *The Times They Are a-Changin'*, with its state-of-the-art protest epics: "With God on Our Side," "Only a Pawn in Their Game," and the roiling "When the Ship Comes In." The album's title track, says Janet Maslin, "crystallized for many the mood of its day, even as it anticipated the spirit of the counterculture."

But Dylan was up to more than crystallizing and anticipating. Reinterpreting Woody Guthrie for a new generation, setting quirky stylistic standards, and renewing folk music's covenant with the left were all intriguing maneuvers, but what really set the staid music scene spinning was the power of suggestion enhancing all this self-invention. The dimensions of Robert Zimmerman's conjuring talents were such that his creation, Bob Dylan, was conceived with a full-blown mythic stature. Dylan didn't develop, at least not in any accepted sense. He simply *arrived*.

Every artist, of course, is obliged to mold his public persona, the intended object of adoration. Thus Jim Morrison, the Electric Shaman, and Mick Jagger, the Devil himself, shared Dylan's self-aggrandizing urge. Beyond the demands of ego, however, comparison fades. For even the most magnetic rock stars, the show's the thing, a good performance its own reward. For Dylan, his consummately crafted alter ego was always a means to an end. Much has been made of his ever-shifting image, a kind of prototype for David Bowie's quick-change career. In Jonathan Cott's Dylan biography, for example, the author goes on at length about Dylan's similarity to the Greek god Proteus, who could take on any form he desired. But Dylan, the real Dylan, always remains the same. The roles are simply instruments of his will, means to an end. They are, in turn, aspects of that most ambitious of all roles: to be the distillation of aspirations.

In the summer of '63, Dylan performed at the Lincoln Memorial during the march on Washington, crowned by Martin Luther King's divinely appointed "I Have a Dream" speech. He was later to join Pete Seeger in Greenwood, Mississippi, to lend his support to a black-voter registration drive. Dylan stepped onto the stage of the civil rights drama as a voice that, like King's own, had already summed up the struggle's spiritual calling. "Blowing in the Wind" was the anthem that rallied white, middle-class kids, not "We Shall Overcome." It was Dylan, the very image of liberation from the strictures they felt so keenly, that would begin to lead youth into the crucible of political awareness. And it was Dylan, finally, who would move beyond, initiating his followers into the politics of consciousness.

For those—and there are many—who have studied Dylan with talmudic thoroughness, no distinct point of departure emerges to mark his complete shift of focus from the external to the internal. It's clear that by early '64, the protest movement was simply irrelevant to him as either a subject for versifying or as a pressing personal concern. "I'm not really a social critic. I knew where to put the song back then, that's all," Dylan is quoted as telling a friend in Anthony Scadutto's book *Dylan: An Intimate Biography*. "When I wrote those songs they were written within a small circle of people. I took the time out to write those things, in little rooms and all." If not a social critic, Dylan was a potent social catalyst, and the dissolution of the equal rights struggle into dissension, drift, and, eventually, violence, coincided with Dylan's own questions about his political calling. "I'm just not gonna be a part of it," he said. "I'm not gonna make a dent or anything, so why be a part of even trying to criticize it?" And more to the point: "I'm hungry and restless and pretty damned wretched. I used to think I was smart, but I don't know anymore. I don't even know if I'm normal."

It had a familiar timbre, that cry of dislocation, the deep doubts not just about the status quo but about threadbare reality itself. It was, after all, 1964. One of the more famous Dylan tales has the folksinger driving through the Rocky Mountains when he hears a Top Ten radio countdown in which eight of the chart toppers are Beatles cuts. "They were doing things nobody was doing," he told Scadutto. "Their chords were outrageous, just outrageous, and their harmonies made it all valid. . . . But I just kept it to myself that I really dug them. Everybody else thought they were for teenyboppers. . . . But it was obvious to me that they had staying power." That summer he would stop by the Delmonico Hotel and personally guide the Mop Tops through the portals of reefer. Dylan himself had gotten particularly attached to the weed's creative enhancements during a tour the year before, and its effects on his music, combined with the singer's own mushrooming horizons, would be startlingly evident on his next album.

One of the greatest works of transition in pop history, *Another Side of Bob Dylan*, had a drolly understated title and an assortment of widely divergent material. The neither-fish-nor-fowl feel of the album perfectly mirrors Dylan's increasing attraction to rock, especially the new, cogent, and self-conscious rock of the English invaders. "Ramona" and "Spanish Harlem Incident" had an erotic pull to them that gave weight to Dylan's handling of a whole new range of emotions. The LP had more than its share of one-off rambles—"Motorpsycho Nitemare," "I Shall Be Free #10"; early signs of the looming surrealism that was shortly to burst forth in radiant display. The strutting piano riff and sly humor of "Black Crow Blues" were in a thinly veiled rock setting. To top off the unmistakable impression that caution was being thrown to the winds, Dylan delivered a new kind of protest song. "Chimes of Freedom" cast the whole human race in the role of the afflicted, with Dylan a helpless observer, caught between "sundown's finish and midnight's broken toe."

"Midnight's broken toe?" That wasn't the half of it. *Bringing It All Back Home* tipped the balance even further in rock's favor. Released in 1965 it was, in fact, the point of no return, yielding a modest Top Forty hit in "Subterranean Homesick Blues," and a smash folk-rock cover with the Byrds' version of "Mr. Tambourine Man." The betrayed ranks of folkies screamed howls of protest, calling Dylan a "freak and a parody." *Sing Out!* magazine railed, "[I]f ever the world was in need of the clear and uncompromising anger and love of the poet, it is now."

Much has been made of Dylan's subsequent appearance at the Newport Folk Festival, when he took the stage in fruit boots, black leather jacket, and electric guitar and was roundly abused by the outraged purists. If courage can be defined as doing the smart thing instead of the stupid, then Dylan's switch to rock can be defined as a courageous act. In fact, Dylan had, by this time, so completely identified with rock 'n' roll, assuming well before the fact the mantle of Rock Star, that anything less than Raybans and a Fender would have been an act of artistic suicide. Yet even as his music began to mutate, Dylan adhered to both the form and content of his original persona. He was, in other words, still a protest singer, and on *Bringing It All Back Home* he brought to the role a savage intensity coiled in thickets of imagery. Of an earlier composition, "Hard Rain's Gonna Fall," he had once remarked that each line could stand as a separate song. Compared to the fireworks set off by numbers like "Gates of Eden" and "It's All Right, Ma, (I'm Only Bleeding)," "Hard Rain" seemed like a nursery rhyme.

By leaping over accepted metaphors for evil—Mississippi sheriffs, warmongers, and hard-hearted women—Dylan was catching up with some really nasty individuals: Vampire lovers, puppet masters, and every degree of spiritual cripple. By shifting the focus from political oppressions and liberations to emotional slavery and intimations of eternity almost too beautiful to bear, Dylan had set foot into a fantastic and uncharted interior world. The ravishing sorrow of "Mr. Tambourine Man" or the clear, bitter truth of "It's All Over Now, Baby Blue" marked a metamorphosis in the expressive potential of pop music. With rock 'n' roll, Dylan had cut through to the bone pain of humanity.

What was heralded in *Bringing It All Back Home* emerged alive and kicking on *Highway 61 Revisited*, the greatest rock album of Dylan's career and one of a handful of the greatest rock albums of all time. Here, the forays into Dylan's dense new world had become a diary of exile. Protest is transformed into a precision scream. Characters and props and sudden whiplash plot turns fill the skyline with random associations, crackling and glowing like hallucinogenic fox fire. This time around, backed by a blistering rock ensemble anchored to Mike Bloomfield and Al Kooper's surgical fills, Dylan the rocker outraces even the quantum leaps of 1965. It's the year of "Satisfaction," *Rubber Soul*, and Frisco's first dances, and here's Bob Dylan, turning over rocks in the rubble at the end of time, prefiguring not just the demise of the sixties but some sort of ultimate extinguishment of hope, love, and body warmth. The stops along *Highway 61*—"From a Buick 6," "Ballad of a Thin Man," "Just like Tom Thumb Blues," "Tombstone Blues"—are more than scenes from an explicit nightmare. They are the summary executions that Dylan, as judge and jury, has ordered up for every metaphysical criminal he has ever encountered or ever fancied that he has encountered. *Highway 61 Revisited*, yielding the Top Five hit "Like a Rolling Stone," established Dylan's visionary imagination as the artistic terminus for the angst and anger of the twentieth century, a repository of all the beautiful fatalism that had followed the ostensible death of God. *"Highway 61 is just too good,"* Dylan himself would remark, while his longtime associate and sometime friend Phil Ochs, marveled, "How can a human mind do this?"

Blonde on Blonde, following in May of 1966, is generally considered, by virtue of its bulk alone, to be Dylan's masterpiece. Like all good masterpieces, it is foreboding and seemingly inpenetrable, yielding its treasures slowly. As a piece of rock 'n' roll, it falls short of the reckless breakthrough achieved on *Highway 61*. A poppier sound prevails, a calliope tilt that clearly points to Dylan's increasing awareness of his role as rock innovator, as well as the influence of producer Bob Johnston, who would continue to shape the singer's sound for years to come. The double LP's fourteen cuts sustain the astonishing output that began on *Bringing It All Back Home*, and in terms of sheer songwriting prowess, these three albums can be considered as one sustained run of genius. The side-long "Sad-Eyed Lady of the Lowlands," the scathing "Just Like a Woman" and the album's haunted soul "Visions of Johanna," are Dylan in effortless command of his secret lan-

guage of signs. The needle set down on any groove un-
covers the same rich texture.

> Ain't it just like the night
>   to play tricks when you're tryin' to be so quiet
> We sit here stranded
>   though we're all doin' our best to deny it
> And Louise holds a handful of rain,
>   temptin' you to defy it
> Lights flicker from the opposite loft
> In this room the heat pipes just cough
> The country music station plays soft
> but there's nothing, really nothing, to turn off

Phil Ochs: "I had an increasing lot of secret fear: 'Oh
my God, what can he do next? He can't possibly top that
one.'" The question never came to that. In late July of '66,
at the pinnacle of his influence, Dylan broke his neck in
a motorcycle accident. It was the end of an era.

Speaking with Jonathan Cott in 1978, Dylan made a remarkable admission about the effects of his near-fatal crash
on his creative faculties. "Right through the time of *Blonde
on Blonde*," he confesses, "I was [writing songs] unconsciously. Then one day I was half-stepping and the lights
went out. And since that point, I more or less had amnesia.
Now, you can take that statement as literally or meta-
physically as you need to, but that's what happened to
me. It took me a long time to get to do consciously what
I used to be able to do unconsciously."

The implications of this sudden snapping of circuits for
Bob Dylan the Character—one of the most inspired fic-
tional creations in or outside literature—was deep and permanent. "I used to think that myself and my songs were
the same thing," he told *Newsweek* in 1968, shortly after

the release of *John Wesley Harding*, the post convalescence album that announced most clearly Dylan's new awareness of his own flesh-and-blood reality. "I don't believe that anymore. There's myself and there's my songs . . ." But if Dylan was not to be found in his songs—where he had said to the world he could be fixed and understood— where was he? Dylan would spend nearly twenty years trying to answer that question.

John Wesley Harding, for all its polished and honed songwriting, proved Dylan's point: he was indeed learning to write all over again. Embodying myth had proved too dangerous and destructive; by attempting to objectify the myth, to shift the burden, as it were, he fashioned an open-ended parable that still begged the question: if Zimmerman wasn't Dylan, who was he? To Scaduto he once remarked, "Before I wrote *John Wesley Harding* I discovered something about all those earlier songs I had written. I discovered that when I used words like 'he' and 'it' and 'they' and talking about other people, I was really talking about nobody but me." Dylan could no longer afford to be so intimately involved with his own creation. He stepped back to take the measure of himself, but in the end, like everyone else, he could only guess.

In as good a reading of this loose-knit concept album as any, Scaduto suggests that the famous western outlaw *John Wesley Harding*, of the title's name was, in fact, more than a "friend of the poor." "He is Christ," ventures the writer, "and he is also Dylan, who was saying that he was cast in the role of Messiah and had come to believe it was real, to believe that he could save people's souls. He never realized that it was all ego, and that he had been caught in a false posture, trapped into believing he was more than a man."

Dylan may have thought he was more than man, but he'd never been caught in a false posture in his life. At

330

least not publicly. *John Wesley Harding* shared the poetic density of Dylan's earlier work but none of its emotional fire or clarifying certainty. Dylan had yet to understand the lessons of his close encounter with death, and this album, with its parable song structures and deeper, more resonant vocal style, had the form of wisdom without the understanding. *John Wesley Harding* was a premature announcement of Dylan's maturity.

A string of late sixties and early seventies albums continued the drift. Living in semiseclusion in upstate New York with his wife and a growing brood of kids, Dylan took pains to present the image of a man at peace with himself. *Nashville Skyline*, *Self-Portrait*, and *New Morning* were genuine enough expressions of the bucolic joys of country hearth and home, but behind it all the void still loomed. By reducing himself to a simple man rooted in traditional values, Dylan served only to aggravate his fans and, more important, move further from any lasting reconciliation with the ghosts of his past or the quandary of his future. "He don't fool me, man," spat Country Joe McDonald.

For all intents and purposes, Dylan simply checked out of the seventies, releasing diffuse and desultory albums that reflected nothing more than the artist's continuing affection for playing and singing. Despite incessant caterwauling by the critics—announcing with each new LP that "the old Dylan" was back—most of these efforts withered on the vine. Even more vigorous blooms such as the 1974 *Blood on the Tracks* were marred by Dylan's weakening grip on his poetic gift. As good and true a song as "Tangled Up in Blue" was, it sat cheek and jowl with the ludicrous and mean-spirited "Idiot Wind," suffering by its proximity. Dylan was no longer singing about himself, no longer singing about us, and no longer singing about the relationship between the two. No one was sure of exactly what he was singing about, as he came, increasingly, to depend on his old magic to perform for him. From 1975 to 1978 no fewer than four albums of old and repackaged material were released; everything from the archival *Basement Tapes* to the abysmal *Dylan at Budokan*. The debacle of *Renaldo and Clara* was waiting in the wings, as was the final blow to the fragile image of inner harmony; the failure of his marriage. By 1978 Dylan had reached a dead end.

Every man has the right to decide for himself the meaning of his life, to point to one or another construct or accomplishment and say, "Here it is. That sums me up." The problem is, some have more of a right than others. Bob Dylan, for example, had almost no right at all.

It wasn't that he had simply forfeited it for the status of legend or that he conceded his own search for identity to the demands of his public. "I came to believe that Dylan was Christ revisited," says one acquaintance. "I felt that everything fit, without being Christian-religious or anything, I felt that what he had to say about living and communication with people was the truest, most honest and most Christ-like thing I've ever heard." So what? Dylan wasn't the first, and certainly won't be the last, elevated to messianic status. People believe what they want: even the famous, victimized by the collective imagination of their public, need to seek their own center.

Dylan, whose isolation was only another facet of his popular image, was bearing another cross entirely. It wasn't a question of freedom of choice, of a flip through the catalog of available destinies, or of even reaching decisions after weighing options and testing waters. From the very beginning, he was hemmed in from all sides, called against his will, his better judgment, and any hope of escape to a desperate quest for the one and final Unattainable. Pursued by the Hound of Heaven, Dylan was driven like a lamb to slaughter into the arms of God. "I wore three links of chain," Dylan sang on his first album, breathing vitality into an old spiritual; "every link was Jesus' name. Keep your hand on that plow, hold on." On that same LP there were no less than three songs that captured his fear and fascination with death and dying, establishing early his reputation as a young man haunted by the grave. In social protest, his music had the Old Testament ring of unequivocal judgment. "Then they'll raise their hands, sayin' we'll meet all your demands," he crowed on "When the Ship Comes In," "But we'll shout from the bow your days are numbered. And like Pharaoh's tribe, they'll be drownded in the tide and like Goliath, they'll be conquered." Calling folk music itself "legend, myth, Bible and ghost" his music teems with religious imagery from the tolling bells in "Chimes of Freedom," to the God in "Highway 61 Revisited" who tells Abraham, "the next time you see me coming, you better run."

Dylan himself ran and ran hard, but for every stride he slipped two steps back toward the altar of Yahweh. The singular and special power of Dylan's music can be attributed to his fated obsession with the mysteries of Jehovah, setting him apart from the ruinous equivocations of Eastern doctrines. As Cott observes, "Exile, redemption, salvation, righteousness, judgment, faith and belief have all been constant concerns and themes in his work. And he had always sung of Jesus—the greatest of Dylan's outlaw heroes." Everywhere he turned, and everywhere his followers turned with him, Dylan confronted the Most High. And what he might himself choose to deny was writ large in the body of his work.

Ask Stephen Pickering, aka Chofetz Chaim Ben-Avraham, Jewish mystic and author of numerous tracts relating Dylan's music to the ancient Hebrew prophetic tradition. In *Bob Dylan Approximately: A Portrait of the Jewish Poet in*

Search of God, Pickering declares, "Bob Dylan's poetry centers upon God, upon Heaven (paths to the Gates of Eden, where man will knock on Heaven's door), upon the extant Jewish-messianic tradition. His sense of impending apocalypse (the dialectical struggle between darkness and light) burns into the Jewish heart. In his moral anger, his ethical monotheism, Bob Dylan is a Jewish voice aware of the struggles that can tear apart the heart: what one ought to do as opposed to what one wants to do. Dylan has, in his 'Wedding Song,' admitted that it was never his 'intention to sound the battle charge.' However, the fire is in him like Jeremiah: he cannot be silent." Avowing elsewhere in his midrash that "Poetry/prayer is the language of Bob Dylan's soul," Pickering made his impassioned interpretation of Dylan's music before the artist became a Born Again Christian. But if there is, as Christians, at least, insist, an unbroken linkage between the Old and New Testaments, between the hope of the Jews and the work of Christ, then Dylan has only strengthened Pickering's argument. Here is a man squarely in the Davidic tradition: poet, leader, apple of God's eye, and archetype.

Dylan's trio of straightforward evangelical albums, the 1979 *Slow Train Coming*, the 1980 *Saved*, and the 1981 *Shot of Love* caused a kind of identity crisis within the rock establishment itself. Had he led them down so long and scenic a road only to deposit them at the foot of the cross? Dylan's announcement of his Christianity was far outside rock's normative dealings with religion. It had no precedent. Some refused to set one. "It is . . . usually best to be reticent about discussing someone's personal religious beliefs," writes Cott before going on to savage Dylan's "preprogrammed, puritanical and often propagandizing form of fundamentalist Christianity." Paul Williams wrote a whole book on the subject, with a title that tells all: *Dylan—What Happened?* To his credit, the veteran rock

334

critic and stubborn Dylan devotee finds reason to be optimistic in the face of this baffling turn of events. "How do I feel about what happened to Bob Dylan?" he writes. "I'm glad he found religion, glad not just for him but for myself and all of us, because Bob Dylan the artist is an international resource, and I feel that resource has just been renewed. Dylan has been recalled to life; and like John Donne and G. K. Chesterton and so many others before him, he may well produce a finer body of work in the second half of his life—after conversion—than he did in the first half, which would be an extraordinary accomplishment indeed."

Extraordinary, certainly, but not yet to be. Had Dylan's music, under the influence of his newly found faith, regained its former ferocious intensity, there is no telling what sainted or sacrificial status might have awaited him, what denomination or cult might have grown up around this new figurehead. As it turned out, Dylan would not produce a "finer body of work" reflecting his Christian fervor. Cott was right: parts of *Slow Train Coming*, almost all of *Saved*, and long stretches of *Shot of Love* were arid and dogmatic. Despite the fact that Janet Maslin, among others, saw Dylan coming "full circle" and once again singing "accusingly from a lonely one-man perch atop the mountain," it was clear that Christianity had not restored his poet's laurels. Later LPs, the '83 *Infidels* and the '85 *Empire Burlesque*, found him drifting away from fire-and-brimstone bluntness back into distracted musings that missed far more often than they connected.

Something strange was afoot here. For Dylan to again find his voice, this time in the service of Jesus, would have had the satisfying inevitability of good melodrama. But Dylan hasn't found his voice again, and whether he's found himself is a question no longer open to public scrutiny. Jesus, it seems, does not need Dylan's astonishing

335

gifts to complete His work, and if Dylan needs Jesus to be complete himself, he has set down the path of the humble and contrite.

Bob Dylan's interpretation of his classmates dream of the upper room was the simple one. Old things are passed away, and all things are made new. Old circuits must be stripped for the cleansing water to flow. Dylan may yet find himself washed in that water where the old man and the legend of the old man fade away. With the last chapters of Dylan's saga still unwritten, he shares a common uncertainty; will his four-score-and-twenty, finally, be graced with the recognition of meaning and purpose? "I am hanging in the balance of the reality of man," he sang in "Every Grain of Sand," his finest postconversion song. It's in that lonely place that Dylan continues to search for himself. If the fateful accident sent him careening headlong into his own mortality, it also opened before him the void that lay behind his genius. In seeking to fill that void, Dylan faced again and again the necessity of demythologizing himself and turned constantly away from the painful task. The final surrender, if it finally comes, may well be his finest moment.

Afterword

What is truth?

—Pontius Pilate

Unlike the history of rock as art, rock as big business or rock as an expression of the popular will, the history of rock and religion can be read as a saga of unfulfilled expectations, betrayed ideals, hollow promises, and thwarted potentials. Perhaps it was never the place of such ephemeral music, no matter how appealing, to bear the burden of truth or brunt of spiritual longings. Perhaps the overweening ambitions of rock stars and the inarticulate needs of rock fans can, in the end, only cancel themselves out, taking the music down with them. Perhaps what matters most is, not what rock 'n' roll can teach us about ourselves and the cosmos but rather what it leaves unsaid, the way it reaches beyond logic and purpose and Big Questions to capture precious moments of transition.

Perhaps. And perhaps, when all the muddled and mistaken paths to enlightenment that rock has taken us down empty out into one lonesome cul-de-sac, it will hardly have seemed worth the journey. Rock 'n' roll, the most powerful music the world has ever known, has a lot to answer for . . . crimes against art and humanity, the spirit and itself.

But for those who have loved the music, all crimes are paid. The power of rock music is kind of a religious mystery itself. It makes people feel really bad and extra good. It brings out some of our noblest and most of our meanest impulses. For those who've been touched by it, it can't be lived without. It continues to grow, or mutate, and yet, at its core, it is immutable.

If all that sounds like religion, then you've hit the nail on the head. It's not because someone proclaimed it so, nor is it the result of a hundred profound, perverse, and preposterous attempts to make it so. Rock 'n' roll is a spiritual force because people hear in it spirits and things of the Spirit. In some way that's both wonderful and awful we receive blessings and curses. Without knowing how or why, people's lives are changed by rock 'n' roll music. It doesn't happen *out there*. It happens *in here*. And if rock 'n' roll never dies, it's because you can't kill something that sounds true in the ear of the believer.

Bibliography

Anderson, Robert Mapes. *Visions of the Disinherited: The Making of American Pentecostalism*. New York: Oxford University Press, 1979.

Baker, Glen A. & Stuart Coupe. *The New Music*. New York: Harmony Books, 1980.

Banks, Russell. *Continental Drift*. New York: Harper & Row, 1985.

Bashe, Phillip. *Heavy Metal Thunder*. New York: Dolphin/ Doubleday, 1985.

Bergman, Billy & Richard Horn. *Recombinant Do Re Mi*. New York: Quill Books, 1985.

Boone, Pat. *Together*. Nashville: Thomas Nelson, 1979.

Booth, Stanley. *Dance with the Devil—The Rolling Stones and Their Times*. New York: Random House, 1984.

Bugliosi, Vincent with Curt Gentry. *Helter Skelter*. New York: Bantam Books, 1974.

Bullfinch, Thomas. *Bullfinch's Mythology*. London: Spring Books, 1964.

Broughton, Viv. *Black Gospel*. New York: Blandford Press, 1985.

Brown, Peter & Steven Gaines. *The Love You Make—An Insider's Story of the Beatles*. New York: McGraw Hill, 1983.

Carr, Roy & Charles Shaar Murray. *Bowie: An Illustrated Record*. New York: Avon, 1981.

Cash, Wilbur J. *The Mind of the South*. New York: Knopf, 1960.

Clarke, Steve. *The Who in Their Own Words*. New York: Quick Fox, 1979.

Clifford, Mike, ed. *The Illustrated Encyclopedia of Black Music*. New York: Harmony Books, 1982.

Coleman, Ray. *Lennon*. New York: McGraw Hill, 1985.

Cone, James H. *Spirituals and the Blues—An Interpretation*. New York: Seabury Press, 1972.

Coon, Caroline. *1988: The New Wave Punk Rock Revolution*. London: Orbach & Chambers, 1977.

Cott, Jonathan. *Dylan*. New York: Rolling Stone Press, 1984.

Courlander, Harold. *Haiti Singing*. Chapel Hill: The University of North Carolina Press, 1939 (reprinted by Cooper Square Publications in 1973).

Davies, Hunter. *The Beatles*. New York: McGraw Hill, 1978.

Davis, Julie, ed. *Punk*. London: Millington, 1977.

Davis, Stephen. *Hammer of the Gods*. New York: William Morrow & Co., 1985.

Dempsey, Michael, ed. *The Bible: Sniffin' Glue*. London: S. G. Publications, 1978.

Dempsey, Michael, ed. *100 Nights at the Roxy*. London: Big O Publishing, 1978.

Dunleavy, Steve. *Elvis: What Happened*. New York: Ballantine Books, 1977.

Durasoff, Steve. *Bright Wind of the Spirit; Pentecostalism Today*. Englewood Cliffs, N.J.: Prentice-Hall, 1972.

Editors of *Rolling Stone*. *The Rolling Stone Interviews*. New York: Rolling Stone Press, 1981.

Frazer, James G. *The Golden Bough: The Roots of Religion and Folklore*. New York: Avenel, 1981.

Gans, David & Peter Simon. *Playing in the Band*. New York: St. Martin's Press, 1985.

Gillett, Charlie. *The Sound of the City—The Rise of Rock and Roll*. New York: Overbridge & Dienstfrey, 1971.

Gleason, Ralph J. *The Jefferson Airplane and the San Francisco Sound*. New York: Ballantine Books, 1969.

Goldman, Albert. *Elvis*. New York: Avon, 1981.

Griffin, Rick. *Man from Utopia*. San Francisco: Calitho Press, 1969.

Hall, Manly P. *The Secret Teachings of All Ages*. Los Angeles: Philosophical Research Society, 1977.

Harrison, Hank. *The Dead*. Berkeley, Ca.: Celestial Arts, 1980.

Hebridge, Dick. *Subculture: The Meaning of Style*. Toronto, Canada: Metheun, 1979.

Henderson, David. *'Scuse Me While I Kiss the Sky; The Life of Jimi Hendrix*. New York: Bantam Books, 1981.

Hersey, Gerry. *Nowhere to Run; The Story of Soul Music*. New York: Penguin, 1985.

Hopkins, Jerry. *Elvis: A Biography*. New York: Warner Books, 1983.

Hopkins, Jerry & Danny Sugerman. *No One Here Gets Out Alive*. New York: Warner Books, 1980.

Hopkins, Jerry. *Bowie*. New York: Macmillan, 1985.

Howard, Thomas. *Evangelical Is Not Enough*. Nashville: Thomas Nelson, 1984.

Hubbard, Don J. & Carol Kalcialoha. *The Role of Rock*. Englewood Cliffs, N.J.: Prentice-Hall, 1983.

Johansson, Calvin M. *Music and Ministry*. Peabody, Mass.: Hendrickson, 1984.

Johnson, Paul. *Modern Times*. New York: Harper & Row, 1983.

Jones, LeRoi. *Blues People*. New York: William Morrow & Co., 1963.

Kagan, Paul. *New World Utopias*. New York: Penguin Books, 1979.

Kramer, Daniel. *Bob Dylan*. Secaucus, N.J.: Citadel, 1967.

Latourette, Kenneth Scott. *A History of Christianity*. New York: Harper & Row, 1975.

Lewis, Myra. *Great Balls of Fire*. New York: Quill Books, 1982.

Lewis, C. S. *The Screwtape Letters*. New York: Macmillan, 1977.

Lewis, C. S. *The Great Divorce*. New York: Macmillan, 1978.

Malone, Bill. C. *Country Music U.S.A.* Austin, Texas: University of Texas Press, 1985.

Mann, May. *The Private Elvis*. New York: Pocket Books, 1977.

Marcus, Greil. *Stranded*. New York: Knopf, 1979.

Marsh, Dave. *Before I Get Old; The Story of the Who*. New York: St. Martin's Press, 1983.

McDonough, Jack. *San Francisco Rock: The Illustrated History of San Francisco Rock and Roll*. San Francisco: Chronicle, 1986.

Michaels, Ross. *George Harrison: Yesterday and Today*. New York: Flash Books, 1977.

Miles, Barry, comp. *The Beatles in Their Own Words*. New York: Delilah/Putnam, 1978.

Miller, Jim, ed. *The Rolling Stones Illustrated History of Rock and Roll*. New York: Random House/Rolling Stone Press, 1980.

Norman, Philip. *Symphony for the Devil; The Rolling Stones Story*. New York: Dell, 1984.

Palmer, Robert & Mary Shanahan. *The Rolling Stones*. New York: Rolling Stone Press, 1983.

Pareles, Jon & Patricia Romanowski. *The Rolling Stone Encyclopedia of Rock and Roll*. New York: Summit/Rolling Stone Press, 1983.

Pickering, Stephen. *Bob Dylan Approximately; A Portrait of the Jewish Poet in Search of God*. New York: McKay, 1975.

Reich, Charles & Jann Wenner. *Garcia: A Signpost to New Space*. San Francisco: Straight Arrow Books, 1972.

Ritz, David. *Divided Soul; The Life of Marvin Gaye*. New York: McGraw Hill, 1985.

Scaduto, Anthony. *Bob Dylan: An Intimate Biography*. New York: Grosset & Dunlap, 1971.

Sculatti, Gene & Davin Seay. *San Francisco Nights; The Psychedelic Music Trip; 1965–68*. New York: St. Martin's Press, 1985.

Sheff, David & G. Barry Golson. *The Playboy Interviews with John Lennon and Yoko Ono*. Chicago: Playboy Press, 1981.

Shore, Michael with Dick Clark. *The History of American Bandstand*. New York: Ballantine Books, 1985.

Sidran, Ben. *Black Talk*. New York: Da Capo, 1981.

Southern, Eileen. *The Music of Black Americans*. New York: W.W. Norton, 1983.

Swaggart, Jimmy with Robert Paul Lamb. *To Cross a River*. Plainfield, N.J.: Logos, 1977.

Swenson, John. *The Who*. New York: Ace Books, 1979.

Synan, Vinson. *The Holiness Pentecostal Movement in the United States*. Grand Rapids, Michigan: Eerdmans, 1972.

Tharpe, Jac L. *Elvis: Images and Fancies*. Jackson, Mississippi: University Press of Mississippi, 1979.

Thomas, Roy & Stan Lee. *The Conquest of Kaluu—Strange Tales #148*. New York: Marvel Comics Group, 1966.

Tosches, Nick. *Country*. New York: Scribners, 1985.

Tosches, Nick. *Hellfire*. New York: Dell, 1982.

Turner, James. *Without God, Without Creed; The Origins of Unbelief in America*. Baltimore: The Johns Hopkins University Press, 1985.

Various. *The Rolling Stones Interviews*. New York: Rolling Stone Press, 1981.

Vermorel, Fred & Judy. *The Sex Pistols*. London: Universal, 1978.

Waller, Don. *The Motown Story*. New York: Scribner's, 1985.

Weldon, Michael. *The Psychotronic Encyclopedia of Film*. New York: Ballantine Books, 1983.

Whitburn, Joel. *The Billboard Book of Top 40 Hits*. New York: Billboard, 1985.

White, Charles. *The Life and Times of Little Richard*. New York: Harmony Books, 1984.

Williams, Paul. *Dylan: What Happened*? San Francisco: And/Entwhistle, 1980.

Index

INDEX

349

About the Authors

Davin Seay is an author and journalist whose work has appeared in the *Los Angeles Times*, *People Magazine*, *California Magazine*, *The Philadelphia Inquirer*, and numerous music publications, including *Contemporary Christian Music*, where he is an editor-at-large. He is the co-author of *San Francisco Nights*, a history of psychedelic music, and has worked in the music industry at Warner Bros. Records and is currently completing his first novel. He has also written for television, radio and film.

Aside from his interest in popular music, David Seay is also actively engaged in military history studies and is the co-creator of Seay's Battlefield Maps. He is a student of Russian culture and contemporary church history. He lives in Los Angeles with his wife and three children.

Mary Neely is founder and chief executive officer of Exit Records, an independent record label she began in 1983, currently distributed through Island Records.

"Perhaps my interest in music developed during extensive travel in Africa, India, and South America through the years 1964 to 1970. The role of music in religion and ritual was integral among primitive cultures. On infrequent visits home to the States, there were clear similarities between what I saw in my travels and what I saw happening here through music.

"Music was becoming the single most powerful thread among the world's youth—a unifying force. These were not just popular songs. They chronicled, as well as influenced, the times." Mary's convictions led to her position as executive producer of "Rock Scope," a radio series carried as special programming by over two hundred rock–formatted radio stations from 1978 to 1983. Through interviews, research, and the music itself, these larger meanings were explored. *Stairway to Heaven* is based on that material.